MACRAMÉ
YOU CAN WEAR

LAURA TORBET

A COMPLETE BASIC COURSE IN MACRAMÉ AND 25 BRAND-NEW WEARABLE PROJECTS
WITH FULL INSTRUCTIONS

Color photos by Mort Engel
Black and white photos by Mark Stein
Book design by Katherine Wendel

A WATSON-GUPTILL / BALLANTINE BOOK, NEW YORK.

© Copyright 1972 by Laura Torbet

All rights reserved. No part of this publication may be reproduced or used in any form or by any means — graphic, electronic or mechanical, including photocopying, recording, taping or information storage and retrieval systems — without the written permission of the publisher.

This edition published by arrangement with Ballantine Books, Inc.

Printed in the United States of America

ISBN 0-8230-2950-6

Library of Congress Catalog Card Number: 70-189185

First Printing: February, 1972

WATSON-GUPTILL PUBLICATIONS
165 West 46th Street, New York, N.Y. 10036

BALLANTINE BOOKS, INC.
101 Fifth Avenue, New York, N.Y. 10003

Table of Contents

Introduction ix

THE BASIC COURSE 1

Equipment **2**

Materials

    Cord **3**, Beads **4**, Findings **4**

Working Methods **5**

Mounting Cords **6**

    Reverse Lark's Head **6**, Lark's Head **6**

The Square Knot (and the Half Knot) **7**

    Sennits **9**, Mounting Cords for Sennits **9**, Half Knot Sennit **9**, Variation of Half Knot Sennit **9**, Square Knot Sennit **9**

The Clove Hitch **10**

    Pinning the Holding Cord **10**, Clove Hitch Bar from Right to left **11**, Clove Hitch Bar from Left to Right **11**, Diagonal Clove Hitch—X Pattern **12**, Closing a Double Bar of Clove Hitches **12**, Vertical Clove Hitch **13**, Vertical Clove Hitch from Left to Right **13**, Vertical Clove Hitch from Right to Left **14**

The Overhand Knot **15**

    Using Overhand Knots to Finish Work **15**

Cutting and Gluing **16**

MORE ABOUT EVERYTHING 17

More About Square Knots **18**

    Square Knot Sennits **18**, Alternating Square Knots **20**, Decreasing Square Knots **20**, Increasing Square Knots **20**, Square Knot Patterns **21**, Square Knot Bobble **21**

More About Clove Hitches **22**

    Double Bar of Clove Hitches Starting in Center **22**, Adding Separate Cords with the Clove Hitch **23**, Random or Asymmetrical Holding Cord **24**, Triple Hitch **24**, Diamond Pattern **25**, Motifs Inside Diamond Patterns **25**,

Chevron Pattern **27**, More Vertical Clove Hitches **28**, Alternate Vertical Clove Hitches **28**, Clove Hitch Sennits **29**, Clove Hitch Patterns **30**, The Angled Technique **32**

Braids, Chains and Sennits 33

Single (Half Hitch) Chains—Right and Left **33**, Alternating Single Chains **33**, Clove Hitch Chain **34**, Alternating Triple Hitch Sennit **34**, Lark's Head Knot and Lark's Head Chains **35**, Alternating Lark's Head Sennits **35**

Two Special Knots 36

The Josephine Knot **36**, Josephine Knot Sennits **39**, The Berry Knot **40**

The Many Uses of the Overhand Knot 41

Overhand Knot Chains **41**, Alternating Overhand Knots **42**, Overhand Knot Used to Secure Braids and Twists **42**, Overhand Knots with Square Knots **42**, Collecting Knot **43**, Overhand Wrap **44**, Coil Knots **44**

Other Methods of Mounting and Starting Work 46

Another Method of Mounting with the Lark's Head **46**, Starting a Macramé Fringe on a Hem **46**, Double Lark's Head **47**, Pinning Cords at Center **47**, Starting in the Middle with a Clove Hitch Bar **47**, Shaping a Garment on a Flat Surface **48**, Mounting on a Ring with the Reverse Lark's Head **48**, Mounting on a Ring with the Clove Hitch **48**, Starting from the Center on a Circular Mounting Cord **49**, Adding Cords from a Central Core to Form Spiral Pattern **50**

Fancy Mountings and Picots 51

Mount with Overhand Knot **51**, Single-Loop Mount **51**, Double-Loop Mount **52**, Loop with Square Knot Mount **52**, Double-Loop Square Knot Mount **53**, Clove Hitch Mount **53**, Pointed Mountings **54**, Corner Mounting **54**, Tassels **54**

Working with Beads, Rings and Feathers 55

Simple Ways of Adding Beads **55**, Adding Beads When Mounting Cords **55**, Beads in Square Knot Patterns **56**, Beads on the Holding Cord of Clove Hitch Bar **56**, Adding a Ring with Square Knots **56**, Adding or Covering a Ring with Clove Hitches **57**, Adding Feathers **57**

Miscellany **58**

Adding Cords When You Run Short **58**, Adding Extra Cords and Joining Two Pieces **59**, Lacing **60**, Other Ways to Finish Work **61**, Working with Beads **62**, Gluing **62**

Working with Color **63**

THE PROJECTS **65**

1. Ring Choker **66**
2. Feather Choker **67**
3. Pin **68**
4. Bracelet **69**
5. Three-Color Fringed Shorts **70**
6. Choker **71**
7. Child's Dress **73**
8. Suspenders **74**
9. Silver Sash **76**
10. Long Necklace **78**
11. Beaded Belt **80**
12. Child's Vest **82**
13. Man's Belt **84**
14. Drawstring Bag **86**
15. Pendant Money Bag **88**
16. Beaded Shoulder Bag **90**
17. Three-Color Man's Tie **92**
18. Bib **94**
19. Bolero **96**
20. Fringed Poncho **98**
21. Pendant Necklace **100**
22. Man's Tie **102**
23. Bib/Apron **104**
24. Dress **106**
25. Bikini **109**

Bibliography **112**
List of Suppliers **113**

Introduction

The most difficult thing about macramé is convincing people how easy it is to do. Intricate as it looks, it is no more than two simple knots tied in an endless number of variations.

There is, of course, much more to be said in favor of macramé: very little working equipment is required and it can be purchased at any five and dime; materials are inexpensive and easy to find. Unlike weaving or embroidery, for example, macramé brings quick results—a finished piece can take just a few hours. Also, once the basic knots are learned, it is not hard to create your own patterns and designs. There is no limit to the possible variations, and you have the freedom to design "as you go"— no need to preplan a pattern. And it's a great feeling to wear something you've made yourself.

I began doing macramé without knowing that I was doing it. I'd had an idea for a long, hanging, beaded necklace (similar to Project 10), and the only way I could think of to work the beads into interesting patterns and to keep them in place was to tie knots between beads and between cords. When I wore the piece, a couple of people remarked about how nice it was that I was doing macramé—a term I'd never heard and which I thought might refer to a little-known form of European meditation or something. Of course, as soon as I got the story straight, I ran right out and bought Virginia Harvey's book, *Macramé: The Art of Creative Knotting,* only to discover that I was already using the two basic knots and had only to enlarge my knowledge of knot combinations and use my imagination to be able to do any number of things with the craft.

Traditionally, macramé has been done by sailors for ships' fittings and by craftsmen for wall hangings and home decorations. I like to wear things I make, and that's what this book is about.

In this era of mass production, one of the few ways we have of expressing our individuality is the way we dress. The desire to be able to make something ourselves has brought about a small revolution in the crafts world, and we take great pleasure in having created something "with our own two hands." There are 25 projects in this book, all meant to be worn. Though the directions are necessarily specific, I hope you'll substitute other materials for the ones suggested if you like, and that as you gain confidence, you'll feel free to change and adapt the pattern here and there as it suits your own taste.

Several very comprehensive books have been written about macramé (the best of which, I feel, are the Virginia Harvey book mentioned previously and a book by Dona Z. Meilach entitled *Macramé: Creative Design in Knotting*). These books go into the history of the craft in some detail, explain many alternate ways of working, and go into very advanced knots and techniques. For the purposes of this book, it did not seem necessary to go into the history of the craft. I have tried several methods of knotting, and I have found the one which works best for me. It is this one only which is presented in this book. As you learn, you will find little tricks and methods which work for you. I have included only the knots and combinations needed to do the projects in the book (and a few extra variations), but they provide quite a complete basic course and you are bound to discover others as you work.

If there is any problem in teaching macramé—especially specific projects—it is that of written instructions. For a while I had a macramé "cottage industry." Friends would duplicate my designs in their homes; I would pay them by the piece and sell them to stores around the country. But they did *not* work from written instructions—they merely copied a sample of the finished piece which they took home with them—for, having learned the basic knots and their variations, they could easily recognize them in the finished piece and see exactly how it was done.

The point here is that I can't stress enough the importance of carefully reading the introductory chapters on the basic knots and their combinations, and the tips on gluing, finishing, mounting, etc., *before* you tackle the projects. Directions are included for samplers which use the basic knots in different combinations. If you take the time to do the samplers, you will be able to tie the knots with ease, and equally important, you will recognize and understand them in the various forms in which they are found in the projects. As mentioned before, the instructions for the projects are very specific, but if you practice the basic knots carefully, you'll be able to do the projects by looking closely at the pictures and checking the written instructions only at points of difficulty.

This book is written for people who like to make things in an age of mass-produced ready-to-wear, people who like things which are a little different, people who like to work with their hands and who like the freedom of a craft where they can create as they go and whose limitations have yet to be found. I hope that you learn to love this simple hand craft, and go on to create your own designs and have many hours of pleasure from just two knots and a ball of twine.

Laura Torbet

Special thanks to: Leonore Fleischer
Kathy Pohl
Connie Holzman
Ron Gilbert
Lillian at Fibre Yarn Co.
Sue Reverby
Vicki Kreznar
John Thamm
And all the "models."

MACRAMÉ
YOU CAN WEAR

THE BASIC COURSE

Words of Importance and Reassurance As You Begin to Knot

This section of the book is about the groundwork of macramé: how to start, how to tie basic knots, and how to finish.

You are probably very anxious to get to the projects. All I can say is, hold your horses. The more time you spend learning the knots and their many variations, and the more practice you allow yourself, the easier it will be to do the projects.

A good way to learn macramé is to set up your knotting surface with 8 to 12 mounted cords of some material—nylon braid, rayon tubular, #2 rattail, or polypropylene cord—that is especially suitable for knotting. Make the cords about 4' long when doubled. Try out each knot and each pattern as you progress. You may want to untie the cords each time and go on to the next pattern, or go from one knot to the next and make a sampler with your mounted cords. (A good habit is to make small samplers with each new type of cord you use and keep them to refer to when choosing cord for new pieces.)

What you will learn in this chapter is very important. It is the basis for all the patterns, knot combinations, fancy headings, etc. found in the following section—so practice it well. Learn to tie the basic knots almost automatically. You will find your own way of working, and practice will teach you to keep your knots straight and of an even tension. Tie firmly, but don't overexert yourself.

Above all, *do not panic.* Written instructions may put you off at first and the involved series of pictures and explanations make macramé seem harder than it really is. As soon as you master a couple of simple knots, you will be reassured, and you will catch on to the next steps even faster.

Note: 1) *When cords are numbered for clarity, they are numbered from left to right. As their order changes, they are renumbered to avoid confusion.*
2) *The small round dots on the knot samplers indicate where pins should be placed.*

Equipment

Macramé requires very little equipment and most of it can be found at any five and dime: a knotting surface, pins, scissors, a crochet hook, a ruler or tape measure, and two C-clamps.

I've found a polyurethane cushion form, available in many sizes, to be the best knotting surface. It is lightweight yet sturdy, and takes the depth of a pin easily. For most purposes a square 3″ or 4″ thick and about 12″ x 12″ is sufficient and very portable. A few projects in this book will require a larger size; if you have a foam mattress or bolster around the house, you're in luck. Other good surfaces, especially for large projects, are two sheets of cork glued together, or a piece of Celotex, available at lumberyards. While almost anything which will take the depth of a pin is usable, your knotting surface is your most important tool and a good one will make your work easier.

Pins are also important. I prefer ⊓-shaped pins, known as upholstery pins or "tidy pins," so that I can pin through the cord or, if the cord is delicate, just inside it, and still hold it in place by pushing the pin all the way down into the knotting surface. Other suitable types are T-pins and glass-head hat pins.

I keep my macramé level and even "by eye," but you may want to pin a measuring tape to the horizontal and vertical edges of your knotting surface to keep your work in line. Another good method is to rule your cushion in 1″ squares with an indelible felt-tip marking pen.

Finally, C-clamps are useful in measuring long cords, as demonstrated on page 5. And a crochet hook is sometimes used to pull cords through tight places and in finishing off work.

1. Here's everything you need: a polyurethane cushion form for a knotting surface, glue, scissors, ⊓-pins, a crochet hook, C-clamps. A ruler or tape measure is also useful.

Materials

Cord

Many materials are suitable for knotting. Cord comes in a wide variety of sizes, shapes, colors, and textures, some better for knotting than others. In general, a good macramé cord has little elasticity, does not fray easily, and has a smooth enough surface so that the cord handles well and doesn't tangle.

It's not terribly important that you know exactly what kind of cord you're using. Some cord is made from natural fibers such as jute, sisal, raffia, polished cotton, navy cord, cotton seine twine, rug wool, and linen. Others are man-made: nylon seine twine, polypropylene cord, tensolite, nylon braid, and the many fancy cords used by the fashion industry—chainette, rattail, guimpe, tubular, ribbon. Some cord is twisted from several smaller pieces or "plys"; some is braided; some is sold by weight, and some by lengths. All you need care about is whether it ties the kind of knots you want.

An index of suppliers for cord, beads, and findings can be found in the back of the book, in case you want to order something specific for a project. Many of these companies will send catalogs or sample cards. My experience has been that with a little research and ingenuity, you can find just about anything just about anywhere. Spend some time checking out your local dime stores, hardware and stationery stores, hobby shops, marine or upholstery suppliers, Army surplus stores, needlecraft sections of department stores. I've learned to buy "interesting" cord as I find it, and figure out later what to do with it. (The same with unusual beads or hardware.) Sometimes the seller doesn't even know himself what kind of cord it is. Finding good knotting cord in colors is a particularly hard task—most cords come in white or "natural" tones only. Just recently a few manufacturers have started to market cord in colors to meet the growing need for good macramé materials. My advice is that when you see a nice cord in a color, buy now—use later.

2. A sampling of the many types of cord suitable for macramé.

Beads

The most important consideration when buying beads is finding them with holes large enough to thread your cord—preferably two cords—through. (Some hints on threading beads are on page 62.)

Crow beads and tile beads can be found in most craft or hobby stores. Tile beads are small, cylindrical, and come in a wide range of colors. Crow beads are larger, rounded, made of glass or plastic, and may be transparent or opaque. Wood beads with large holes, round and tubular, are commonly available. Such things as small curtain rings, nuts (as in nuts and bolts), washers, and other hardware can be substituted for beads. Again the rule holds: keep your eye out for beads (or anything) with large holes and buy now.

Findings

Findings is just a general classification for hooks, closings, jump rings, fasteners, buckles, buttons, or hardware usable in macramé. Most standard jewelry findings are available at hobby or craft stores. Hardware stores are my favorite sources of unusual things; also, I like starting a piece of macramé on a nice, firm hardware base, such as a ring or bar. Learn to keep your eyes and your imagination working as you shop. You'll find all sorts of things to use in this craft.

3. Beads and rings are available in many sizes and colors. Just be sure the holes are large enough for one or two cords. The most commonly available types are crow beads (in glass in foreground) and tile beads (in glass at left in rear).

4. Findings refers to buckles, jump rings, fasteners, pin backs, clasps, wire, eyelets (shown with eyeletting tool), and any miscellaneous hardware which might be suitable for macramé.

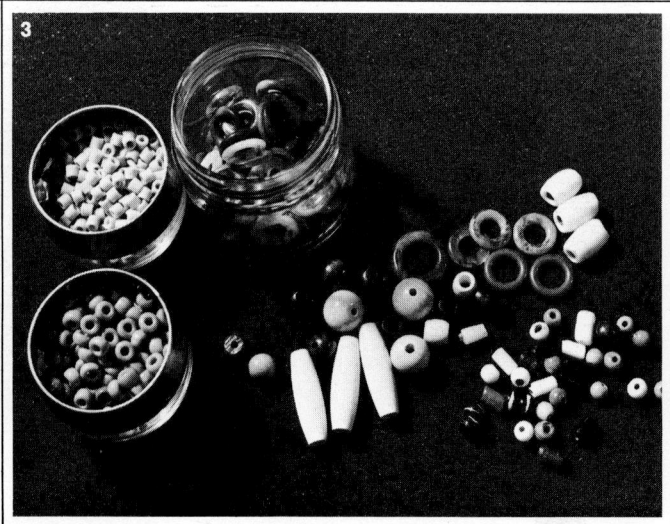

Working Methods

There are many little tricks to doing macramé. Many working techniques will come to you with practice, and these are easier learned than explained. But there are some facts worth knowing.

Generally, cords should be cut 8 to 10 times the length of the finished piece, so that when doubled and mounted they are 4 to 5 times the finished length. It is better to have extra cord than to be caught short. It's inevitable, though, that you will run short occasionally; methods for adding cords are shown on pages 58 and 59.

If a piece is small, I find it easiest to cut one cord to the proper length and then cut the rest of the cords along the length of the first, by hand. When there are many cords, when the cords are very long, or when the cord tangles easily, C-clamps are useful. Tighten one C-clamp upside-down at the end of a table or counter and the other at a distance *half* the desired length of the cord. Then, tying one end of the spool cord to a C-clamp, wind the cord back and forth until you have the number of cords needed. Cut the cords at *one* end and they will already be doubled and ready to mount.

Keeping long cords, or many cords, from tangling can also be a problem. Long ends can be wound on small cardboard bobbins, or made into "butterflies" as shown (Ill. 6), or held with elastic bands and pulled out as cord is needed. My own feeling is that winding bobbins is a pain and that the bobbins get just as tangled as the loose long threads; so unless you're working on a very involved project with extremely long cords, my advice is to forget it.

Pinning is a simple but important part of keeping your macramé even. The rule is, if the work pulls out of position as you knot—*pin it down*. As you'll see, pinning is absolutely *essential* in some cases. It's also important to pin *exactly* where you want the cord to be. Use your pins freely and firmly—push them in all the way.

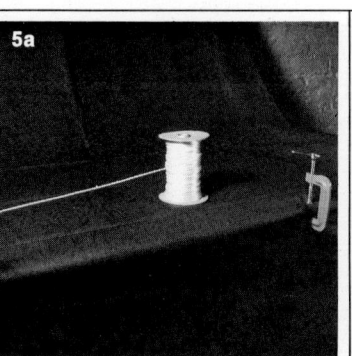 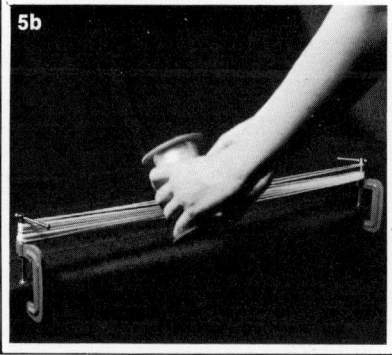 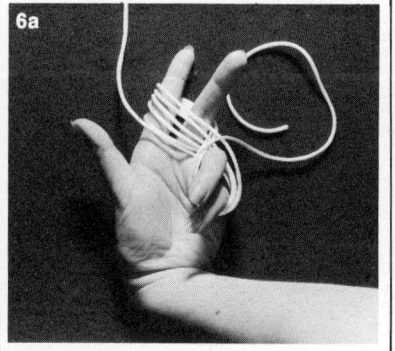 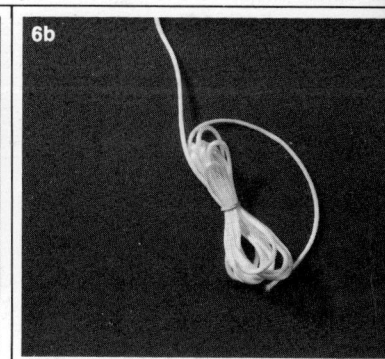

5. A. Tighten the 2 C-clamps *upside-down* at a distance half the length of the cut cord (the doubled length of the cord). Tie one end of the spool to the C-clamp.

   B. Wind the cord around the C-clamp as many times as the number of cords needed. Cut through all the cords at one end and they'll be doubled and ready for mounting.

6. A. Extra-long cords can be wound in a figure-8 pattern through your fingers from the top of the cord *down* to the end.

   B. Fasten with an elastic band and pull more loops out as needed.

Mounting Cords

Macramé involves knotting lengths of cord together in a pattern. Work is begun by mounting the cords to be worked on a taut cord, a bar, on the hem of a garment, or whatever is suitable to the piece.

The Lark's Head and the Reverse Lark's Head are the mounting knots. (I prefer the Reverse Lark's Head because the "loop" ends up on the back of the work.)

Here is a chance to start your practice sampler. Mount 8 to 12 cords (you'll get double that number of working strands) on a bar or on a tightly pinned cord of the same material, using one of the two methods shown, and you'll be ready to knot.

7. Reverse Lark's Head

A. Double cord and put loop under the mounting bar so that it sticks up over the top.
B. Bend the loop down over top of mounting bar.
C. Pull 2 cords through loop, so that loop is behind cords (D).
E. Tighten. Continue this process with each cord. When all cords are mounted push them closely but not tightly together.

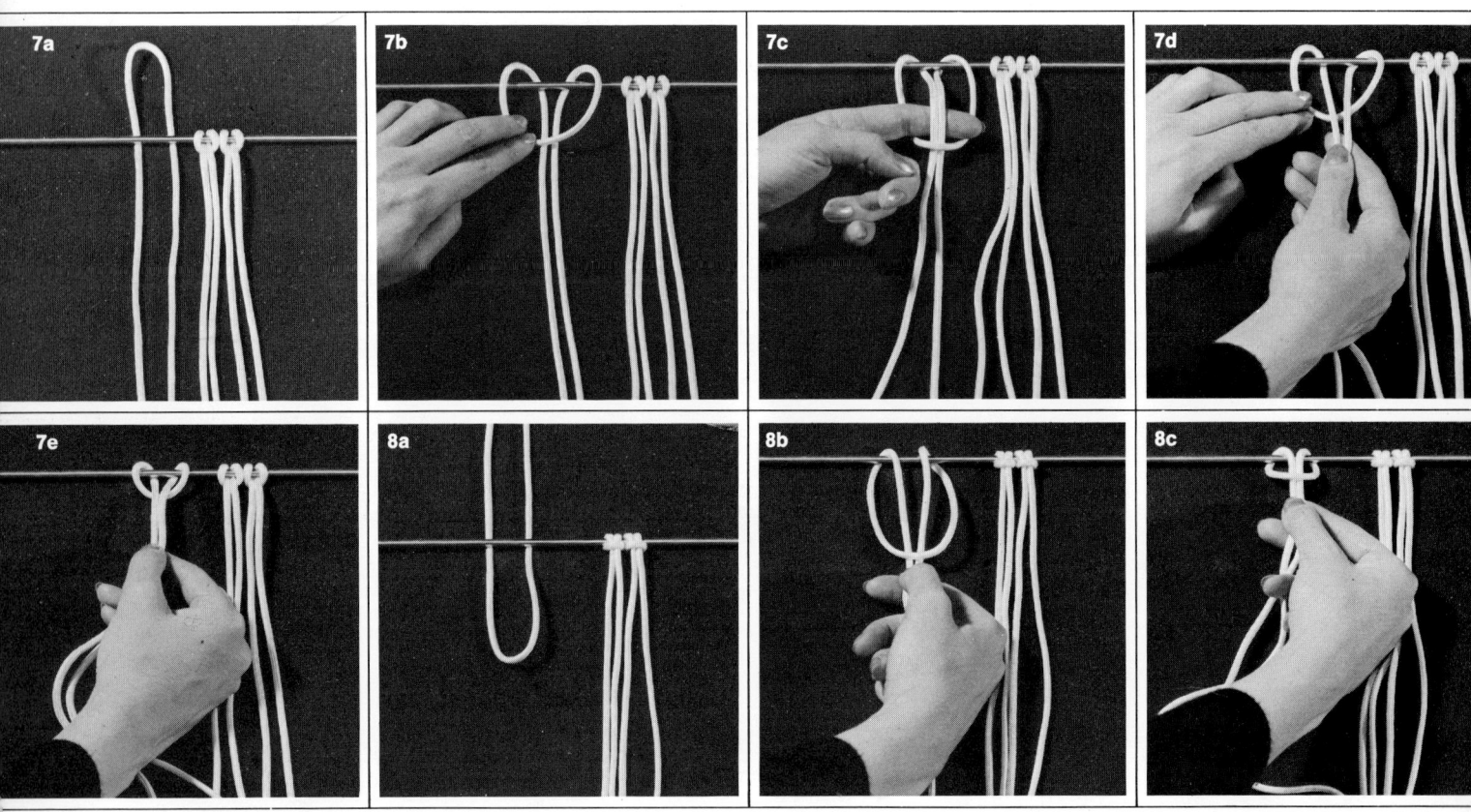

8. Lark's Head

A. Double cords and put loop under mounting bar from the top.
B. Bring cords down over top of mounting bar and pull them through the loop so that loop is on top.
C. Tighten.

The Square Knot (and the Half Knot)

Here is one of the two basic knots of macramé. Learn it well and practice it till it becomes automatic.

The basic Square Knot is made with 4 cords, the two outside cords doing the work of tying over the 2 center cords, which are held taut.

The Square Knot can be tied in endless varieties and patterns, can be tied close together or far apart, or can be tied in all-over designs as filler. It can be tied with several cords over 2 center cords, or 2 cords over several center cords. It can be tied one over the other. Many variations and patterns are shown on pages 18–21.

There are several methods of tying this knot, all of which give the same results. I'll show only one method; if you already know another, stick to it.

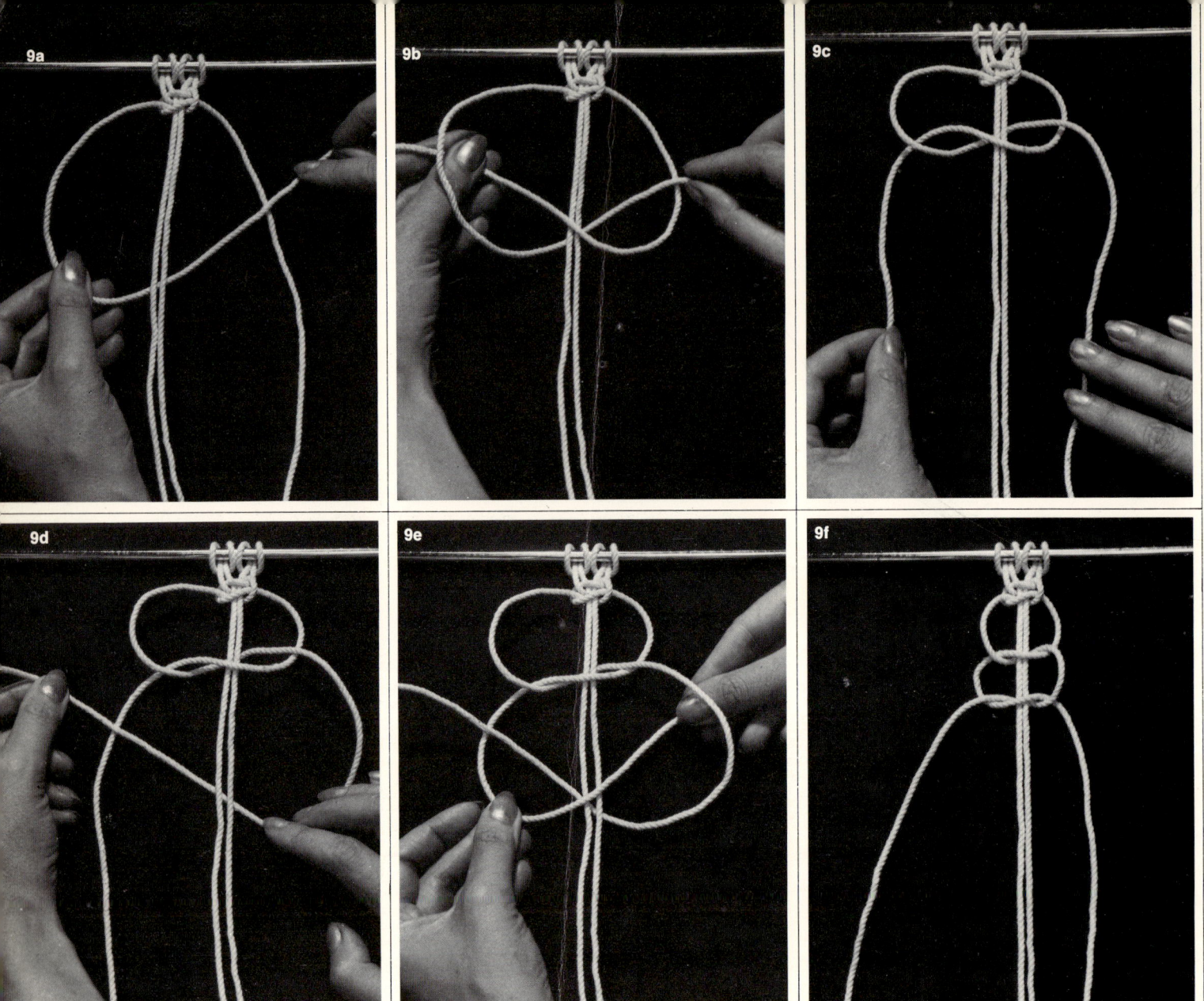

9. The Square Knot is tied with 2 outside cords over 2 center cords. Center cords should be kept taut. This can be accomplished by pinning the center cords to the working surface. I prefer to lean against them (if I am working standing up) or loop them under my pillow (if I am sitting). Some people keep center cords taut with a paper clamp attached to their pillow or by hooking cords through their belt or between their knees, etc. You'll find your own way. Likewise you'll find your own preferred way of manipulating the cords as you tie which is most convenient for you.

- A. Put the left-hand cord *under* the 2 center cords and *over* the right-hand cord.
- B. Put the right-hand cord *over* the 2 center cords and *under* (through) the left-hand cord.
- C. You have now completed the first half of the Square Knot. This knot is known as the *Half Knot*. As you'll see, tying a series of Half Knots results in a twisted braid often used in macramé.

  Now reverse the above process (A and B) for the second half of the Square Knot, remembering to keep the center cords taut.

- D. Put the right-hand cord *under* the 2 center cords and *over* the left-hand cord.
- E. Put the left-hand cord *over* the 2 center cords and *under* the right-hand cord.
- F. Completed Square Knot.

    Note: Remember the Square Knot this way:
    Left cord under and over; right cord over and under; right cord under and over; left cord over and under. In case you lose track, the cord coming out on *top* of the loop just tied goes *under* the center cords next.

Sennits

A braid or chain made with a repeat pattern of knots is referred to as a sennit. Many sennit variations will be found on pages 18–19, 29, 33–36, 39 and 41. For now, two simple and commonly used sennits —repeat patterns of the Half Knot and the Square Knot.

10. Mounting Cords for Sennits

When tying most sennits, the outside cords will be used up at about 4 times the rate of the center cords. Make allowance when mounting by folding the cords accordingly.

11. Half Knot Sennit

By tying just the first half (or the last half) of the Square Knot, you are tying the Half Knot which, when tied in succession, automatically causes a twist pattern or spiral to the left or right (depending on which half of the knot you tie). This sennit, twisting to the right, was made by tying the first half of the Square Knot.

Note: About every 7 Half Knots, the sennit will make a full twist, so just turn over the center cords, reversing the order of the outside cords and continue the sennit. Otherwise the sennit will twist of its own accord and you'll lose track of the order of outside cords.

12. A Variation of the Half Knot Sennit

Tying 7 "left side" knots and 7 "right side" knots alternately will give the *illusion* of a twist and eliminate the necessity of reversing the cords every 7 knots, and keep the sennit from twisting.

13. Square Knot Sennit

Tying Square Knots in succession produces the braid illustrated here. This sennit and others shown in the book are good as headbands, waistbands, key chains, guitar straps, etc., as well as being standard motifs of macramé.

When tying a sennit of any kind, it is easiest to pin the center cords to the knotting surface, since they will remain stationary all the time. When just tying one or two Square Knots with a group of cords, it is quicker just to lean against them or anchor them in a more temporary way.

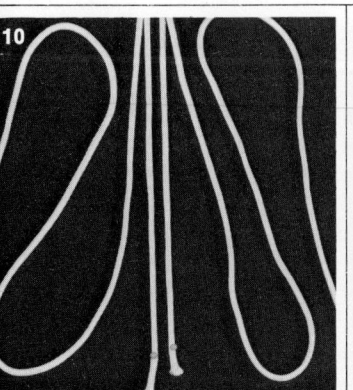 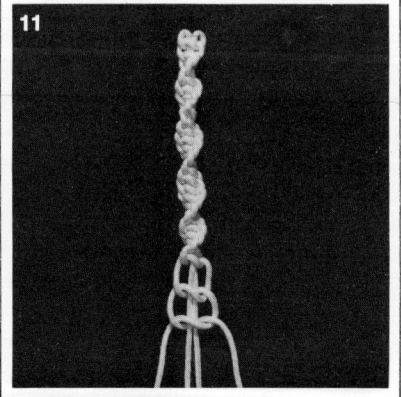 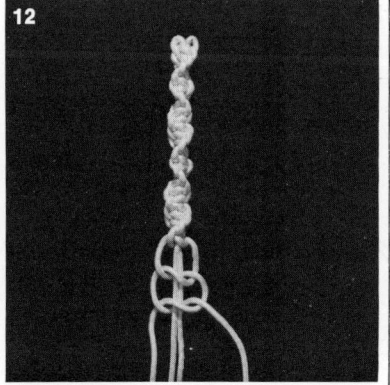 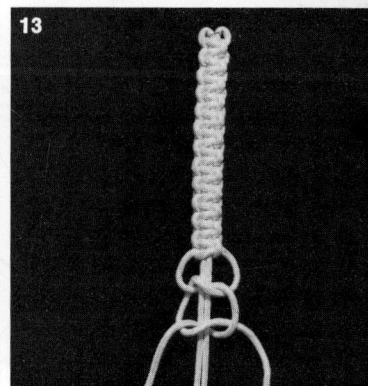

The Clove Hitch

The Clove Hitch is the other basic knot of macramé and probably the most versatile. It is used in making lines and bars, and it adds a strong design element to your pieces. It can be tied horizontally, diagonally, vertically, and in an endless variety of patterns.

Basically it is formed by tying 2 loops over a holding cord, which controls the direction of the line, and tying as many cords in a succession of double loops over the holding cord as needed for your pattern.

Practice this basic knot until you can make straight lines of fairly even tension. It is not hard to do and the knot is easily recognized in its many variations. Soon you'll be "reading" macramé just from looking at the pictures.

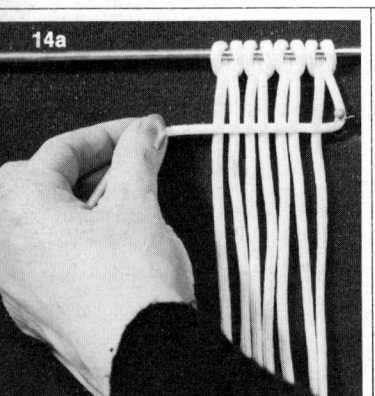 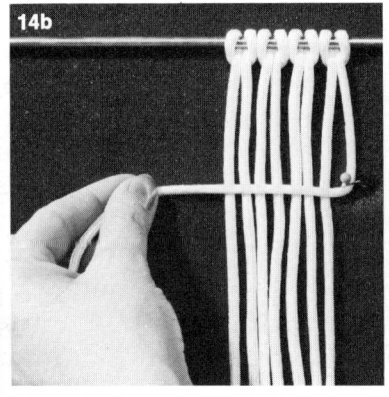 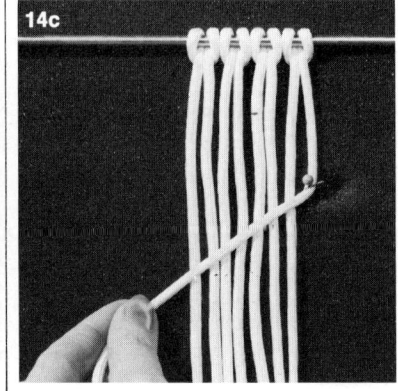 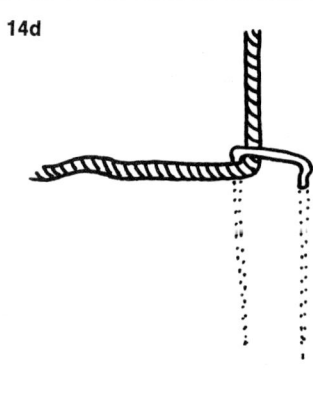

14. Pinning the Holding Cord

I cannot stress enough the importance of pinning the holding cord exactly where you want the line of Clove Hitches to start and then holding the holding cord *taut* and in exactly the direction you want the knots to go. The outside cord (left or right) is usually used for a holding cord. If you have several bars in a piece, this cord will be used up quickly, so when mounting cords, allow for it. However, adding new cords is simple. Several methods of adding new cords are discussed on pages 58–59.

A. If you want a row of Clove Hitches an inch below your mounting bar, you must pin the holding cord 1" from the bar and hold the cord straight across the *top* of the other cords (which are your tying cords).

B. See how pin determines where bar will start.

C. See how direction in which holding cord is held determines the direction of the line of knots.

D. If you are using ⊓-pins, place the pin just inside the point where you want the cord to be and push it all the way into the knotting surface.

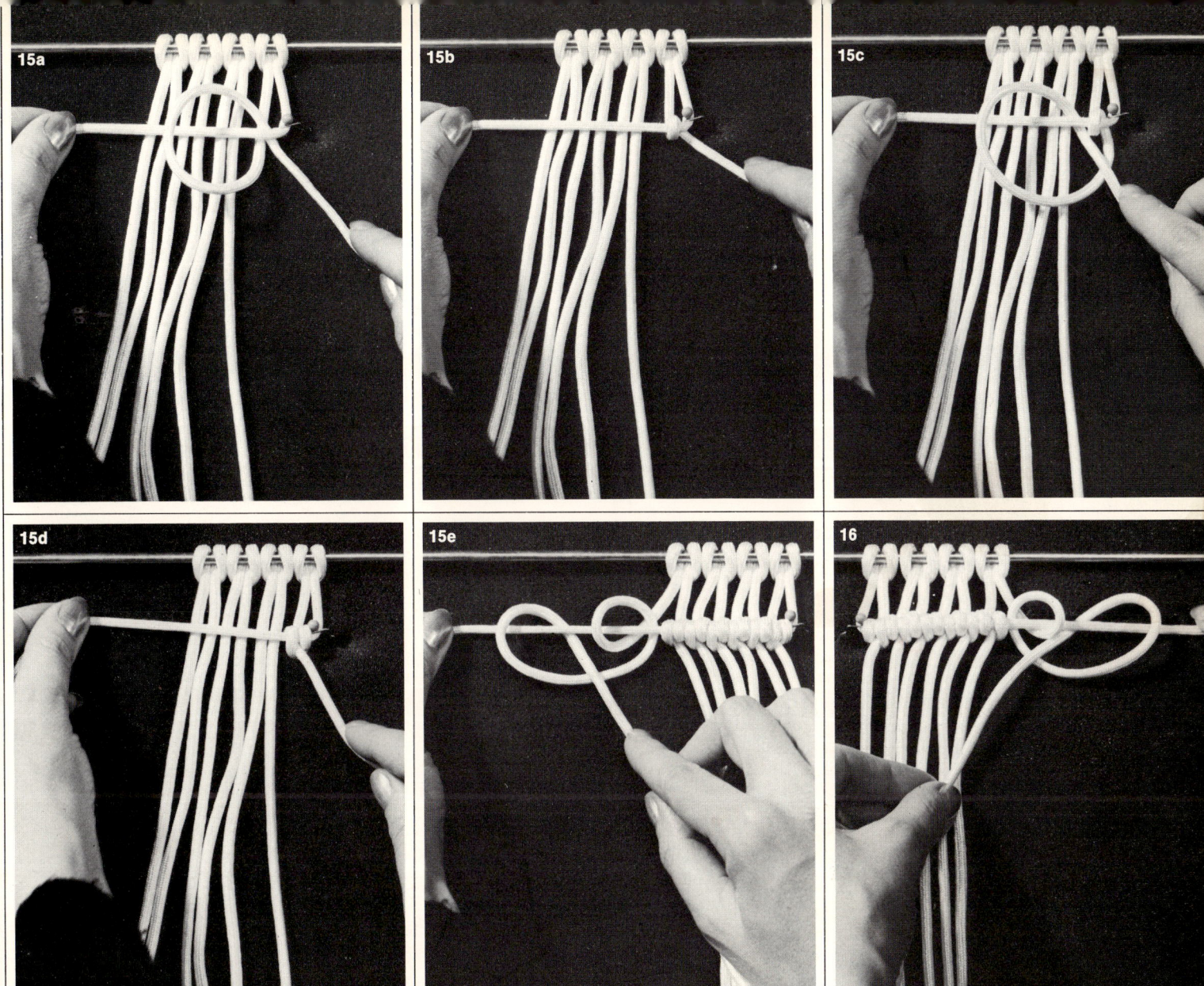

15. Clove Hitch Bar from Right to Left

The Clove Hitch requires tying 2 loops with *each cord in order* over the holding cord.

- A. Grasp the holding cord firmly in left hand and hold it parallel to the mounting bar over the top of the cords. Loop the next cord over the holding cord and back through the loop, pulling toward the right.
- B. Pull this knot somewhat tight.
- C. Make a second loop with the same cord.
- D. Pull it tight and secure the double loop.
- E. Continue across, making a double loop with each cord in succession.

16. Clove Hitch Bar from Left to Right

The procedure for making a Clove Hitch bar from left to right is the same. Here the right hand keeps the holding cord taut and the left hand ties, this time tying the loops toward the left. Practice tying the Clove Hitch in both directions until you can do it effortlessly.

- Note: If you make a mistake in a row of Clove Hitches—either by getting cords out of order or by tying too loosely—you can just pull the *holding* cord out from the beginning of the row instead of untying each knot. If your knots are tied properly, the holding cord can be pulled back and forth with little trouble.

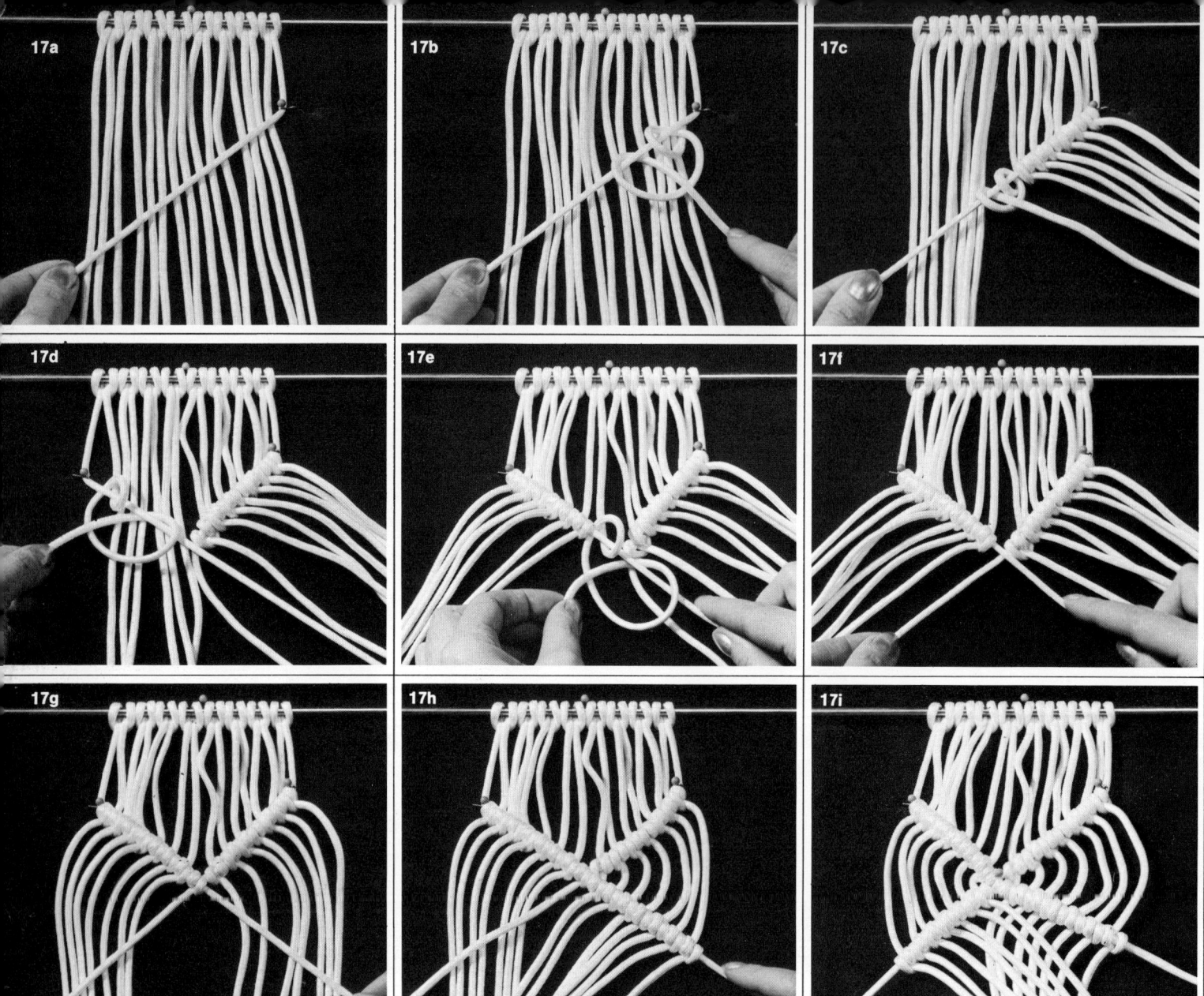

17. Diagonal Clove Hitch; X Pattern

There is nothing new to learning the diagonal Clove Hitch. It's all in maintaining the holding cord at the proper angle.

A. Pin your right-hand cord and hold at angle desired.

B. Tie Clove Hitches from right to left with each cord in succession, until you reach center of work (C).

D. Pin left-hand cord *exactly opposite* right-hand cord and tie Clove Hitches from left to right with each cord in succession until you reach center (E).

F. Crossover can be accomplished by tying the left holding cord in a Clove Hitch over the right holding cord, or vice versa. Here the left-hand cord is on top and will serve as holding cord.

G. The center knot is tied with the right-hand cord looped over the left.

H. The left cord continues to act as holding cord, and the remaining cords continue the X from left to right.

I. The right-hand holding cord is retrieved, and the rest of the cords are tied over it to complete the X.

18. Closing a Double Bar of Clove Hitches

When you complete a double row of Clove Hitches, one end of the bar is closed and it is sometimes desirable to close the other end.

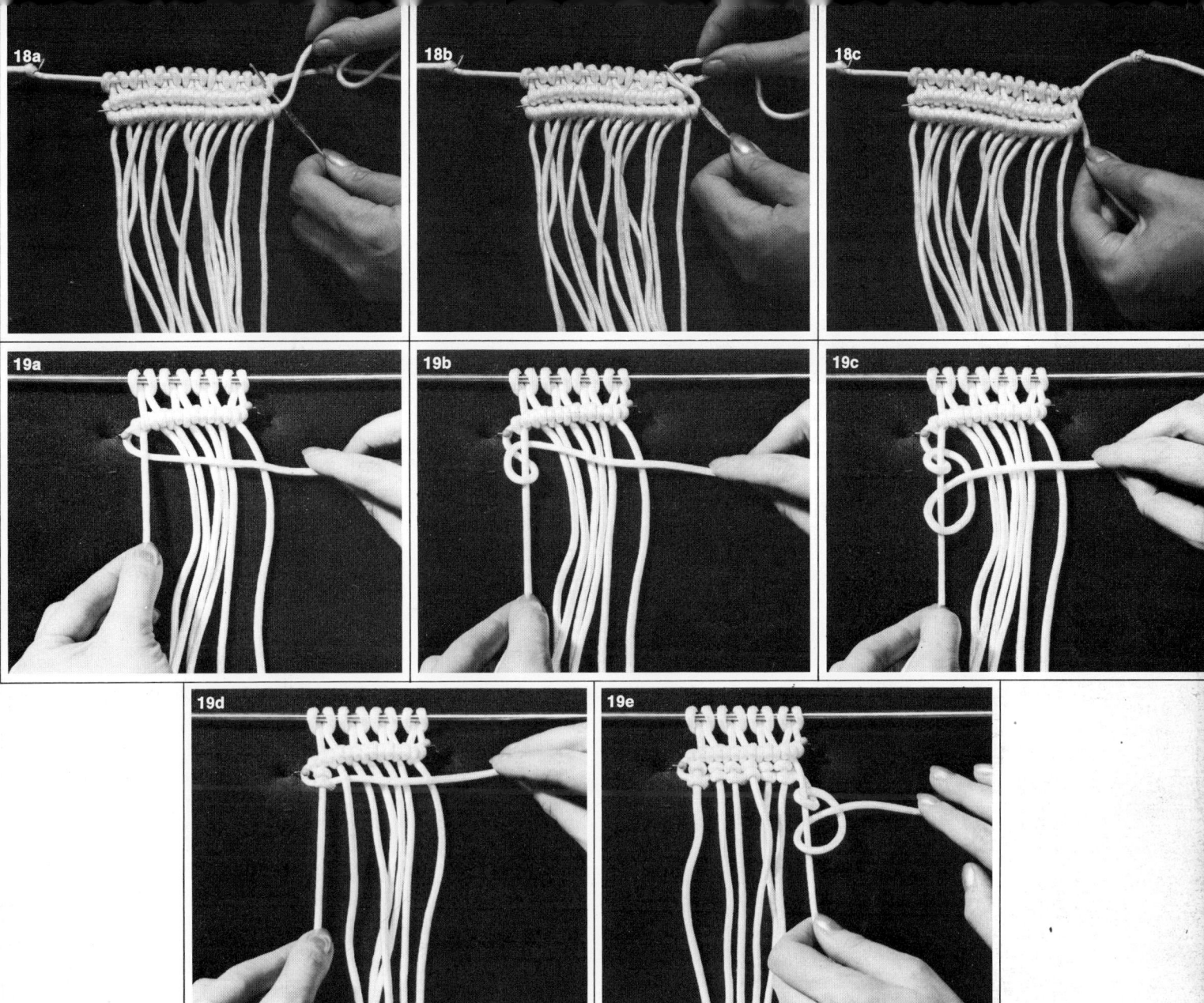

A. A crochet hook is useful here. With the hook, reach up through the first Clove Hitch of the top row from back to front.

B. Grasp the holding cord used for the double bar with the crochet hook.

C. Pull it through.

Vertical Clove Hitch

In the vertical Clove Hitch, one cord—formerly the holding cord—does all the tying and the other cords become the holding cords in turn as the bar is formed. The tying cord will be used up very quickly, so allow for this when mounting.

19. Vertical Clove Hitch from Left to Right

A. Pin the tying cord as for a row of regular Clove Hitches, but put the cord *under* the cord *next* to it.

B. Holding the vertical cord taut in your left hand (it is now the holding cord), loop the tying cord behind and through the loop toward your right with your right hand, pulling upward.

C. Complete the double loop.

D. The completed knot.

E. Continue across row, putting tying cord *under* the holding cord before starting each knot.

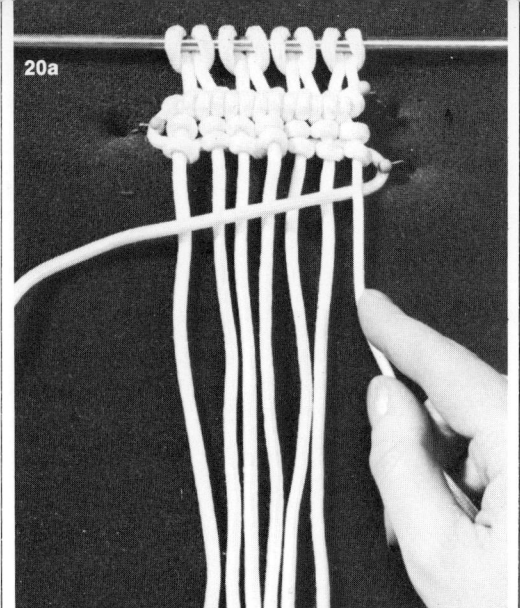
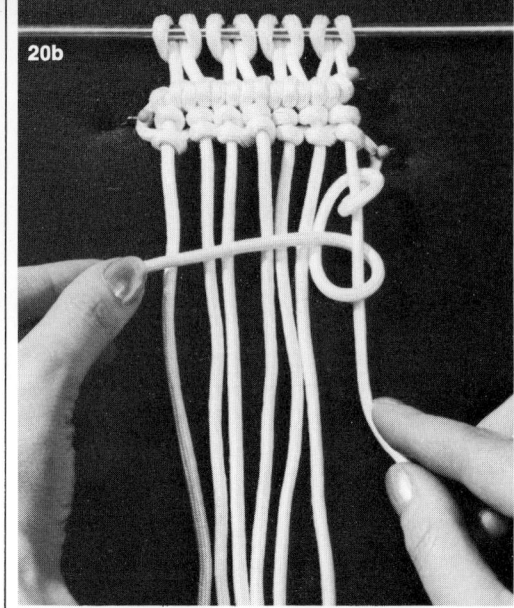
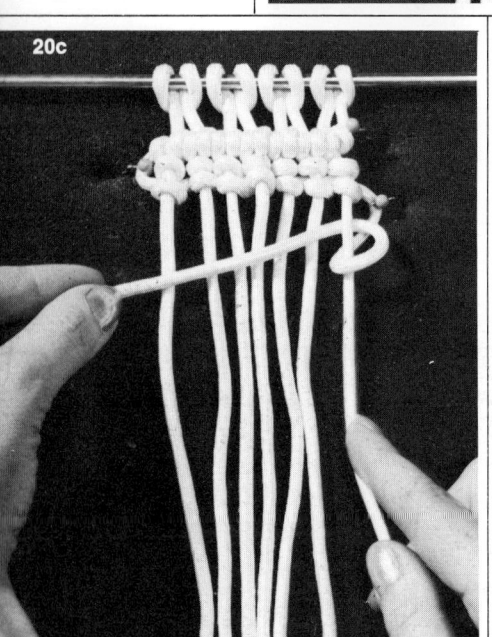
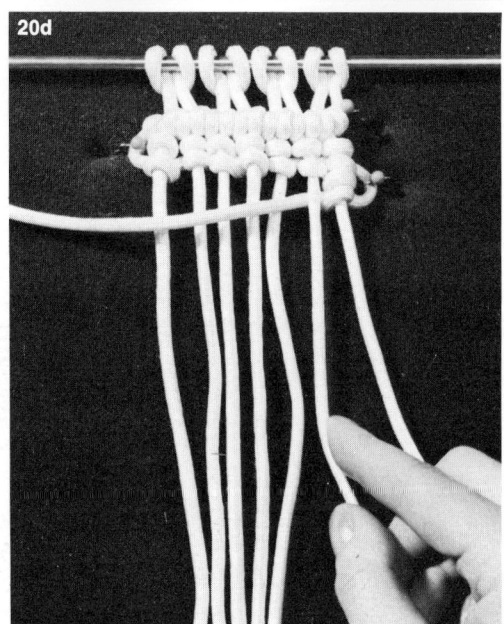
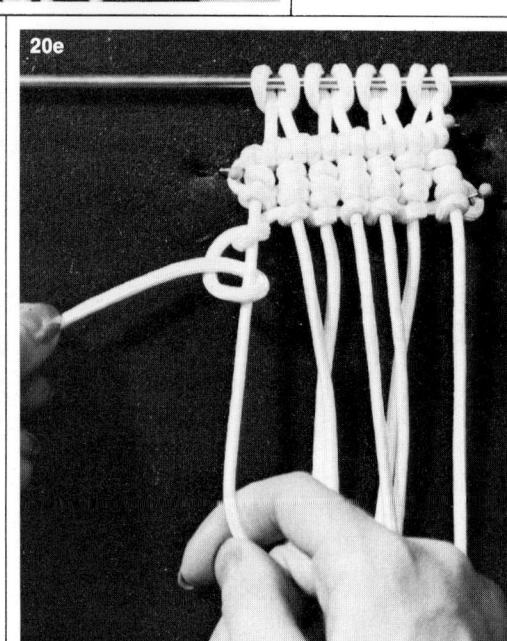

20. Vertical Clove Hitch from Right to Left

    A. Pin the tying cord and place it *under* the first holding cord, holding it taut with your right hand.

    B. Loop the tying cord behind the holding cord and through the loop to your left with your left hand, pulling upward.

    C. Finish the knot with a second loop.

    D. The completed knot.

    E. Continue across row. Remember to start each knot *under* the holding cord and hold each cord taut.

The Overhand Knot

This simple knot, which you've tied hundreds of times before, has many practical uses in macramé as an aid in mounting and finishing work, and also as a design element.

21. A. Overlap the ends of the cord.
    B. Pull the right end under the overlap and through the loop.
    C. Tighten.

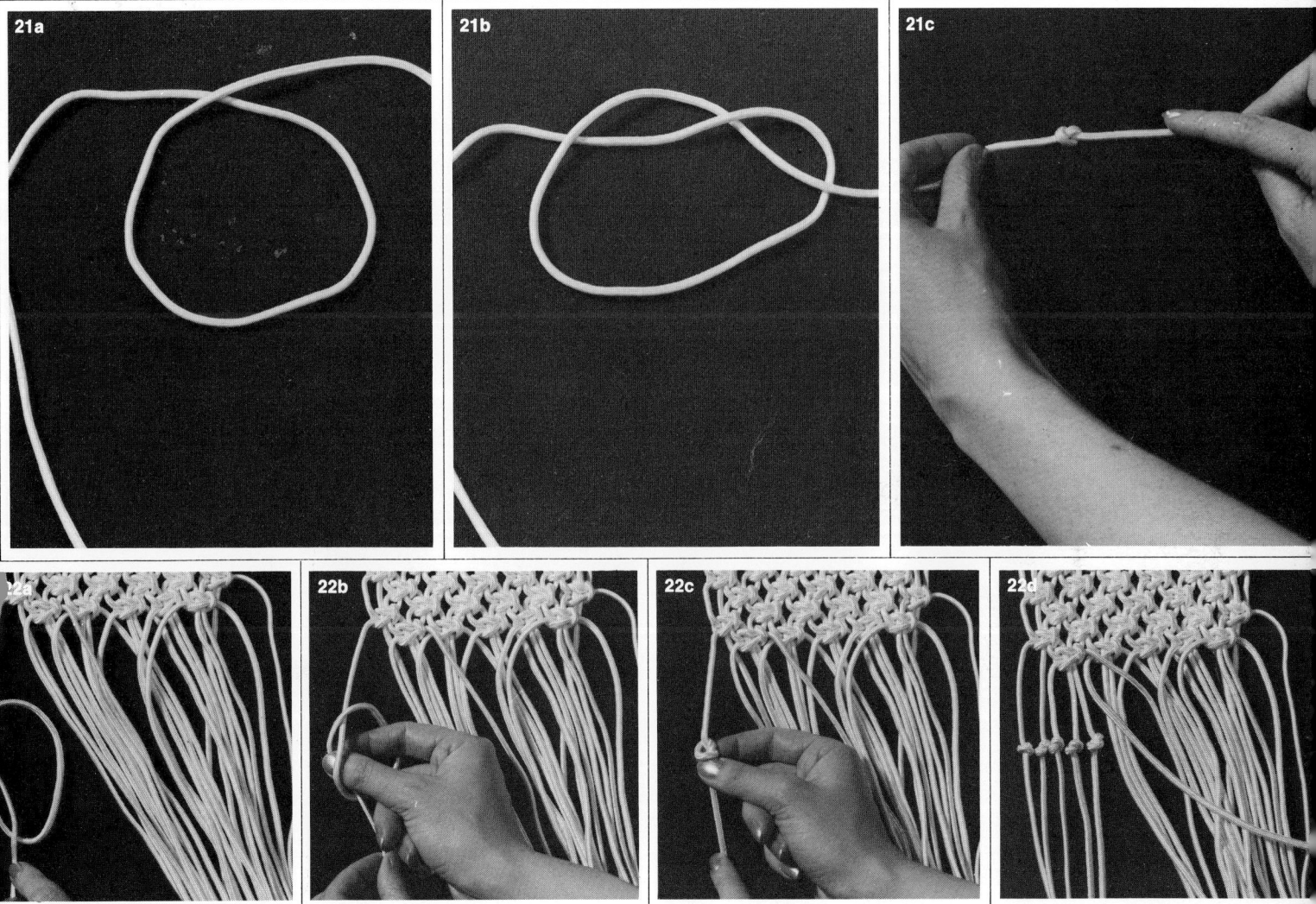

Using Overhand Knots to Finish Work

22. A. Overhand Knots are often used to finish a piece. With a little practice they can be tied to any position desired, such as a straight line or curve.
    B. The secret is to keep your thumb inside the loop as you push it into place.
    C. Then it can't tighten until you release it.
    D. An even row of overhand knots.

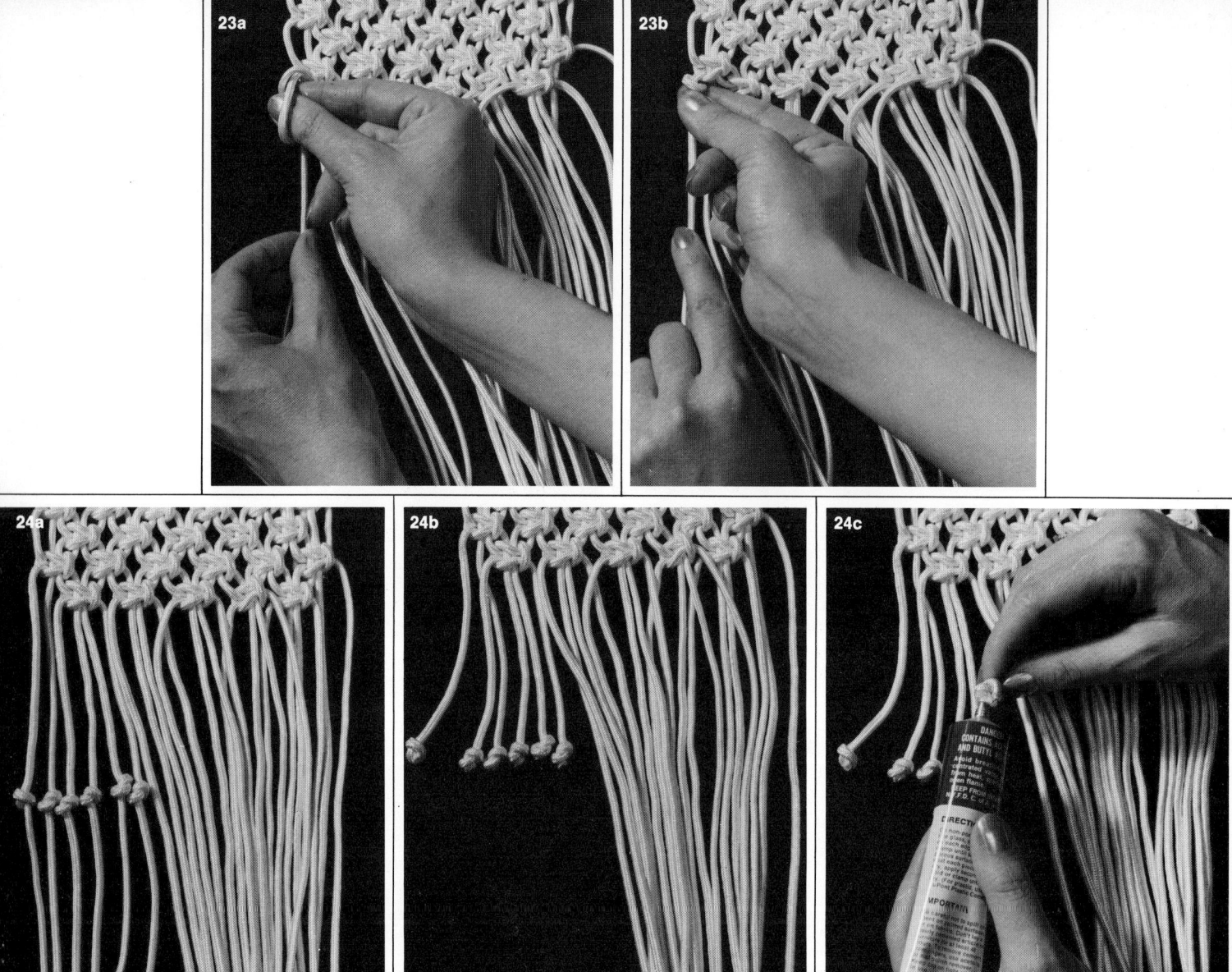

23. Another way of finishing a piece is to tie Overhand Knots in the cord and push them tightly against the piece, if a fringe is not desired.

    A. Be sure to keep the end of your thumb inside loop as you push it along.

    B. Release and tighten against work at last minute.

Cutting and Gluing

24. A. An even row of Overhand Knots is a nice way to end a piece.

    B. Cut the ends just below the knot (especially if the cord is of a type that will fray).

    C. Put a dab of glue on the end of the knot to prevent untying.

    Note: In a finished piece, especially in a fairly heavy hanging, it helps to reinforce it on the back with glue in strategic places—Josephine Knots, long double bars of Clove Hitches, etc.—any place where there is extra stress.

MORE ABOUT EVERYTHING

Everything Else You'll Need to Know to Do the Projects

Now you know how to do macramé. In this section you'll learn many new combinations of the basic knots, a couple of new knots, new ways to start macramé pieces, how to use beads and rings, and ways to finish and fringe macramé. Almost everything in this section will be used in at least one of the projects.

I'll say it again: don't be in a big rush to get to the projects. Keep working with your sampler cords, and duplicate each pattern as you go. The more practice you get now the easier the projects will be later. Besides, detailed instructions for each new step are given in this section; the directions for the projects will just refer you back here.

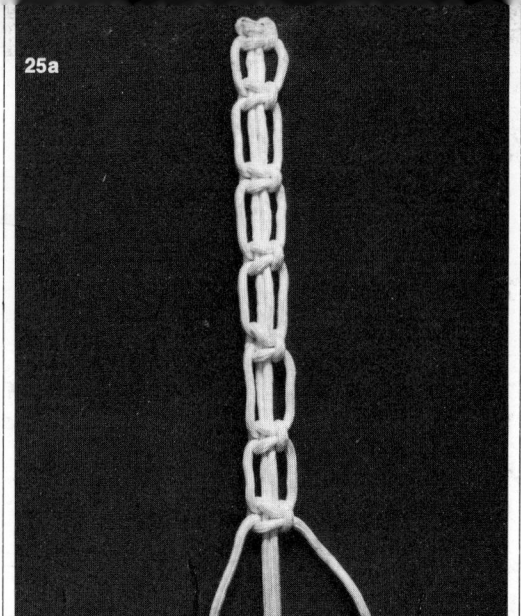
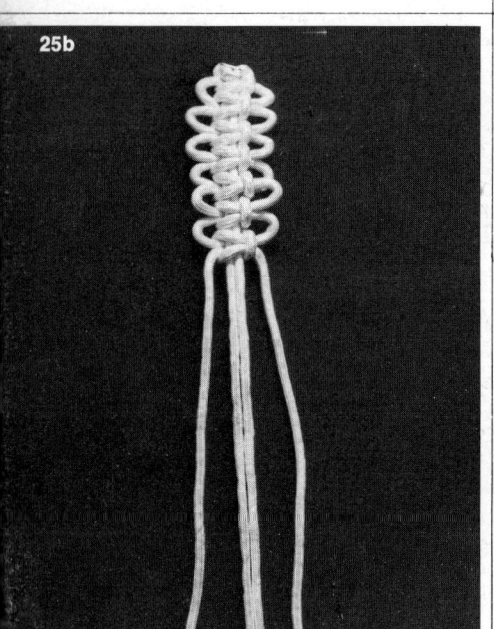
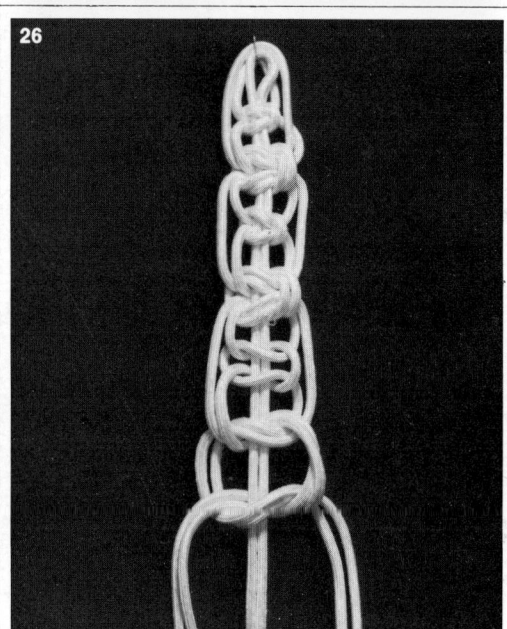
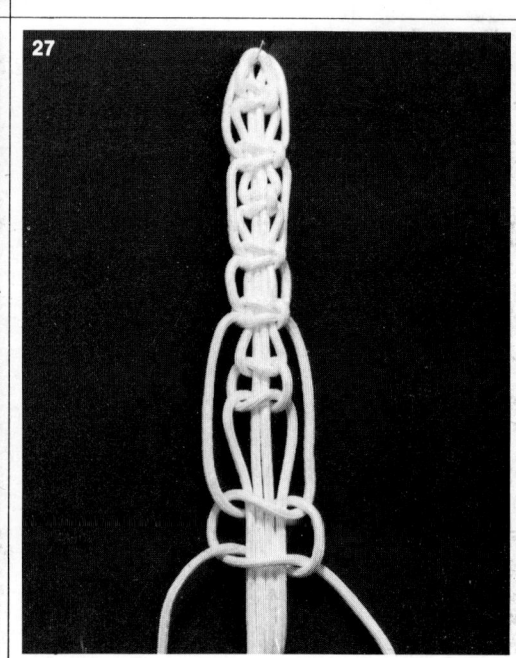

More About Square Knots

On the following pages you'll see the Square Knot in many of its most common sennits and patterns. Learn to recognize them.

Square Knot Sennits

25. A. The distance between Square Knots is easily controlled as you tie. Be sure to tie a complete Square Knot before leaving a space.

    B. Spaced Square Knots will slide easily up and down the center cords. Sennit A gives a loop-edged effect if the knots are pushed tightly together on the center cords.

26. Here is a sennit made by alternately tying a Square Knot with 6 cords—2 on each side over 2 center cords—followed by a regular 4-cord Square Knot with the 4 inner cords (the outside 2 cords "circling" the small Square Knot).

27. This sennit also uses 6 cords. A Square Knot with one cord on each side is tied around 4 center cords, then a regular 4-cord Square Knot is tied with the 4 inner cords (the outside 2 cords again "circle" the small Square Knot).

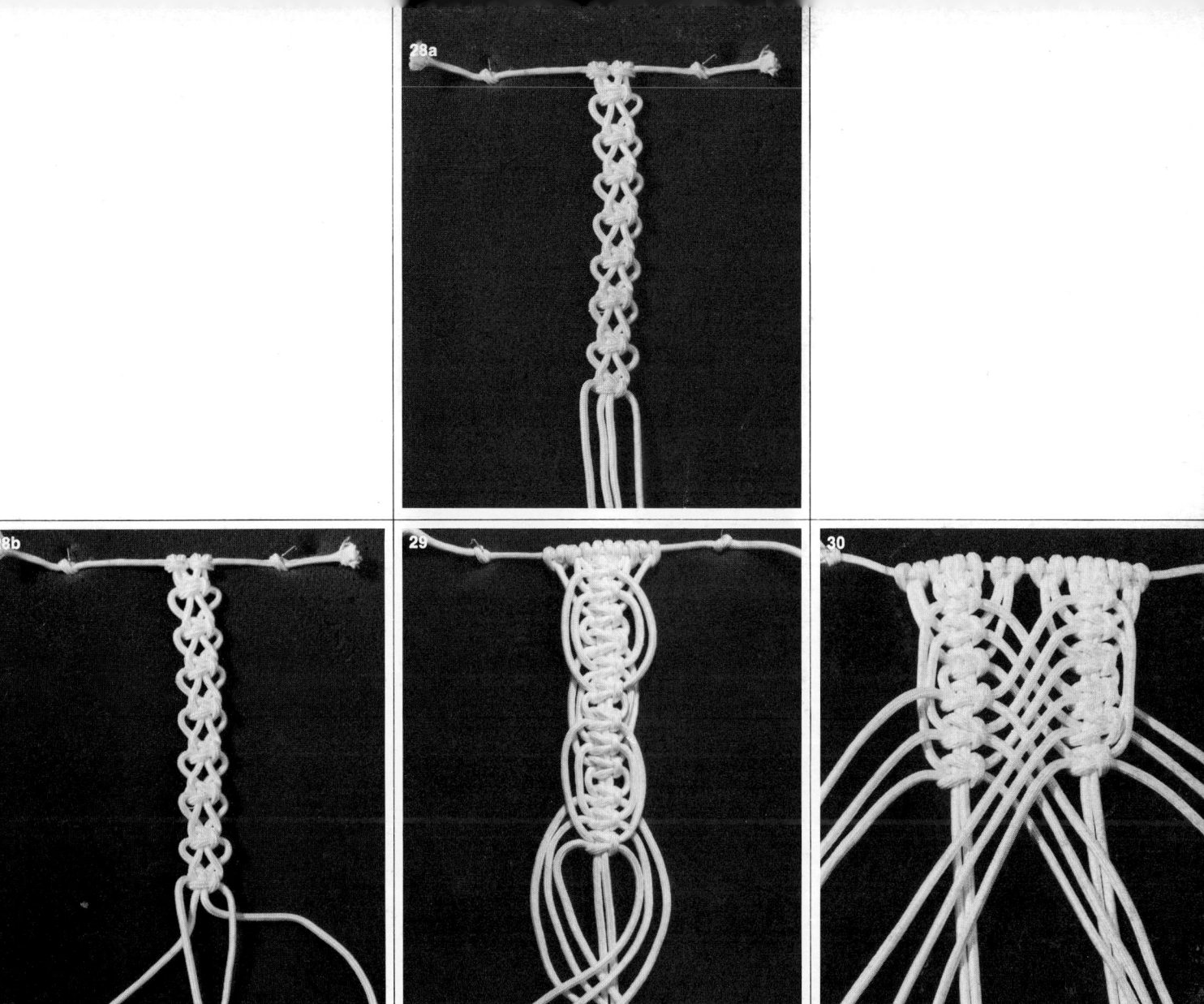

28. A. In this Square Knot sennit, the inside and outside cords are switched with each knot, the tying cords of the first knot becoming the center cords of the second knot, and so on.

    B. Besides being attractive, this is a useful braid when you want to use up cord lengths equally or haven't allowed for longer cords on the outside of your braid.

29. This lacy Square Knot sennit is tied with 8 cords.

    Tie a Square Knot using the four center cords (3, 4, 5, 6).

    Keeping 4 and 5 as the center cords, now tie a Square Knot with the next two cords closest to the center four (2 and 7), leaving a little loop around the outside of the previous knot.

    Still with 4 and 5 as center cords, finally tie a Square Knot with the outside two cords (1 and 8), again leaving a loop. Cords 1 and 8 are now closest to the center.

    Continue the pattern by taking the cords now closest to the center cords (1 and 8) and tying a Square Knot. Continue this sequence. Each three Square Knots will form one section of the pattern. Of course it can be made with any number of cords.

30. This pattern is made the same way as the previous one, but with two groups of 8 cords.

    Tie one section of 3 knots in each sennit, as instructed for the previous pattern. Then switch the inside 3 tying cords on each side and continue the pattern as before, being sure to keep the cords in order. Each time you tie a section of 3 knots, switch the inside 3 cords again.

31. Alternating Square Knots

A lot of basic information about Square Knot patterns can be learned from doing this sampler of 16 cords.

Alternating Square Knots are a basic macramé motif.

Tie 1 Square Knot using each 4 cords in succession so that you have 1 row of 4 Square Knots.

Now leave the 2 cords on the left and tie a Square Knot using each of the remaining 4 cords in succession. The 2 cords on the right will be left over and you will have tied knots using 2 cords each from the knots above.

To continue pattern, repeat the first step, tying a row of 4 Square Knots; each alternate row then leaves the 2 outside cords on each side hanging.

Decreasing Square Knots

To start, do the first two steps of the alternating Square Knot pattern, so you have a row of 4 and a row of 3 Square Knots. Now, just leave 2 more cords hanging on the left and right and you will have a row of 2. Leave 2 more cords left and right and you will have 1 Square Knot.

Increasing Square Knots

Tie a Square Knot with the center 4 cords (the same cords as the last Square Knot of your decreasing pattern).

Now, take 2 cords to the left of the cords used and the 2 left-hand cords of the Square Knot just tied, and tie a Square Knot. Do the same with the 2 right-hand cords and the next 2 cords to the right. Continue increasing each row by using the 2 closest cords to the left and right of the knots just tied.

Try tying the knots at even intervals apart to practice spacing your work.

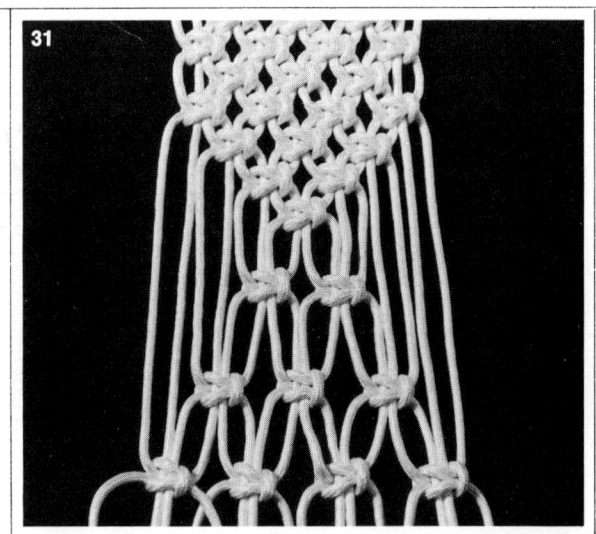

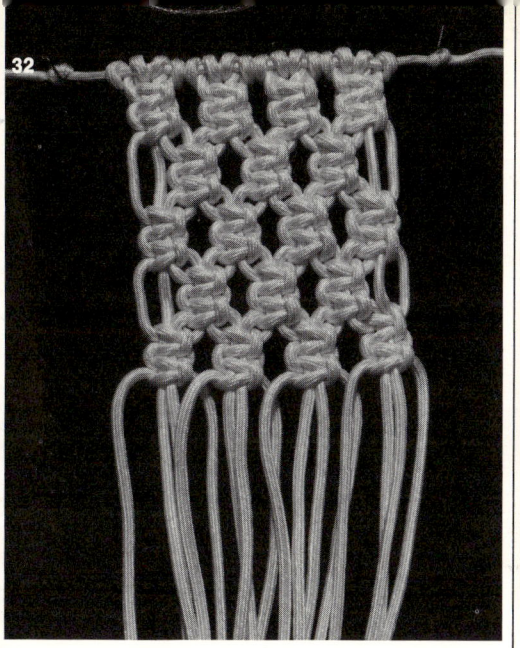 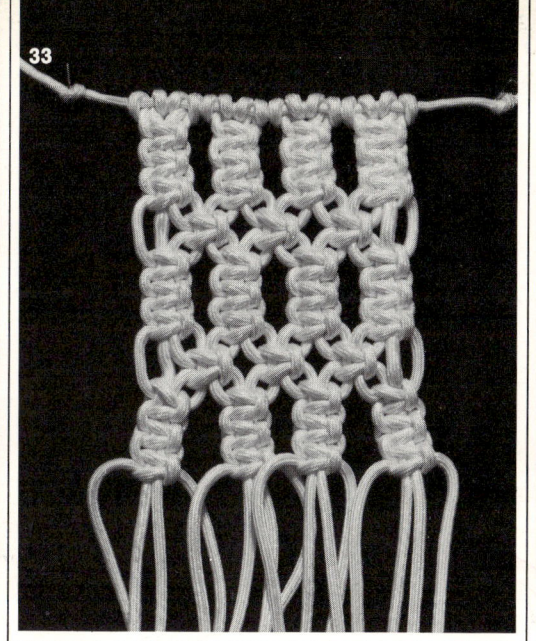 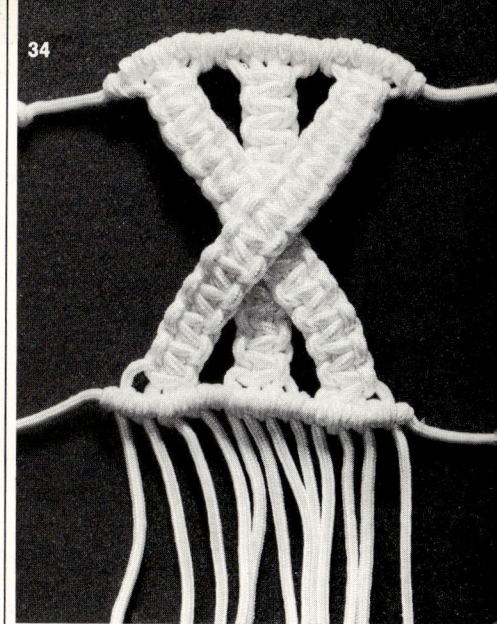

Square Knot Patterns

32. This is just the basic alternating Square Knot pattern, but with 2 knots tied each time in each row (2 rows of 4 Square Knots alternated with 2 rows of 3 Square Knots).

33. Here the Square Knots are alternated in a pattern of a row of 3 rows of 4 Square Knots followed by 1 row of 3 Square Knots.

34. Here 3 Square Knot sennits are made, then the outside 2 sennits are crossed over each other. A new cord is added for a row of Clove Hitches to hold the pattern in place. Be sure to keep your cords in order when tying the bottom row of Clove Hitches.

35. **Square Knot Bobble**

    Here is a simple decorative "button" made with the Square Knot.

    A. Depending on how large you want your button to be, tie a sennit of 4 to 6 Square Knots. *Important note:* the bobble will end up at the point where you tie the *first* Square Knot, so place it carefully.

    B. Take the center cords and put them through the center of the 4 cords, above the first knot.

    C. Pull the cord through and down tightly behind so that the sennit loops back over itself, forming a button.

    D. Tie one more Square Knot *tightly* up against the bobble to hold it in place.

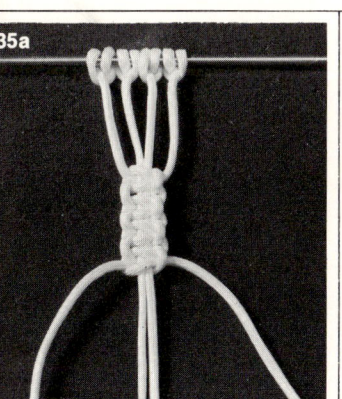 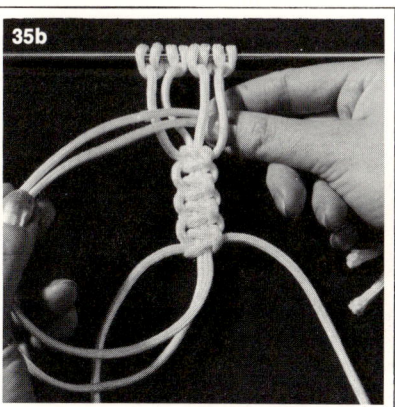 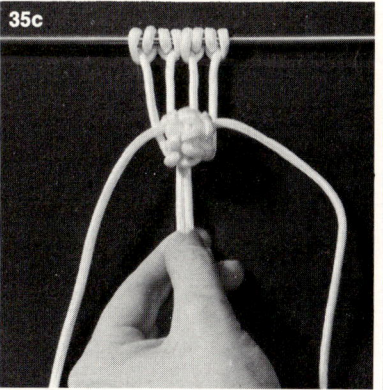 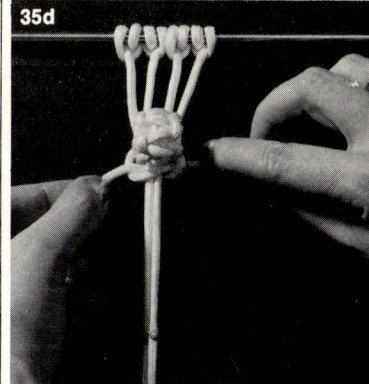

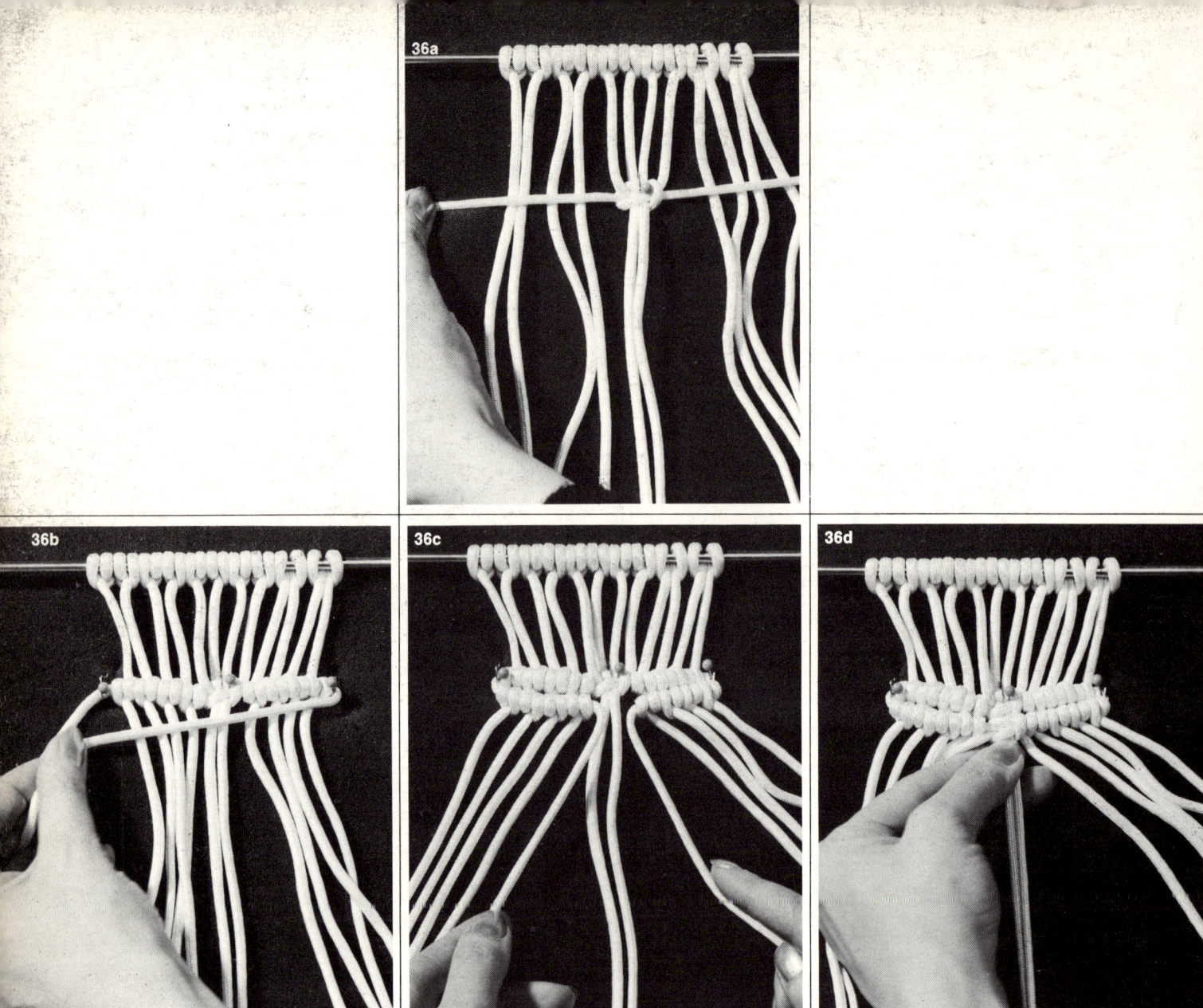

More About Clove Hitches

Now you'll really see the versatility of this knot! Bars, diamonds, sennits, solid patterns, and chevrons are all the work of this double loop.

36. Double Bar of Clove Hitches Starting in Center

A. When making 2 rows of Clove Hitches, especially long rows, I find it easier to start from a Square Knot in the center, leaving the center cords hanging.

B. Tie a row of Clove Hitches out to each side and pin.

C. Tie row of Clove Hitches back to the center on each side, again letting the center cords hang.

D. Use the holding cords from both sides to tie a Square Knot over the 2 center cords. Tie this knot tight and push it right up into the row of Clove Hitches. In this way both ends of the double bar are closed.

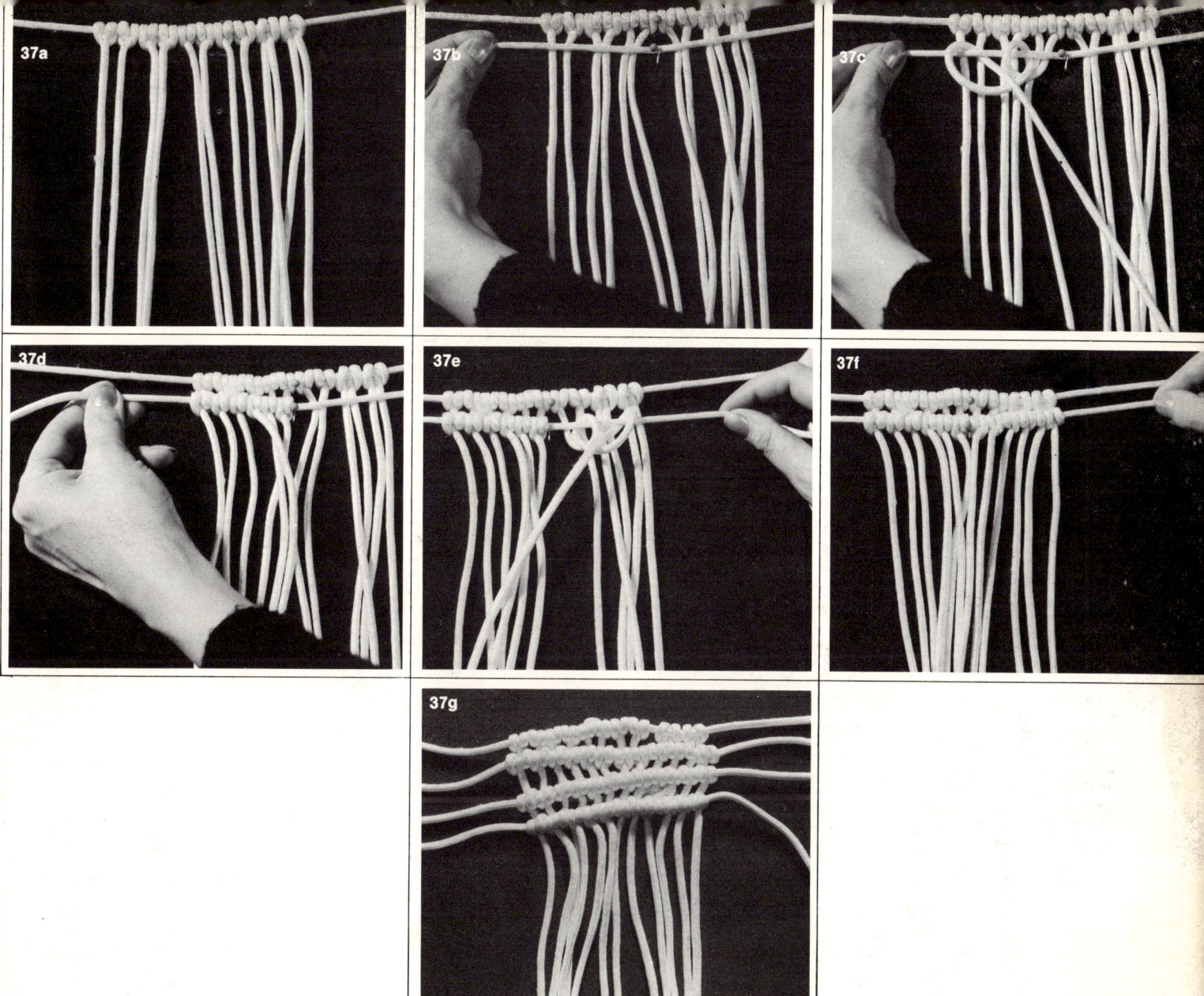

37. Adding Separate Cords with the Clove Hitch

Besides being one way of adding a cord, this is a good motif for several purposes: the added cords can be a choker to be knotted around your neck, can form the center of a belt, or be added as a waistband. This method is used in several projects.

A. Mount cords by the Double Lark's Head method shown on page 47.

B. Pin a second cord close to the first holding cord at the center of the work and to the right of the knots.

C. Tie a row of Clove Hitches from the center to the left side (D).

E. Move the right-hand pin to the left side and tie a row of Clove Hitches from the center to the right (F).

G. Add as many rows as you wish. I prefer working from the center because it's easier to maintain an even appearance, but all the Clove Hitches can be done from one side or the other.

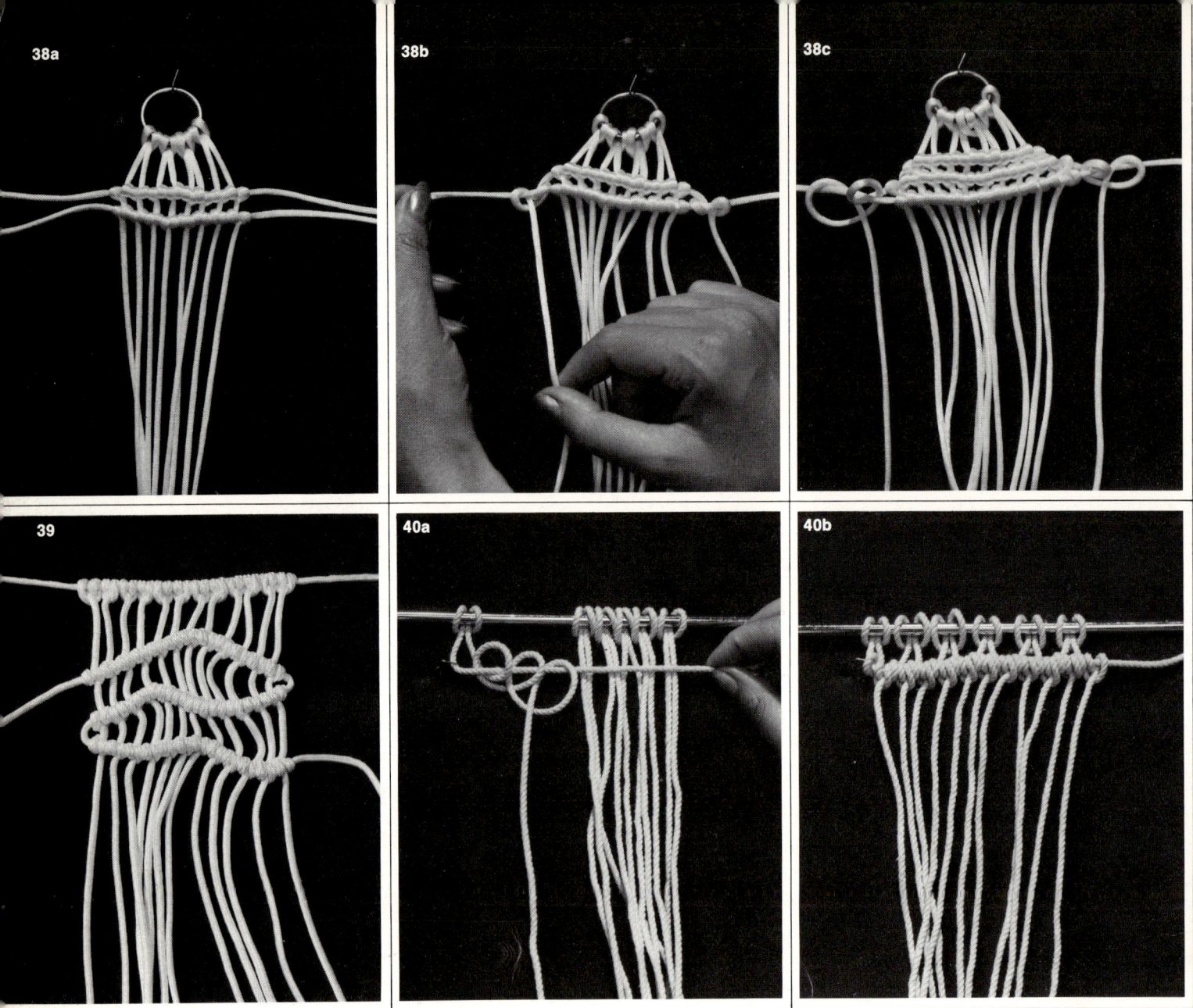

38. A piece is widened with new cords by Clove Hitching them on at the center point and incorporating the new cord by Clove Hitching on the cord above on each side as each new cord is added.

39. Random or Asymmetrical Holding Cord

Clove Hitches can be tied in random asymmetrical patterns by holding or pinning the holding cord in different directions as you work.

40. Triple Hitch

The Triple Hitch is just the Clove Hitch with an extra loop—3 loops are tied with each cord. It is especially useful when you want to widen a piece without the use of beads or new cords.

Diamond Pattern

Another basic motif of macramé, the diamond, is simply the diagonal Clove Hitch using the 2 center cords as holding cords, tying a row of Clove Hitches out to the sides, and pinning and tying diagonal rows back into the center using the same holding cords.

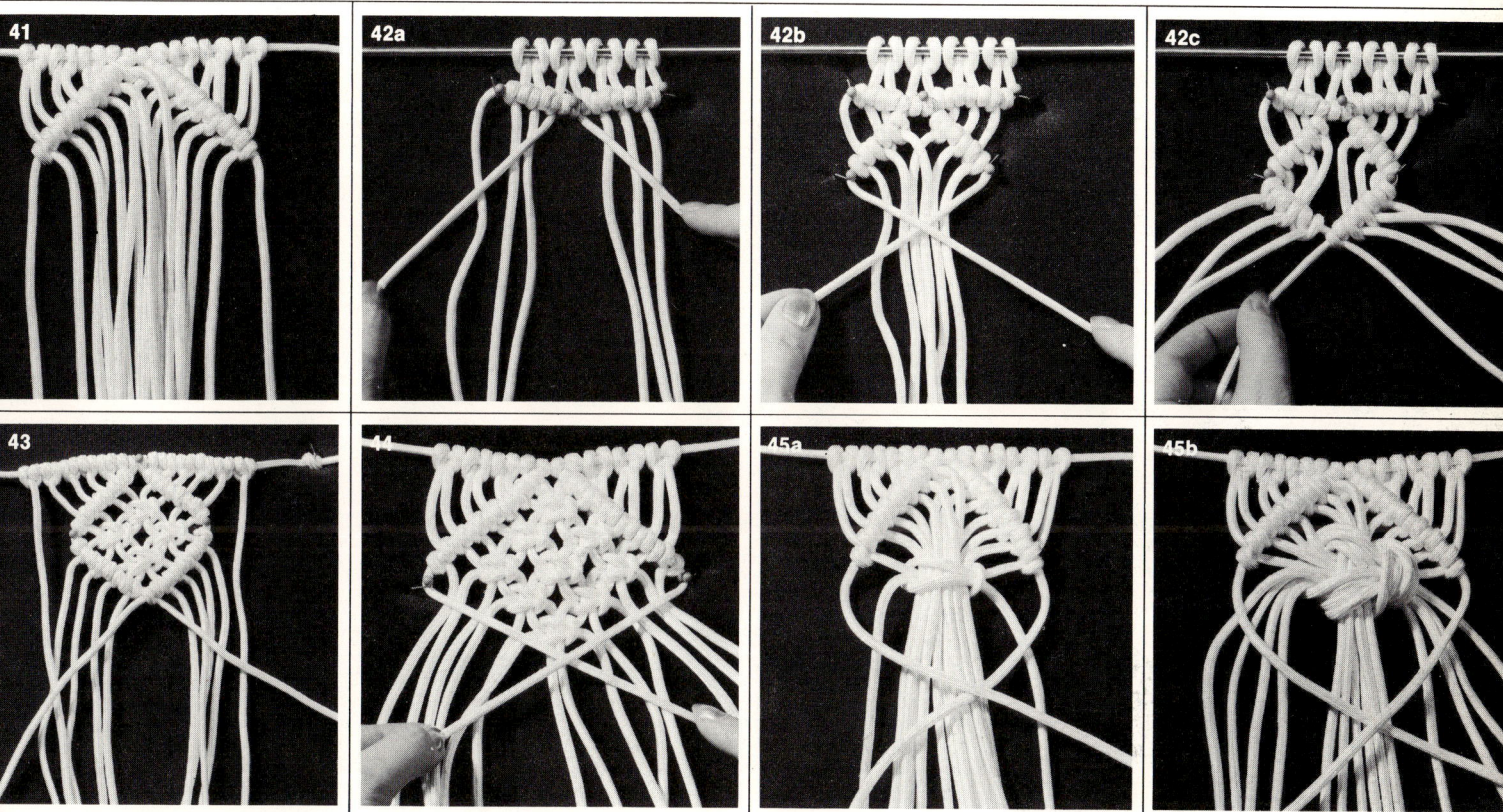

41. If any design is to appear inside the diamond, it of course has to be knotted at this point.

42. Here is a small diamond pattern using 8 cords.
    A. Use the 2 center cords to tie a row of diagonal Clove Hitches out to each side.
    B. Pin the holding cords at the outside point and tie a row of diagonal Clove Hitches back to the center.
    C. Close the diamond by using 1 holding cord to tie a last Clove Hitch over the other.

Motifs Inside Diamond Patterns

43. Infinite variety can be achieved inside the diamond pattern. Here is a pattern of alternating Square Knots: 1, 2, and 1.

44. More alternating Square Knots inside a larger diamond pattern: 1, 2, 3, 2, and 1.

45. A. Cords inside a diamond caught with a large Square Knot tied with 1 outside cord on each side.
    B. The same pattern but using 4 outside cords on each side of the Square Knot.

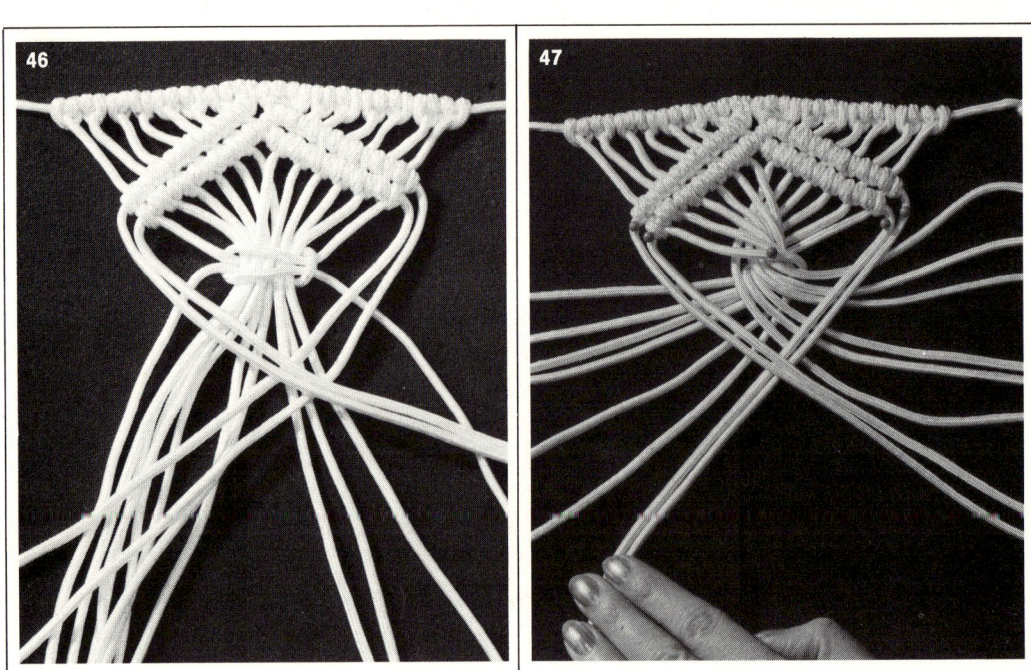

46. The beginning of a double bar diamond with a Square Knot in the center.

    A double bar diamond is started in the same way as a single diamond, with the 2 center cords as holding cords. The inside diamond is formed with the 2 inside cords which remain *after* the outside diamond is formed—the right-hand inside cord acting as holding cord for the left side, then vice versa.

    When knotting the bottom of the double diamond, the inside diamond is of course knotted first and crossed over where the two sides meet. Then the outside holding cords are knotted, and the holding cords from the inside diamond are incorporated. It sounds much more complicated than it is. Just try it.

47. Another diamond motif simply involves twisting the left-hand cords around the right-hand cords (or vice versa), bringing the cords back to their original side, and Clove Hitching them back into the bottom of the diamond pattern in order. If you are careful in making the twist, the cords do not have to be exactly in order to give the *illusion* of being so.

    Note: Before beginning to Clove Hitch the bottom of the diamond, pin the twist in place firmly so it will not pull out of position as you tie.

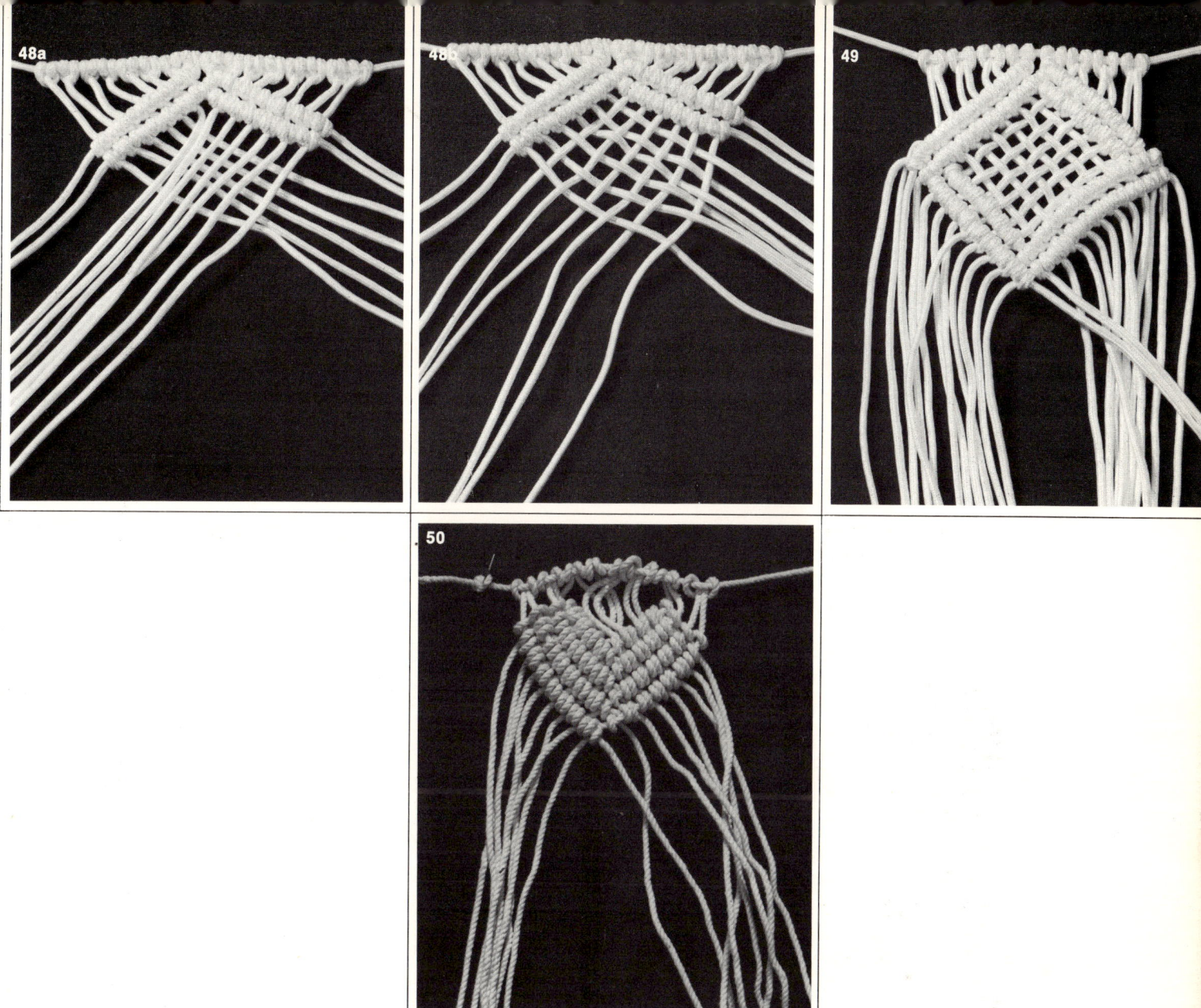

48. Here are two more interesting diamond patterns.

   A. Cross the cords inside the left of the diamond over the cords from the right (or vice versa).

   B. Or, weave the left and right cords together in a simple over-and-under pattern. This can easily be done by hand or with a crochet hook.

   Note: One simple way of weaving is to Clove Hitch the cords from one side into the bottom of the diamond, then weave the cords from the other side through them while the cords are taut.

49. Completed double diamond with woven center design.

50. Chevron Pattern

Consecutive V's of diagonal Clove Hitch bars will form a chevron pattern. There's no trick to it, but always Clove Hitch either the left to right bar or the right to left bar first, and make the crossover in the same manner each time so the overlap is consistent.

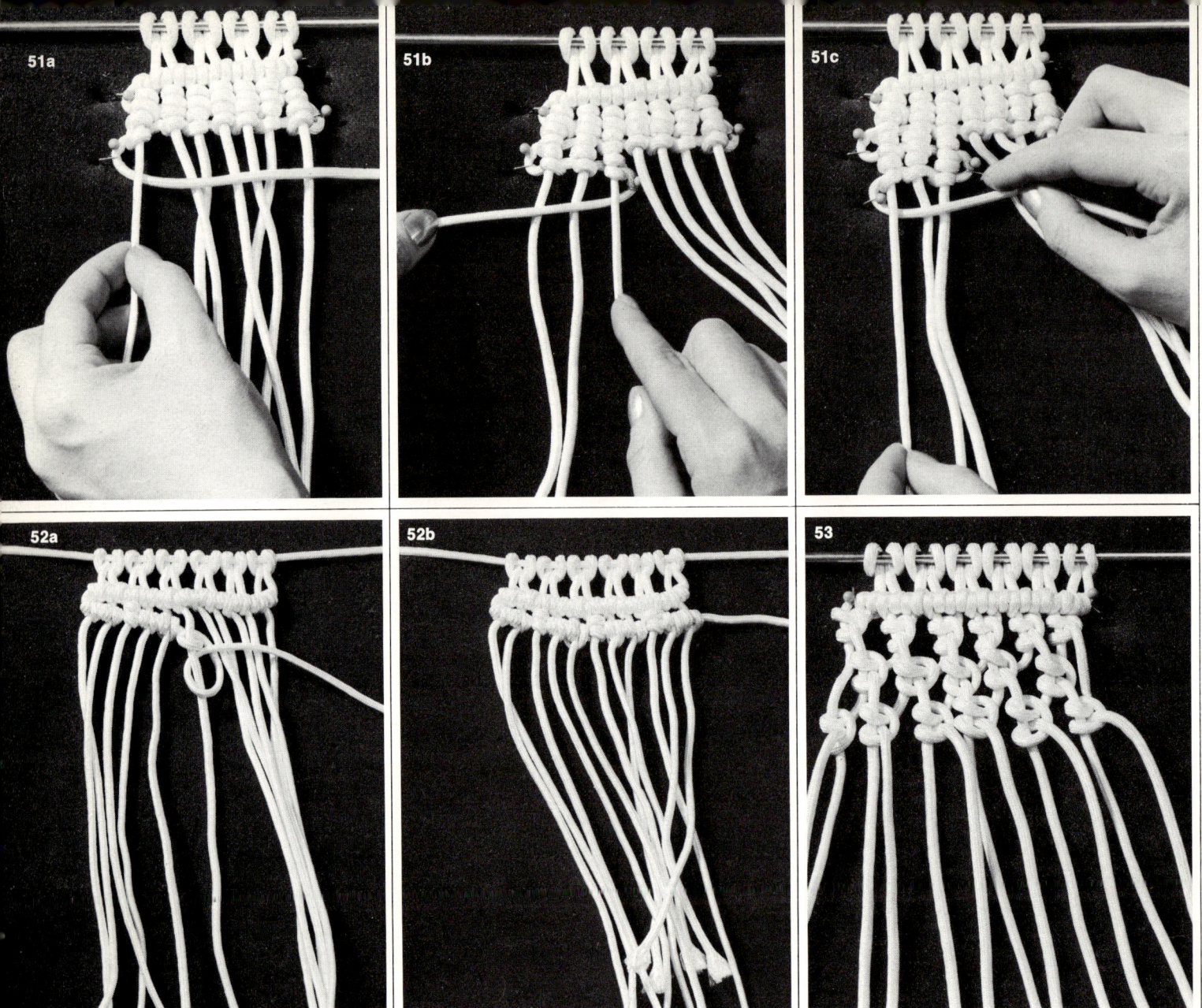

More Vertical Clove Hitches

51. This sequence shows how you can go back and forth with vertical Clove Hitches just by pinning and turning the tying cord where you wish.

52. A. In the middle of a row of Clove Hitches, a vertical Clove Hitch is tied—the holding cord becomes the tying cord by placing it under the cord.

    B. The row is completed with regular and vertical Clove Hitches. Of course any variation or number of Clove Hitches can be used in a particular row.

    Note: This is a particularly useful trick when working with color; see pages 63–64.

53. **Alternate Vertical Clove Hitches**

    Here, Vertical Clove Hitches are tied with each 2 cords across a row, the left cord tying over the right cord. Then the outside cord is dropped, and 1 cord from each knot in the row above is used to tie the second row, the left cords again acting as tiers.

    This of course is the same idea as alternate Square Knots, except with 2-cord groups instead of 4-cord groups.

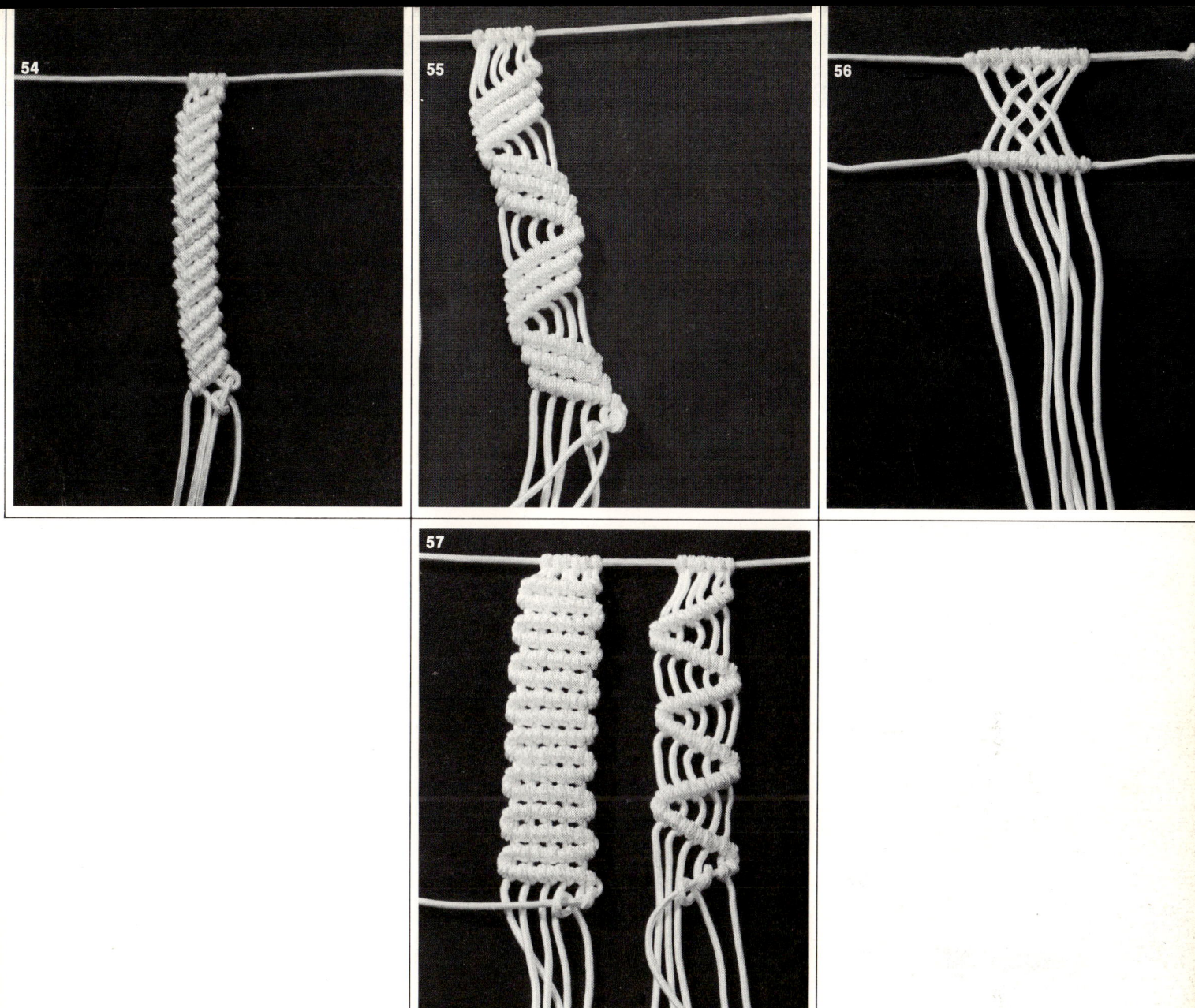

Clove Hitch Sennits

54. Here is a sennit of Clove Hitches tied with 4 cords.

    The right-hand cord always becomes the holding cord for the next row, and the holding cord from the previous row (now on the left side) is Clove Hitched in. Rows are tied close together for this solid pattern, but could be spaced at even intervals with pins.

55. Here, 3 rows of diagonal Clove Hitches are tied from right to left—the right-hand cord always acting as holding cord and the holding cord from the previous row always Clove Hitched in as the last knot in the row. Then 3 rows are tied from left to right in the same manner.

56. Crossed vertical cords—or braided or woven, or whatever—can be held in place with the next row of Clove Hitches: watch the order of the cords to get them straight.

57. The sennit at left of photo is tied using one holding cord winding from left to right—you have to allow for this long holding cord when mounting, of course.

    The sennit at right of photo is tied in the same way except the holding cord is held at an angle for diagonal Clove Hitches.

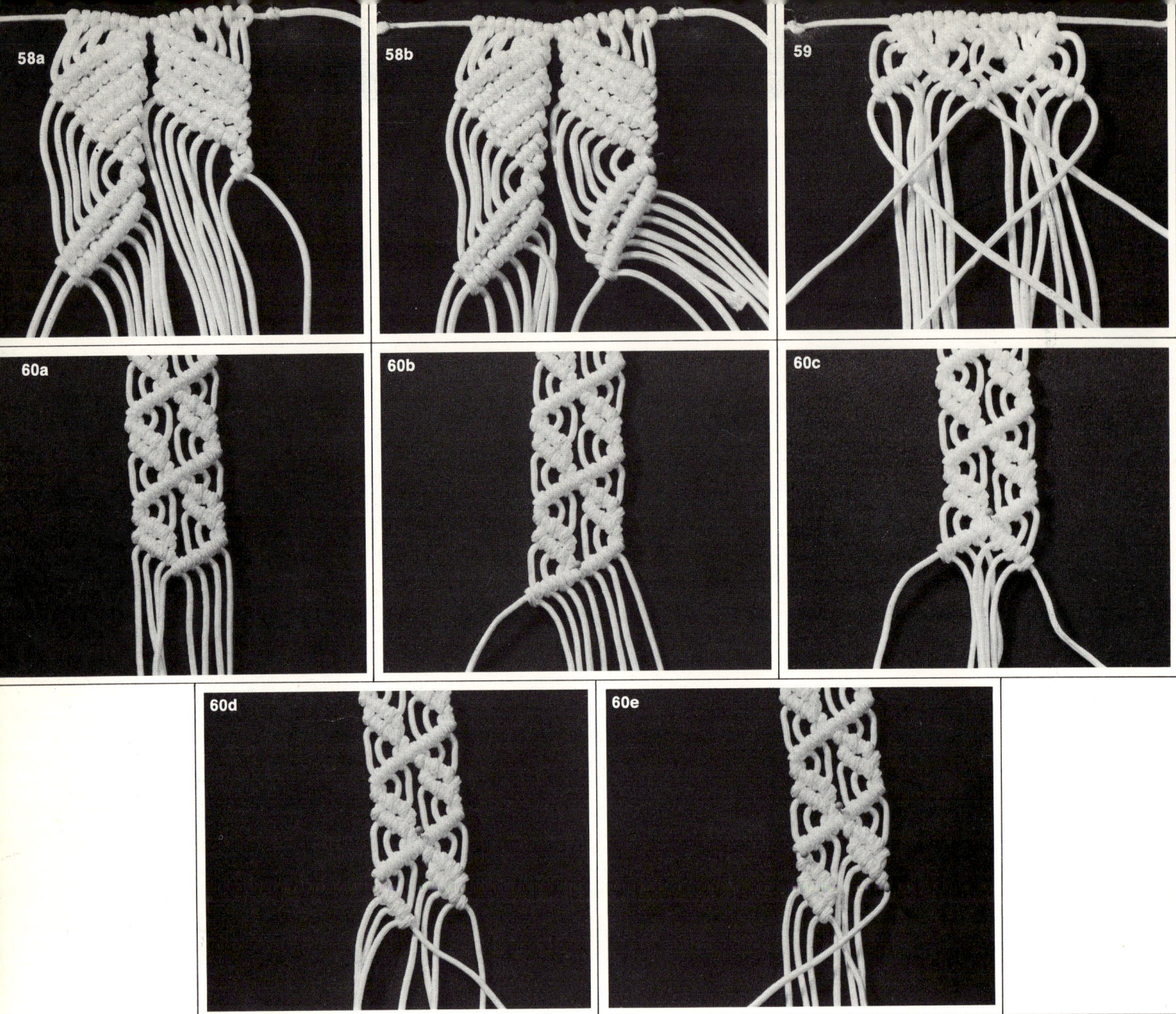

Clove Hitch Patterns

58. The pattern on the left in 58A and 58B is made with consecutive rows of diagonal Clove Hitches using the right-hand cord as the holding cord each time, and *leaving out* the holding cord from the row above. The pattern is repeated exactly the same.

   The pattern on the right in each photo is the same—consecutive rows of diagonal Clove Hitches using the left-hand cord as holding cord each time, but *including* the holding cord from the row above as the last knotting cord in each row. The pattern is repeated in the other direction by taking the holding cords from the *right* for the next sequence.

59. A double X pattern is created by having the holding cords from the left X and right X cross over.

60. A. Here is a variation of the diamond or X pattern—single bars from right to left, and double bars from left to right. It is shown step by step to show you more about creating new motifs.

   B. Completed single bar from right to left.

   C. First of 2 bars from left to right.

   D. Second of the left-to-right double bars completed, and the first of the lower double bars completed.

   E. Second of the lower left-to-right bars completed. The holding cord is in place for the next right-to-left single bar. Practice (and a close look at these pictures) will teach you which cord to use for the holding cord.

61. Here is an X pattern with double inside bars. The top bars of the top of the X and the bottom bars of the bottom of the X are knotted exactly as usual except they are *not* crossed over.

62. A double bar X is about to be followed by a double bar diamond. Look at the picture carefully and you'll be able to see how it works.

63. If the lines of the double bar X pattern are curved—and this just takes a little practice—a flowerlike pattern is formed. The holding cords and knots are exactly the same as in the previous pattern.

64. To make this crosshatch pattern, divide all the cords into even groups of 6, 8, or 10 cords. Although the pattern result is the same, a crosshatch made with 6 cords will be a smaller hatch than one made with 8 or 10. This pattern is made with groups of 6 cords.

    Using cord 1 as the first holding cord, use each sixth cord, counting from the left, as holding cord for a diagonal row of 5 Clove Hitches, from left to right.

    Let the first 3 cords on the left dangle. Counting cord 4 as cord 1, use it as the first holding cord of the next row. Continue across row, using each sixth cord (counting cord 4 as cord 1) as holding cord, and tie diagonal rows of 5 Clove Hitches from right to left. Note that you will get half rows on the outsides of the pattern.

    These two rows form the sequence; repeat them as often as the pattern demands.

65. A flower pattern with alternating leaves. It's just a matter of choosing the right holding cords and practicing the curve.

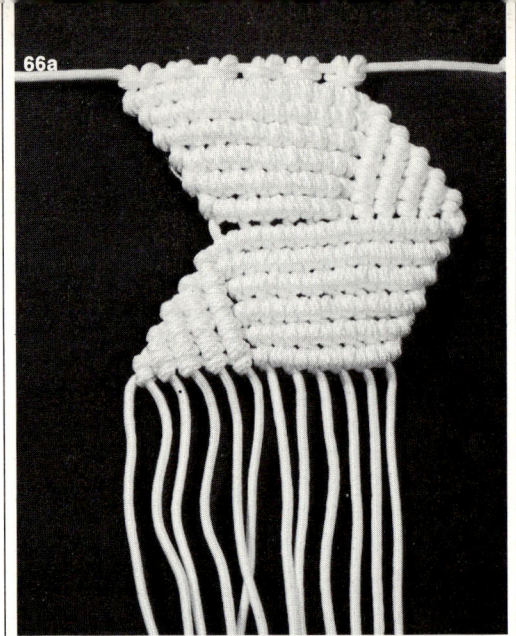
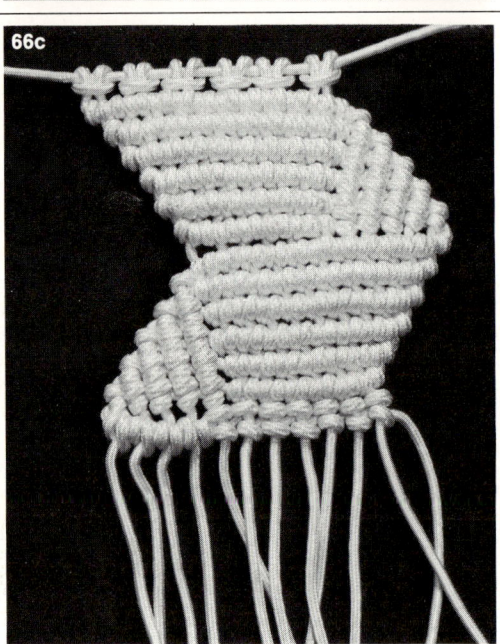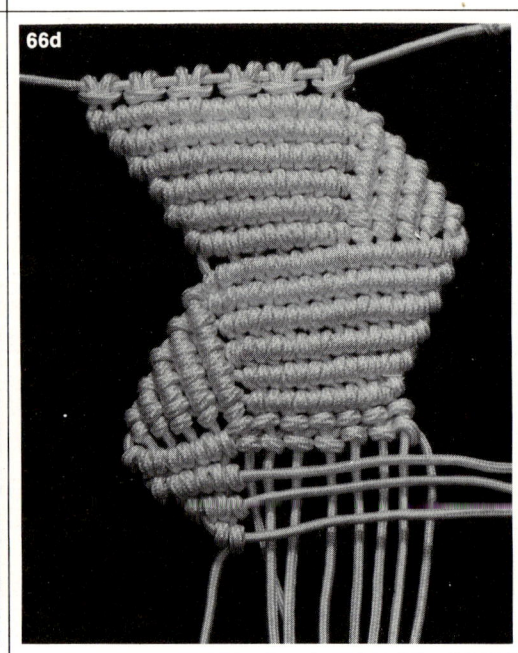

66. The Angled Technique

This method of shaping solid areas is more easily seen than taught with complicated instructions. If you've been practicing your regular and vertical Clove Hitches, you can probably see how it is done.

Basically, to angle from left to right, make consecutive rows of Clove Hitches from left to right, taking the left cord as holding cord for each row, leaving the holding cords from the previous rows untied.

Then take the top holding cord, pin, and angle it vertically. Tie the rest of the holding cords over it in Clove Hitches, or use the cord as a tying cord and tie *vertical* Clove Hitches.

Then take each remaining holding cord in succession, angle it vertically, and do the same. The angle or the choice of vertical or horizontal Clove Hitch can be changed at any time, so there's no sense in going into any more detail. Try it and you'll see how variable and clever a technique this is—and simple.

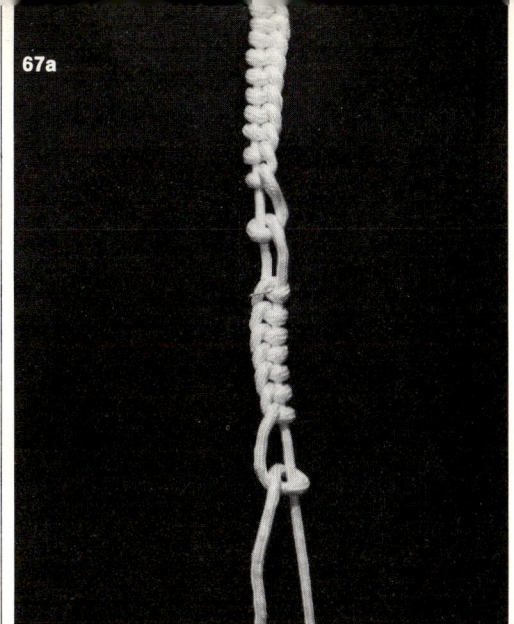
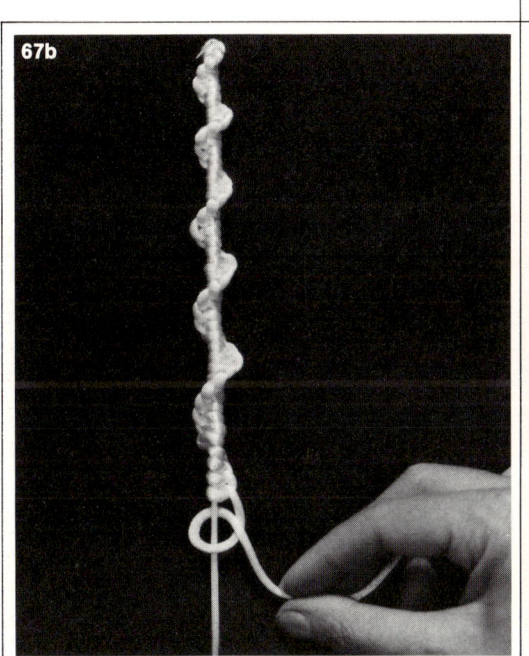
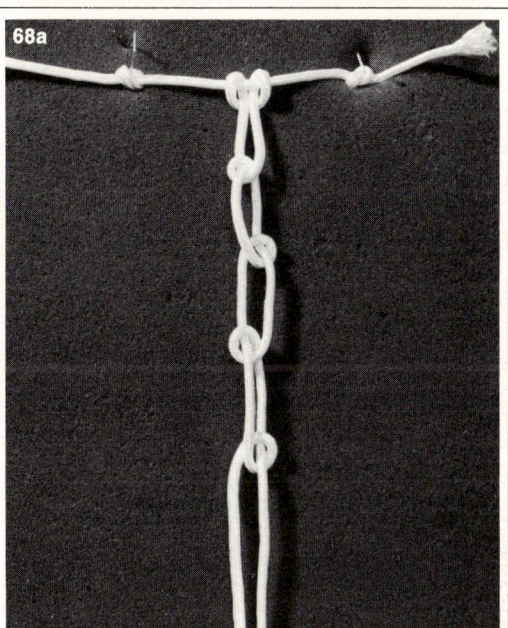
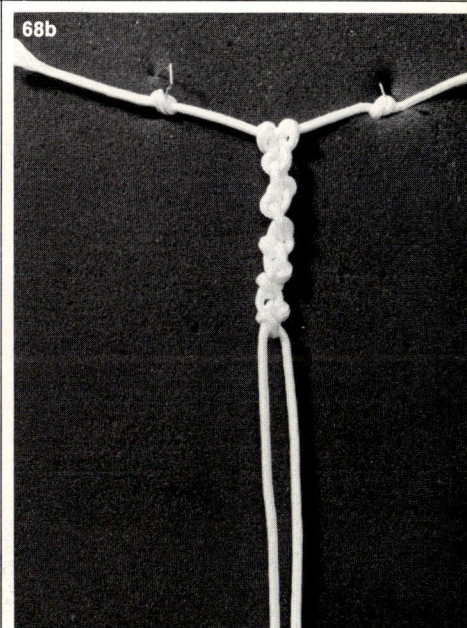

Braids, Chains, and Sennits

Repeat patterns of Clove Hitches and their variations have an endless number of uses—not only as decorative elements in a piece, but by themselves as neckpieces, straps, braids, chains, shade pulls, etc. The patterns shown here are only a few of the many possibilities. New ideas will come to you as you work.

67. Single (Half Hitch) Chains—Right and Left

A. In the upper half of this photo, Half Hitches (a Half Hitch is just *one* loop of the Clove Hitch) are tied continuously over the right cord with the left-hand cord.

In the lower half, the situation is reversed and the left cord ties over the right.

B. If this particular sennit (tied left or right) is tied tightly, it will create a lovely spiraling effect.

Alternating Single Chains

68. Using 2 cords, a single loop of the vertical Clove Hitch is tied alternately one over the other. That is, first the right-hand cord is the holding cord and the left cord ties the loop; then the left cord is held while the right cord ties.

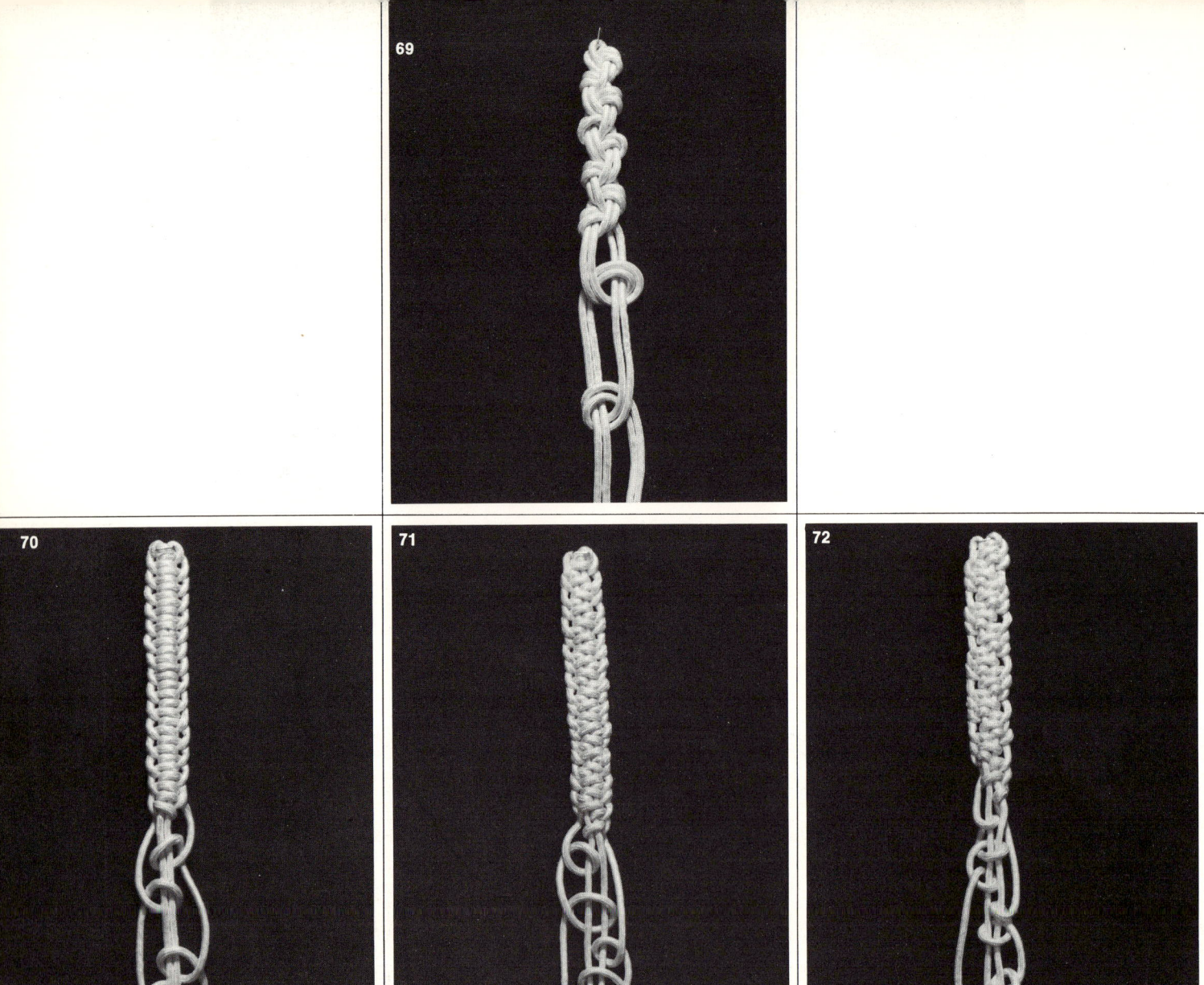

69. The alternating chain can be tied with any even number of cords.

70. When tied around 2 center cords, the alternating single chain forms a flatter braid.

71. Clove Hitch Chain

Here is an alternating Clove Hitch chain. The left cord loops first around just the left center cord and then around both center cords. Then the right cord loops first around just the right center cord and then around both center cords.

72. Alternating Triple Hitch Sennit

The left-hand cord loops around the left center cord, around both center cords, and again around the left center cord.

Then the right-hand cord loops around the right center cord, both center cords, and again around the right center cord.

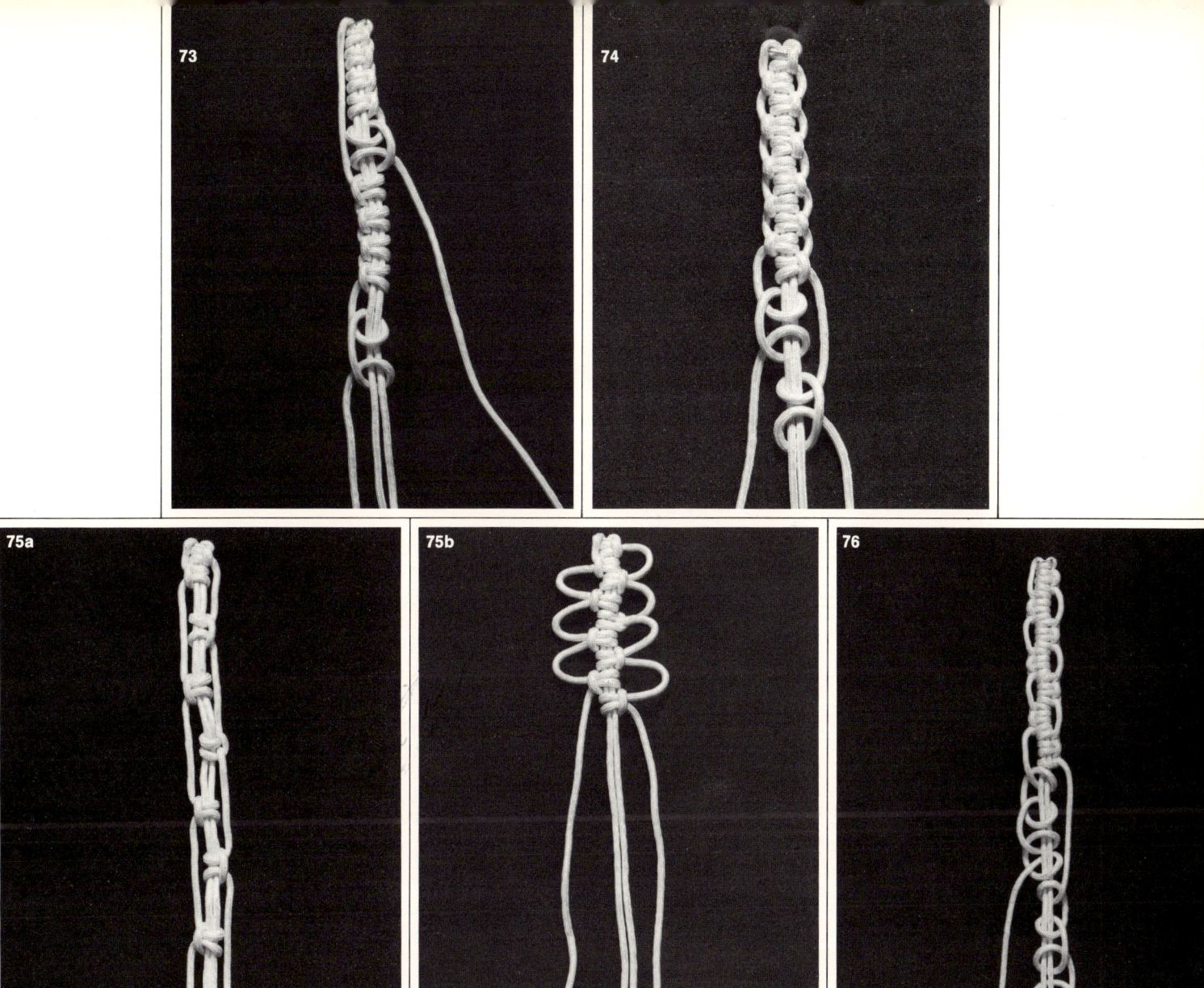

73. Lark's Head Knot and Lark's Head Chains

This is the knot used to start your cords on the mounting bar, actually a variation of the Clove Hitch.

It is made with 2 loops like the Clove Hitch. The first of the 2 loops is tied exactly like the Clove Hitch.

For the second loop, the cord starts *under* the center cords, loops over them and back inside the loop thus formed.

The top half of this sennit is made with consecutive Lark's Heads tied with the right-hand cord over the center cords. The bottom half is tied with the left-hand cord.

Alternating Lark's Head Sennits

74. Tie a Lark's Head over the center cords with the left- and right-hand cords alternately.

75. Alternating Lark's Heads are tied with space between the knots, then tightly pushed up the center cords, forming a loop effect on the sides (B).

76. Alternating double Lark's Heads: 2 each with the left- and right-hand cords.

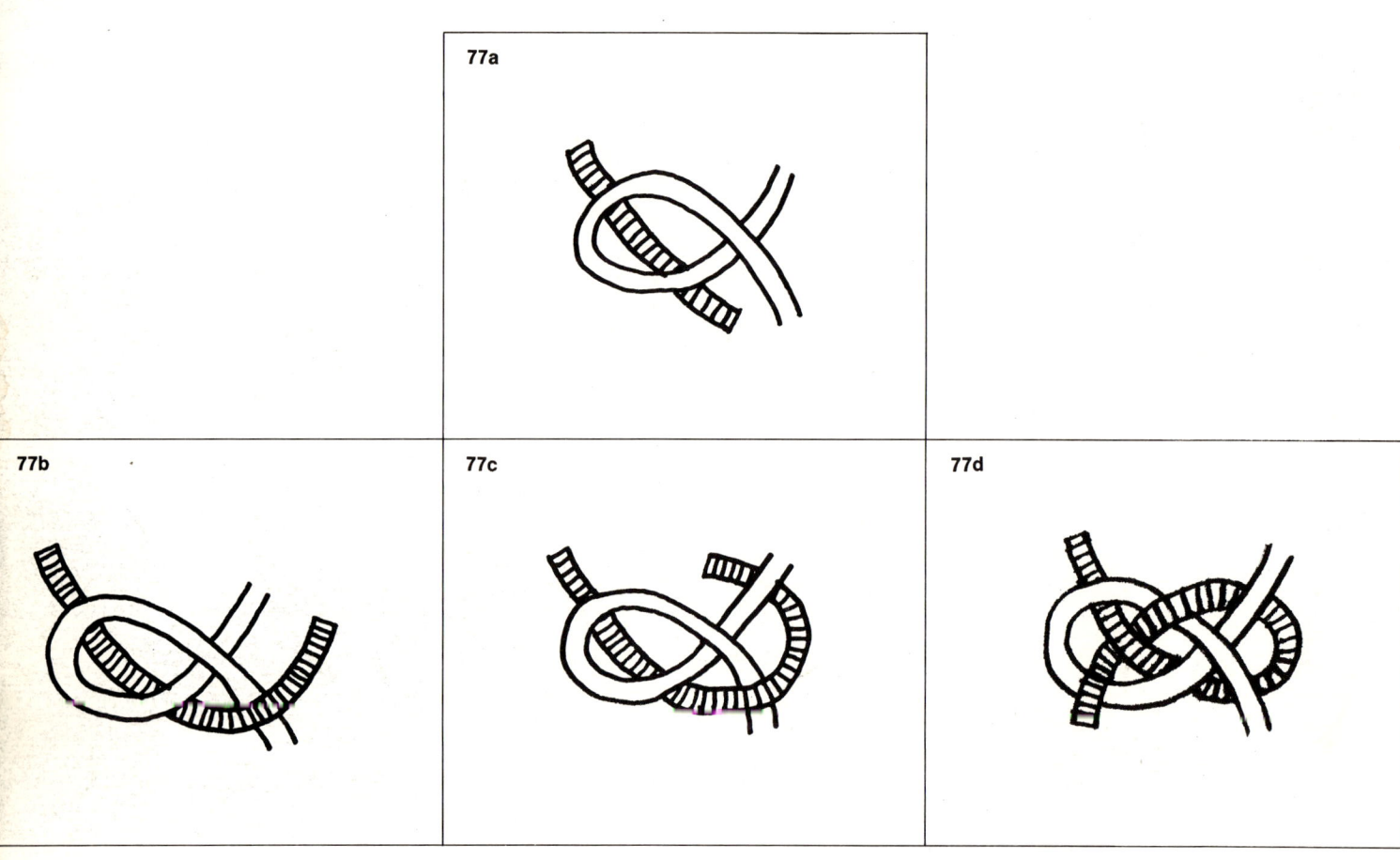

Two Special Knots

The Josephine Knot

This graceful knot looks rather like a pretzel and has many decorative uses. It looks difficult and written instructions are absolutely infuriating, but if you look closely and follow the photos, you should be able to master it after a few tries.

A couple of notes: Having tied the knot, tighten it carefully, pulling evenly on both sides, or you'll lose track of the knot and it will tangle. It is useful to learn to tie it both ways shown—left-hand loop first, and right—for when you make a sennit of Josephine Knots, it tends to twist unless you alternate them. It can be tied with any number of cords. The object is to fan the cords out flat. A dab of glue on the back of finished knots will keep them in place.

77. This is a case where a diagram is helpful in visualizing the "path" of the cords. Look at the sketches to see how the cords intertwine. Follow the photographs to learn how to manipulate the cords and actually tie the knot.

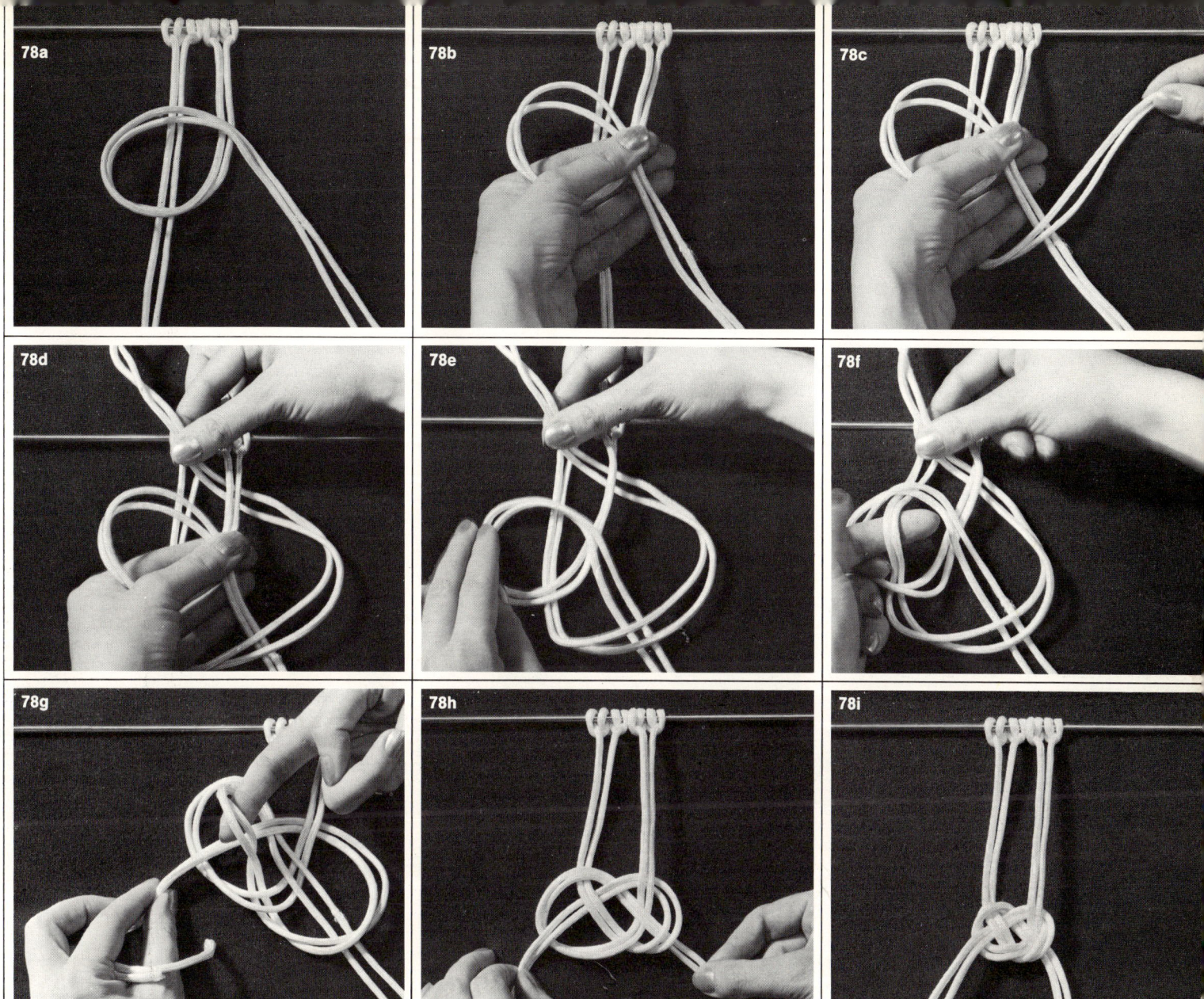

78. Here is my method of doing the Josephine Knot. You will develop your own way.

   A. Make a good-sized loop with the right-hand cord, overlapping on top.

   B. Hold the loop in your left hand at point of overlap and rest the back of your hand firmly on the left-hand cord to hold it in place. *This left-hand cord does all the tying*.

   C. Take the left-hand cord and put it *over* the right-hand cord below the loop.

   D. Now put the left-hand cord *under* the right-hand cord above the loop.

   E. Lay the loop formed by the right-hand cord down *gently in place,* so that the left cord can easily be seen running under the loop.

   F. G. To complete the knot, put the tying cord down through the loop, *under* the left-hand cord from right to left; and out the side of the loop again.

   Note: Any multiple of cords can be used to tie the Josephine Knot. They should be kept as flat as possible for a decorative look.

   H. To tighten the knot, pull out and down evenly on both sides. This takes a little practice.

   I. Completed Josephine Knot.

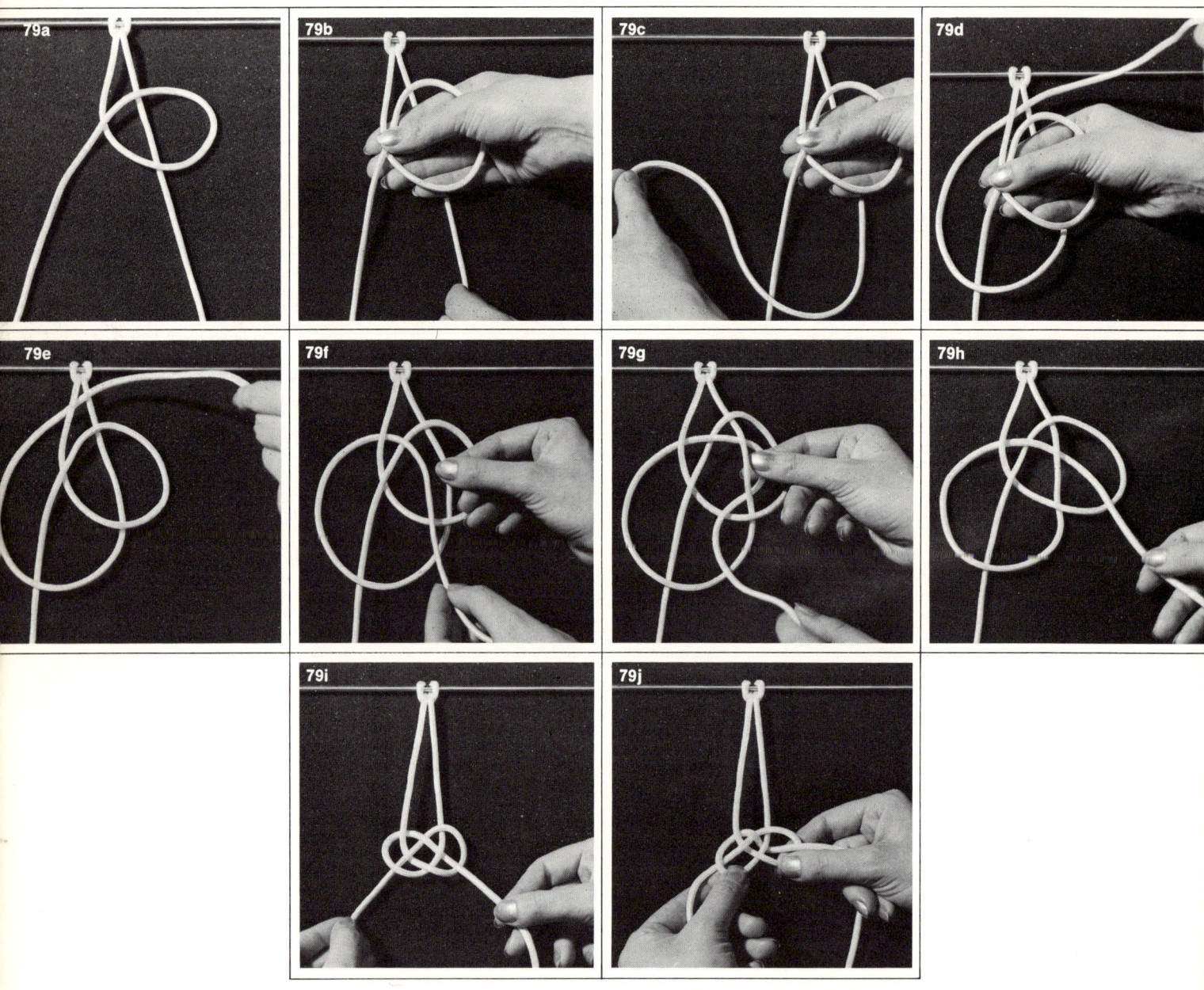

79. A.–I. The Josephine Knot tied in the opposite direction. Be sure to learn both ways.
    J. To raise knot or change its position, loosen it from the bottom as shown.

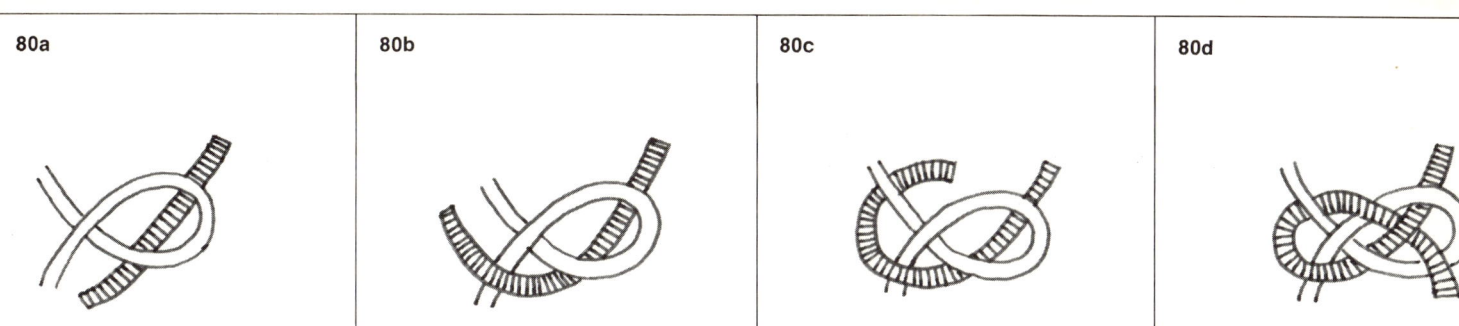

80. Here is a sketch of the Josephine Knot with a right-hand loop.

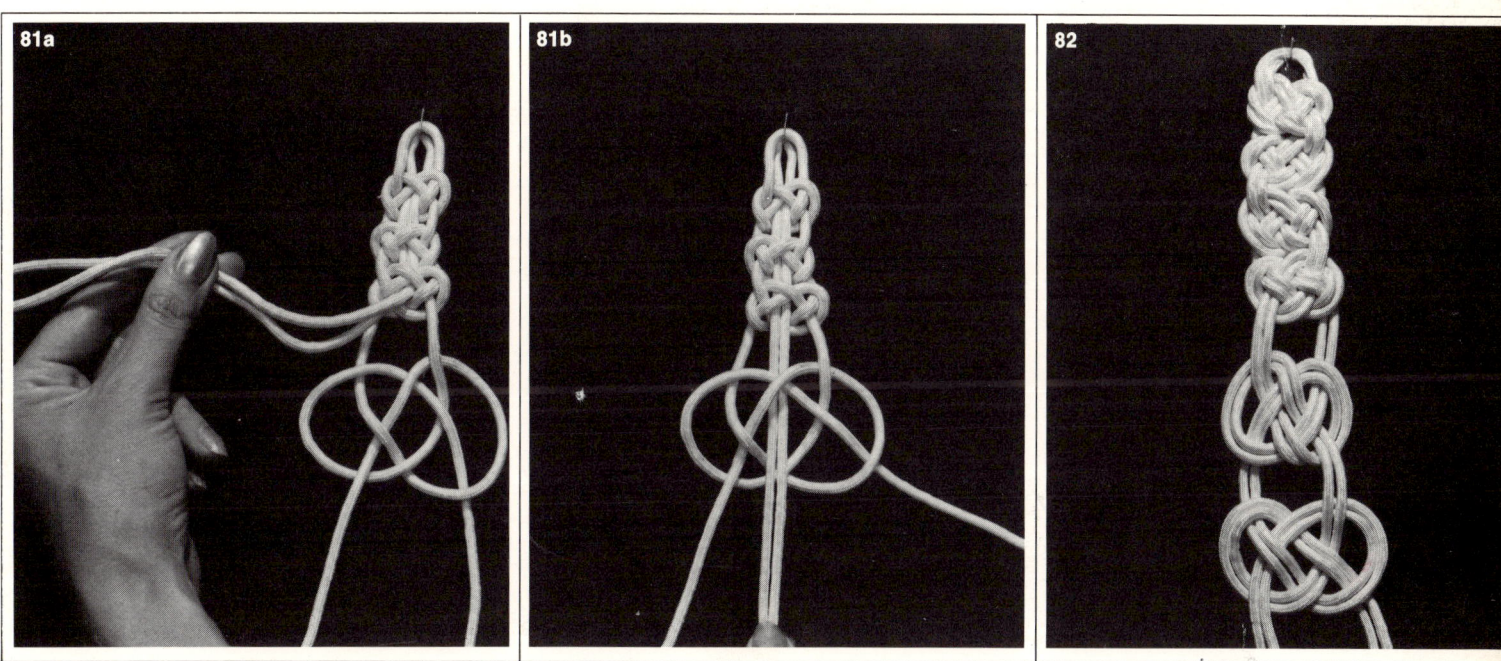

81. Sometimes it is useful to put center cords through a completed Josephine Knot. Beads can be put on the center cords for textural effect.

   A. Make the knot, leaving the center cords aside.

   B. Put center cords under the top of the knot and up through the middle over the bottom of the knot (B).

82. Josephine Knot Sennits

   A sennit of Josephine Knots, tied alternately with left and right loops.

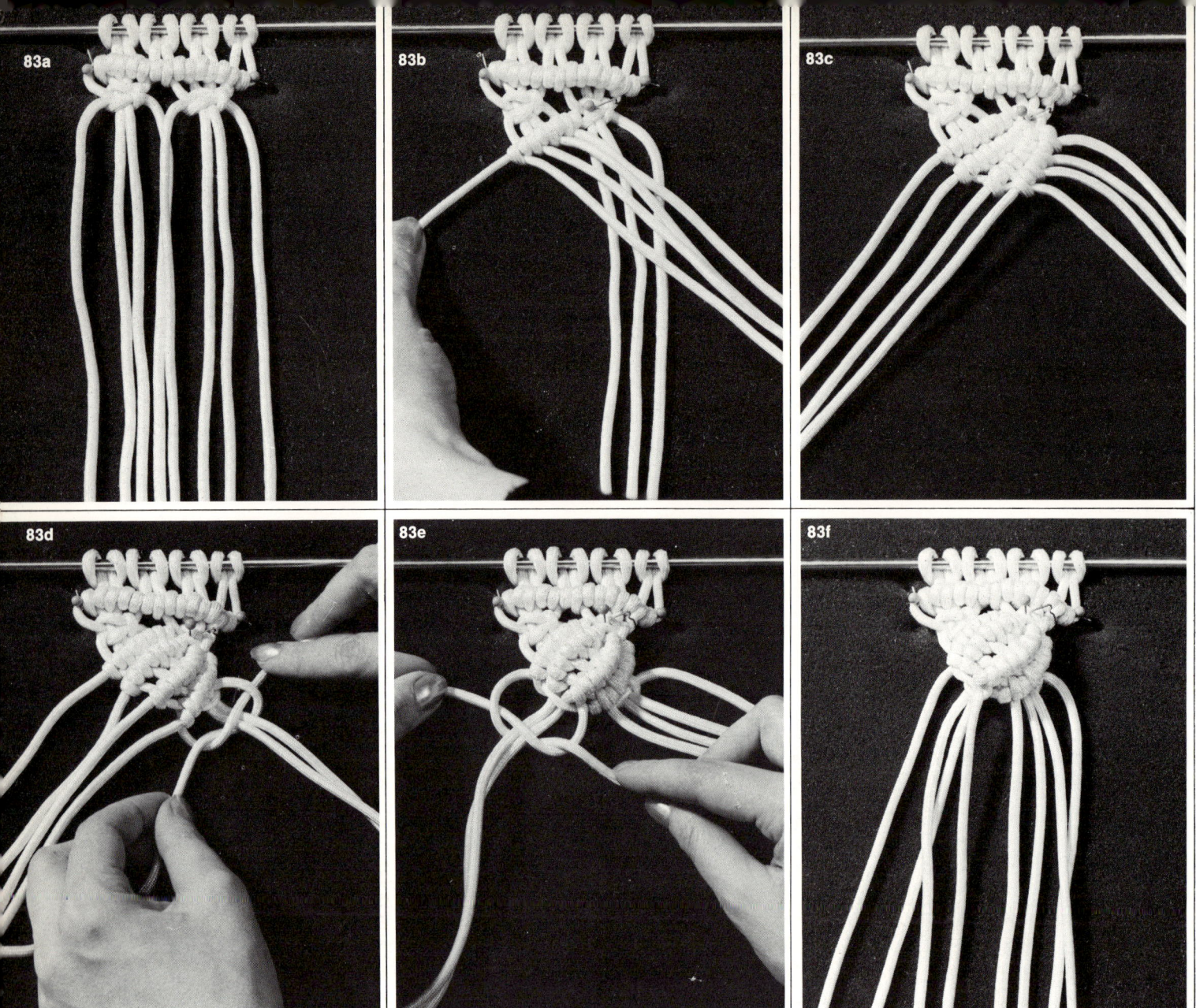

The Berry Knot

Here is a beautiful knot made by bunching up a series of diagonal Clove Hitch rows by tying Square Knots tightly against them.

83. A. Using a group of 8 cords, tie 2 Square Knots side by side and pin in place.
    B. Take the first cord in the right-hand Square Knot and use it as a holding cord to tie a diagonal row of tight Clove Hitches with the 4 left-hand cords.
    C. Make 3 more rows of diagonal Clove Hitches, using the other 3 right-hand cords in succession as holding cords.
    D. Tie a Square Knot with the 4 right-hand cords *very tightly* against the 4 rows of Clove Hitches.
    E. Tie a Square Knot with the 4 left-hand cords *very tightly* against the 4 rows of Clove Hitches so that they bunch up to form a rounded "berry."
    F. Completed knot. Of course this can be done in reverse, with the rows of Clove Hitches going from left to right.

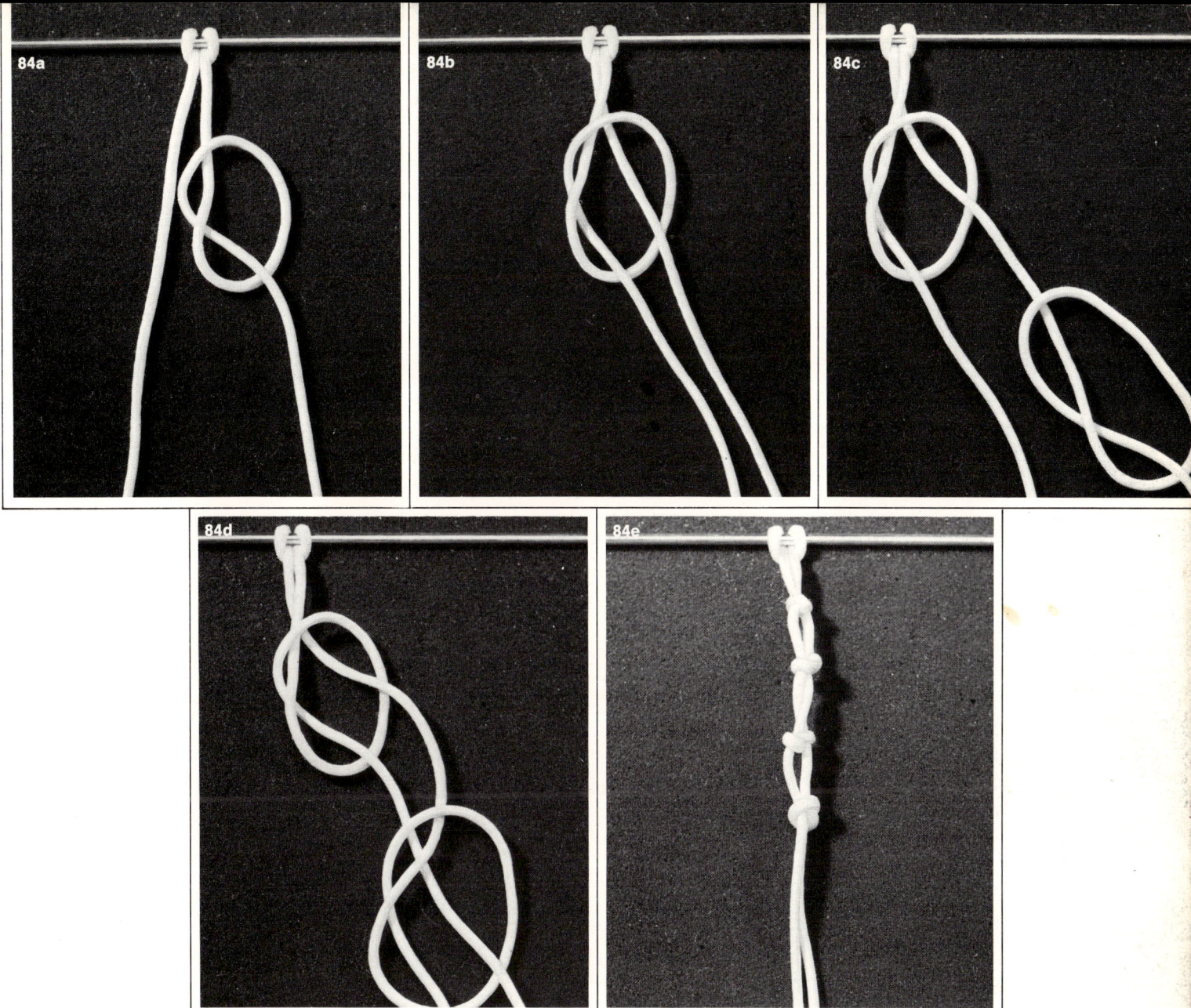

The Many Uses of the Overhand Knot

As you'll see, the Overhand Knot can be both decorative and functional, and it combines well with other knots.

Overhand Knot Chains

84. Here, Overhand Knots are made with the left and right cords around the opposite cord. (Or the knot can be completed and the other cord pulled through before tightening.)

   A. Overhand Knot tied in right cord.
   B. Pull left-hand cord through knot.
   C. Tie knot in left cord.
   D. Pull right-hand cord through knot.
   E. Tighten knots and continue sequence.

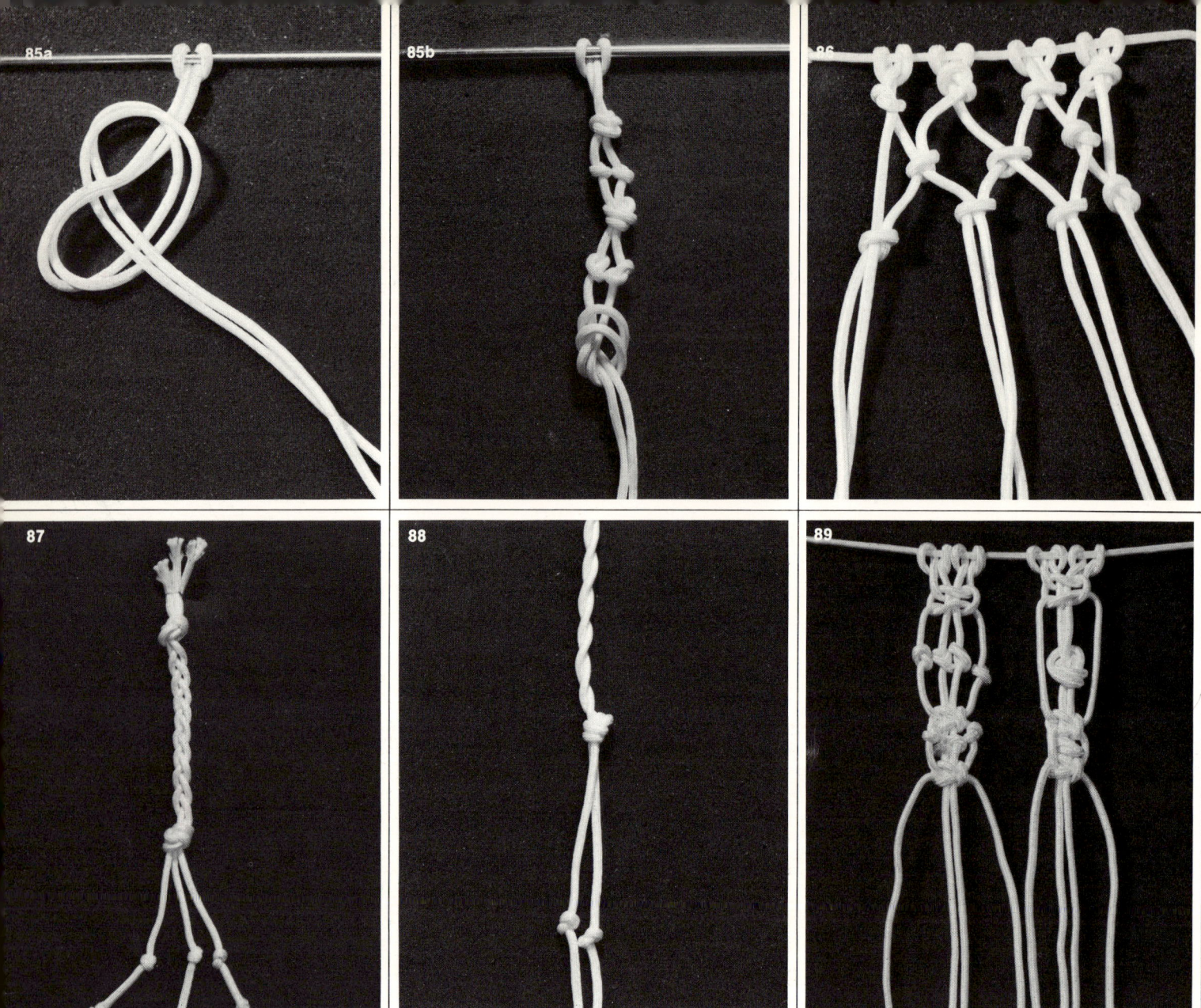

85. A. Overhand Knot with 2 cords.

   B. Overhand Knot tied alternately with 1 and then 2 cords in sequence.

86. Alternating Overhand Knots

Overhand Knots are tied with groups of 2 cords (left over right or right over left) as in Ill. 84.

Then the outside cord is dropped, and knots are tied with 1 cord from each of 2 adjoining knots above, just as with alternating Square Knots or vertical Clove Hitches.

Overhand Knot Used to Secure Braids and Twists

87. Overhand Knots keep a braid from unraveling at top and bottom, and are a decorative element in the fringe.

88. Two cords are merely twisted and held with an Overhand Knot.

89. Overhand Knots with Square Knots

At left of photo, Overhand Knots on the outside cords add interest in a Square Knot sennit.

At right, an Overhand Knot is tied in the center cords between Square Knots.

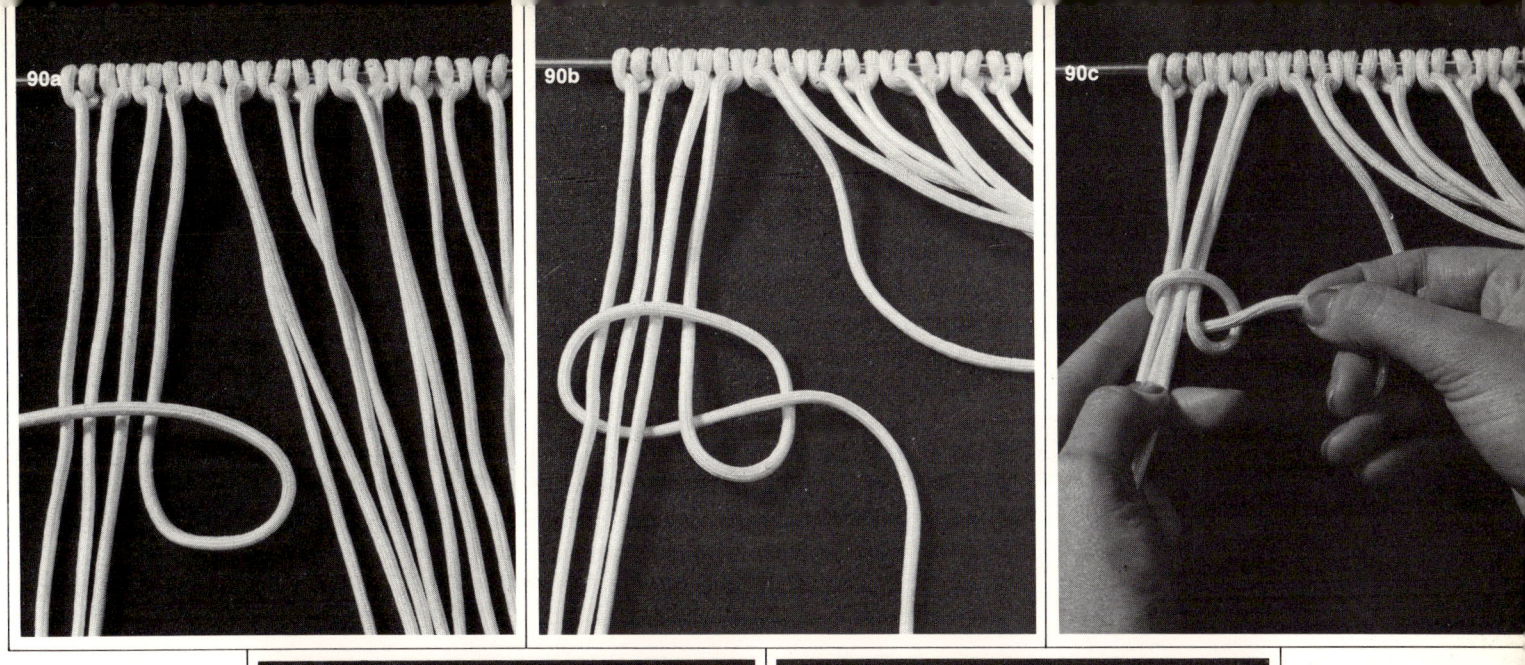
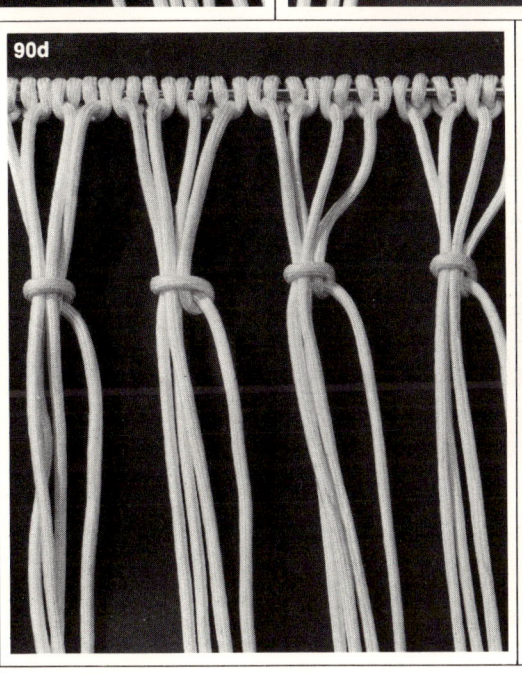
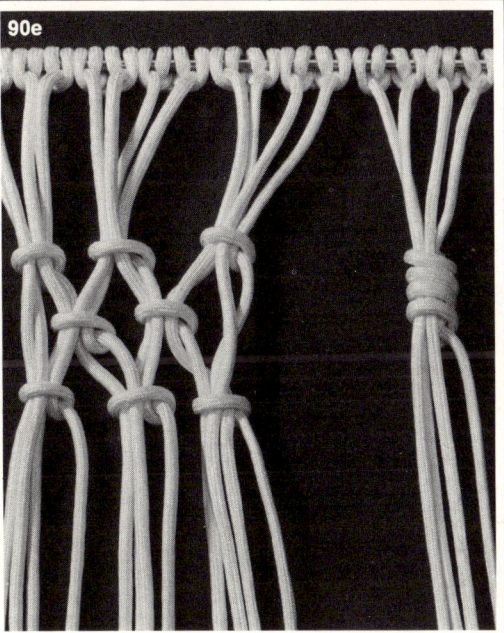

90. Collecting Knot

The Collecting Knot is actually an Overhand Knot used to gather cords together, usually at the end of the pieces as a method for fringing.

A. Take a group of cords; make a loop with the right-hand cord and lay it over the other cords.

B. Put the cord behind the remaining cords and back through the loop.

C. Tighten.

D. A row of Collecting Knots.

E. At left of photo, alternating Collecting Knots. At right, a series of Collecting Knots tied with 1 cord.

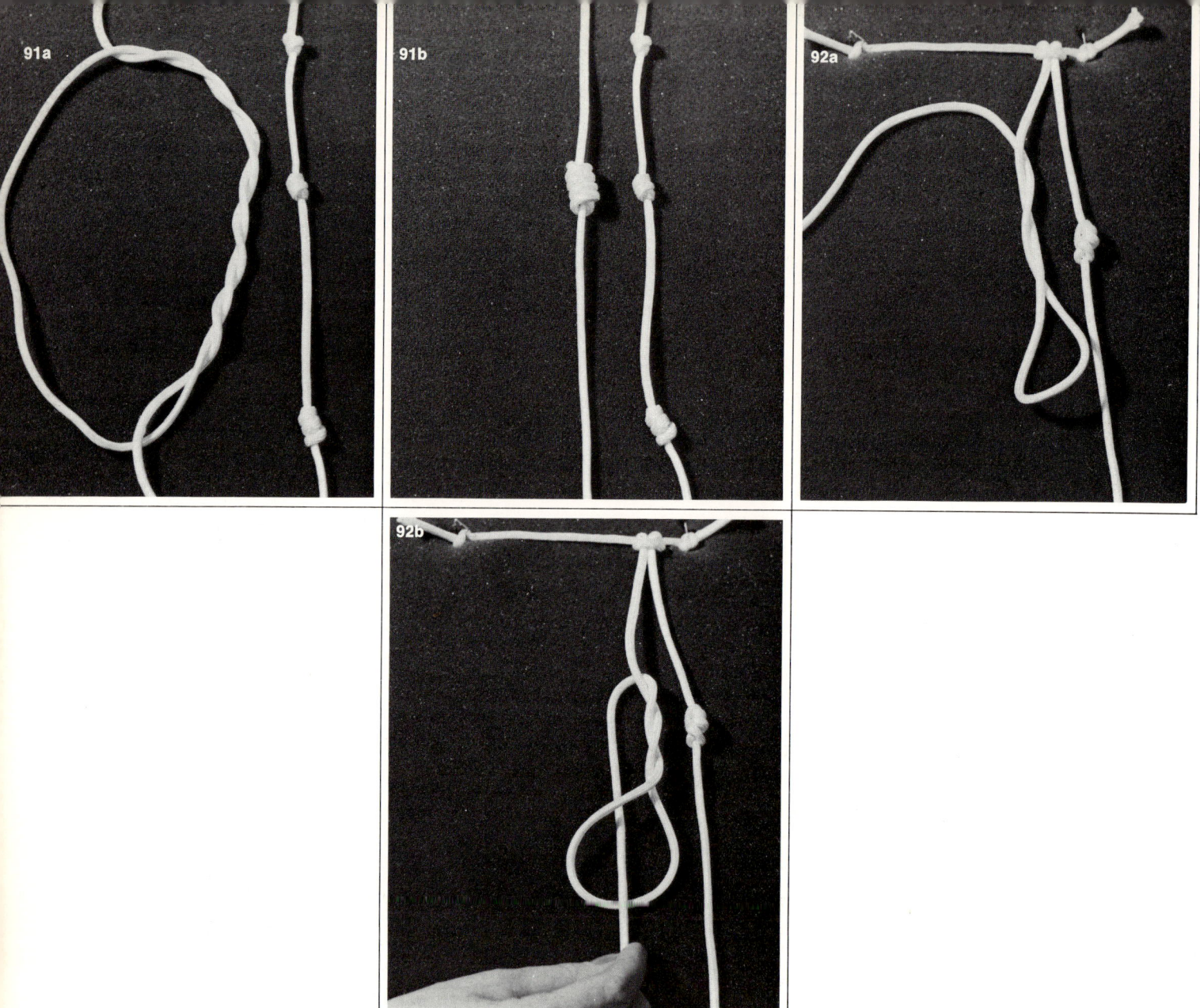

91. Overhand Wrap

    A. Tie an Overhand Knot in a cord; continue wrapping the overhand loop.

    B. Pull tight; the size of the knot will depend on the number of wraps.

Coil Knots

92. A. Make loop in end of cord, wrapping it *up* length of cord several times.

    B. Bring end down back of wraps and through to front of loop to tighten.

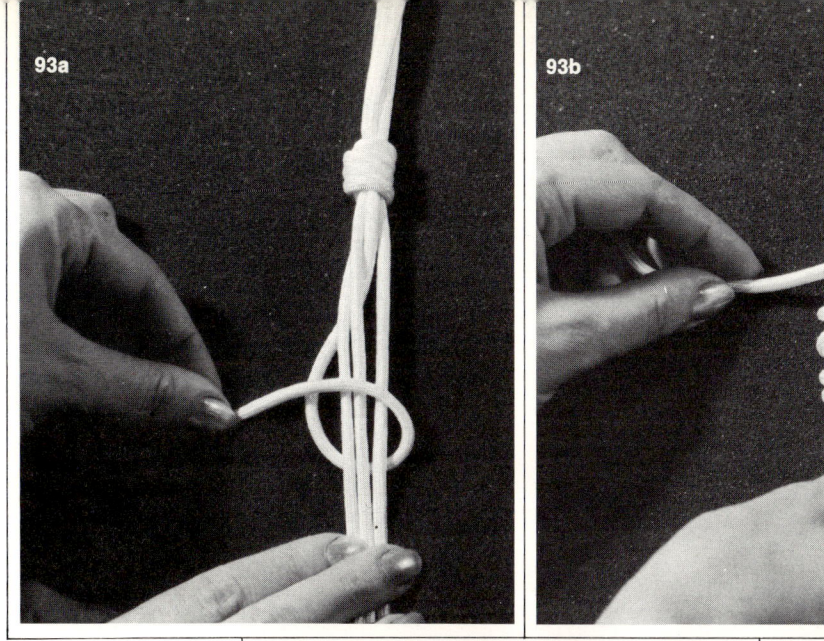
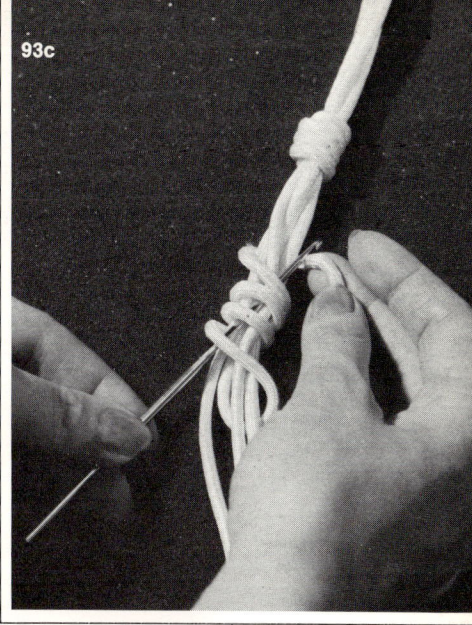
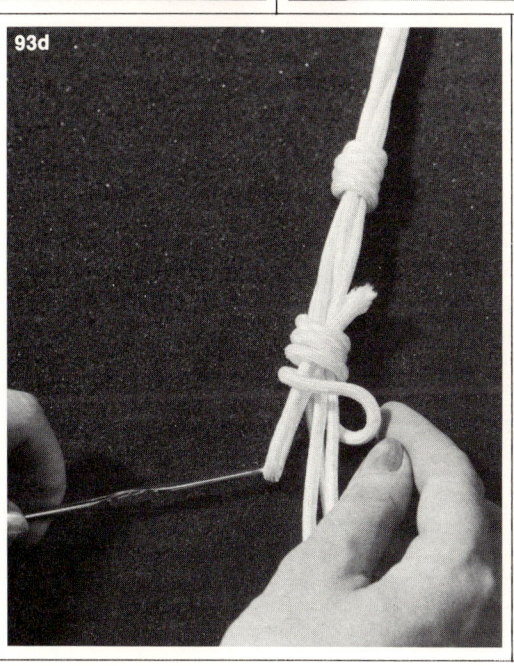
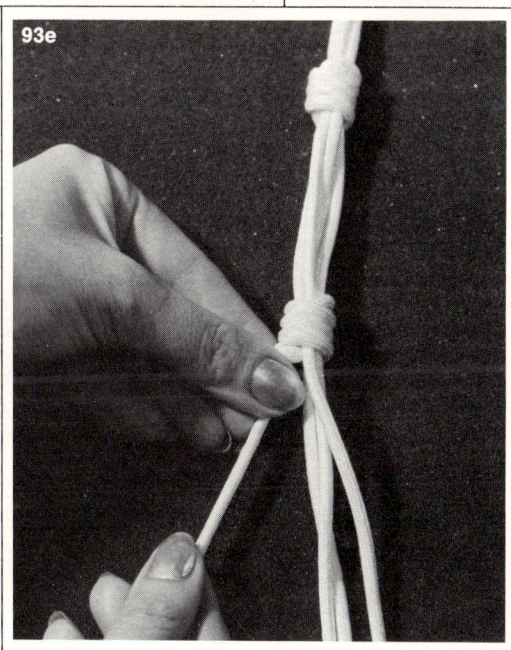

93. Here is a Coil Knot made around several cords.
    A. Loop 1 cord around the others and back across itself.
    B. Continue wrapping cord *up* and around the other cords.
    C. Put crochet hook up through the coil from bottom to top.
    D. Pull end of cord through coil to bottom with crochet hook.
    E. Tighten.

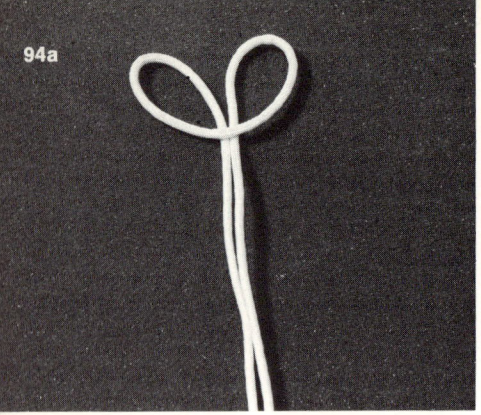 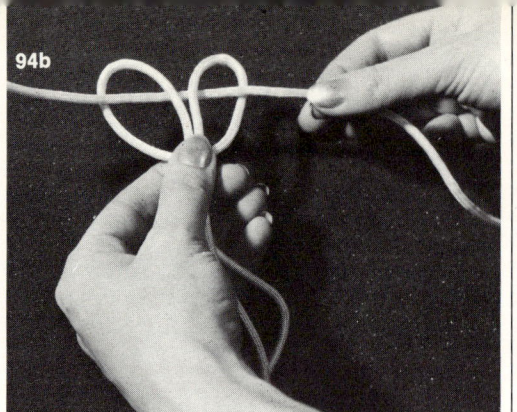 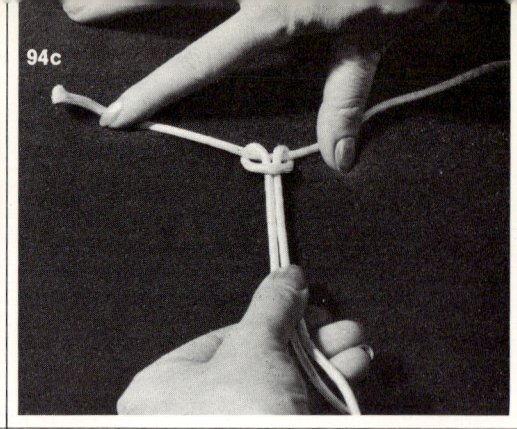

Other Methods of Mounting and Starting Work

94. Another Method of Mounting with the Lark's Head

With stiff cords it is possible to do the Lark's Head in your hand.

A. Double cord and bend loop forward over cords.

B. Hold in position with thumb and forefinger. Take holding cord and run it down into the first loop, *under* the 2 cords and out the top of the second loop.

C. Tighten, and continue adding cords in this manner.

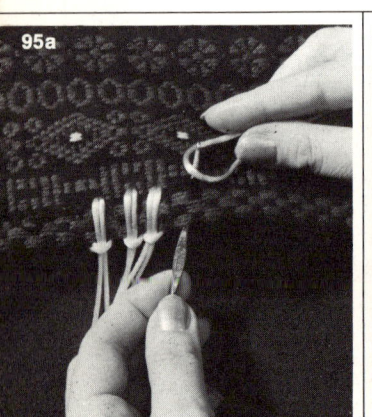 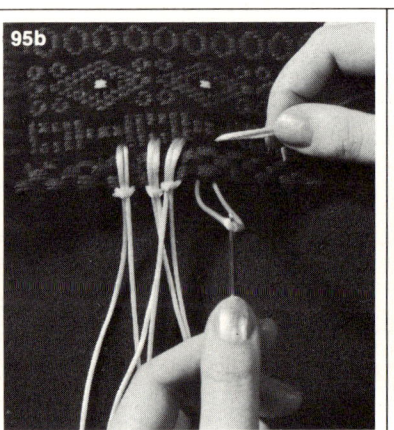 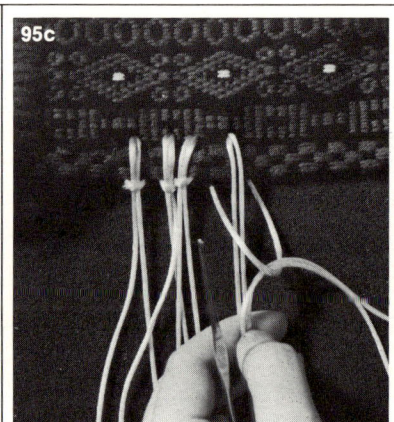 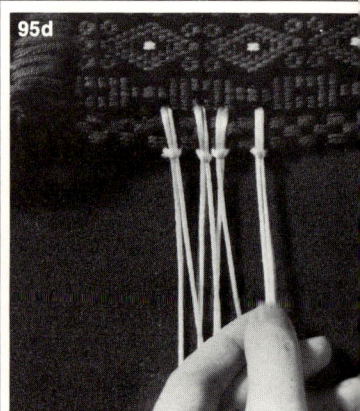

95. Starting a Macramé Fringe on a Hem

Beautiful fringes and borders can be put on a finished garment with macramé. To mount cords on a material hem, mark off the border on the reverse side of the material at approximately ⅜" intervals, depending on the thickness of the cord and the elaborateness of the fringe desired. Try to have a multiple of 4 cords for ease of working.

A. Poke crochet hook through from back of hem where you have marked it. Hold doubled cord on top of material.

B. Grasp loop with crochet hook and pull through from front to back.

C. Complete regular Lark's Head. Pull cords through loop.

D. Tighten.

96. Double Lark's Head

This mount is good for filling out or for covering the mounting bar and evenly spacing the cords. It is also good when adding extra cords on a row of Clove Hitches, as it looks almost the same as the Clove Hitch.

A. Mount cord as in regular Reverse Lark's Head procedure. Take the right-hand cord, loop it behind mounting bar and to the left through the loop, toward the center of the Clove Hitch.

B. Take the left-hand cord, loop it behind mounting bar and to the right through the loop.

C. Repeat with all cords, tighten, and push together.

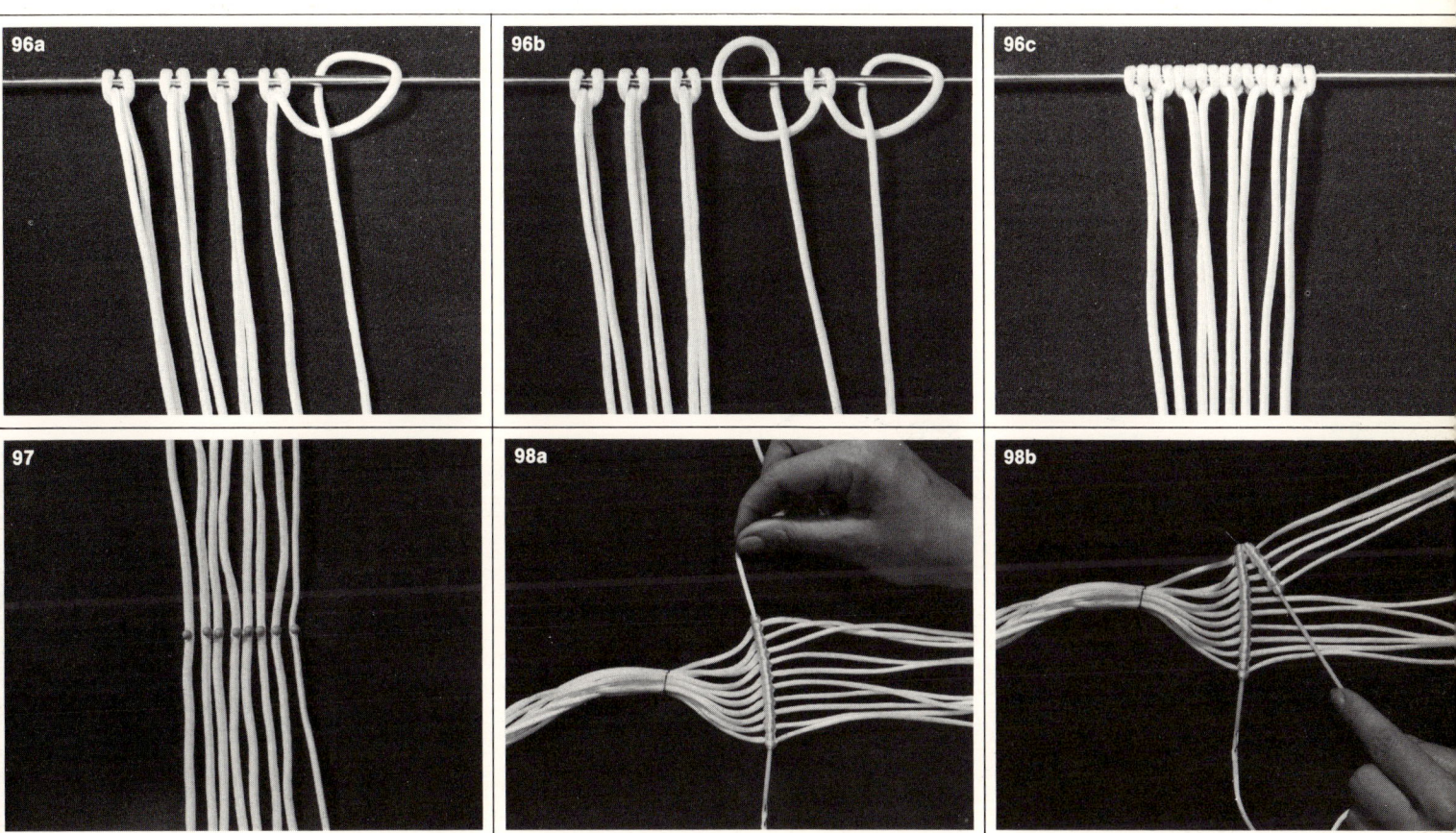

97. Pinning Cords at Center

One way of starting a piece in which both sides are the same—such as a choker, a belt, or the shoulder straps of a vest or dress—is to take the cords, line them up evenly on your knotting surface, and just pin them at the center. Start knotting from either side out to the ends; no mounting bar is needed.

98. Starting in the Middle with a Clove Hitch Bar

A piece is started in the center by using one of the tying cords as holding cord for a Clove Hitch bar. The other working strands are temporarily pinned at one side of the center to the knotting surface, and the middle of the holding cord is Clove Hitched to the middle of the rest of the cords. The knotting can continue on either side of the holding cord, and the holding cord can continue to serve as a knotting cord on both sides of the starting row.

99. Shaping a Garment on a Flat Surface

If you want to make a garment on a flat surface yet shape it to your figure, outline the garment on your working surface with a piece of the cord to be used. Pin it *very firmly* to the working surface. Mount the cords (and end them) on this "framework" as needed.

Of course, if you sew and are fortunate enough to have a dressmaker's form, you can knot garments directly on the form, pinning as you go.

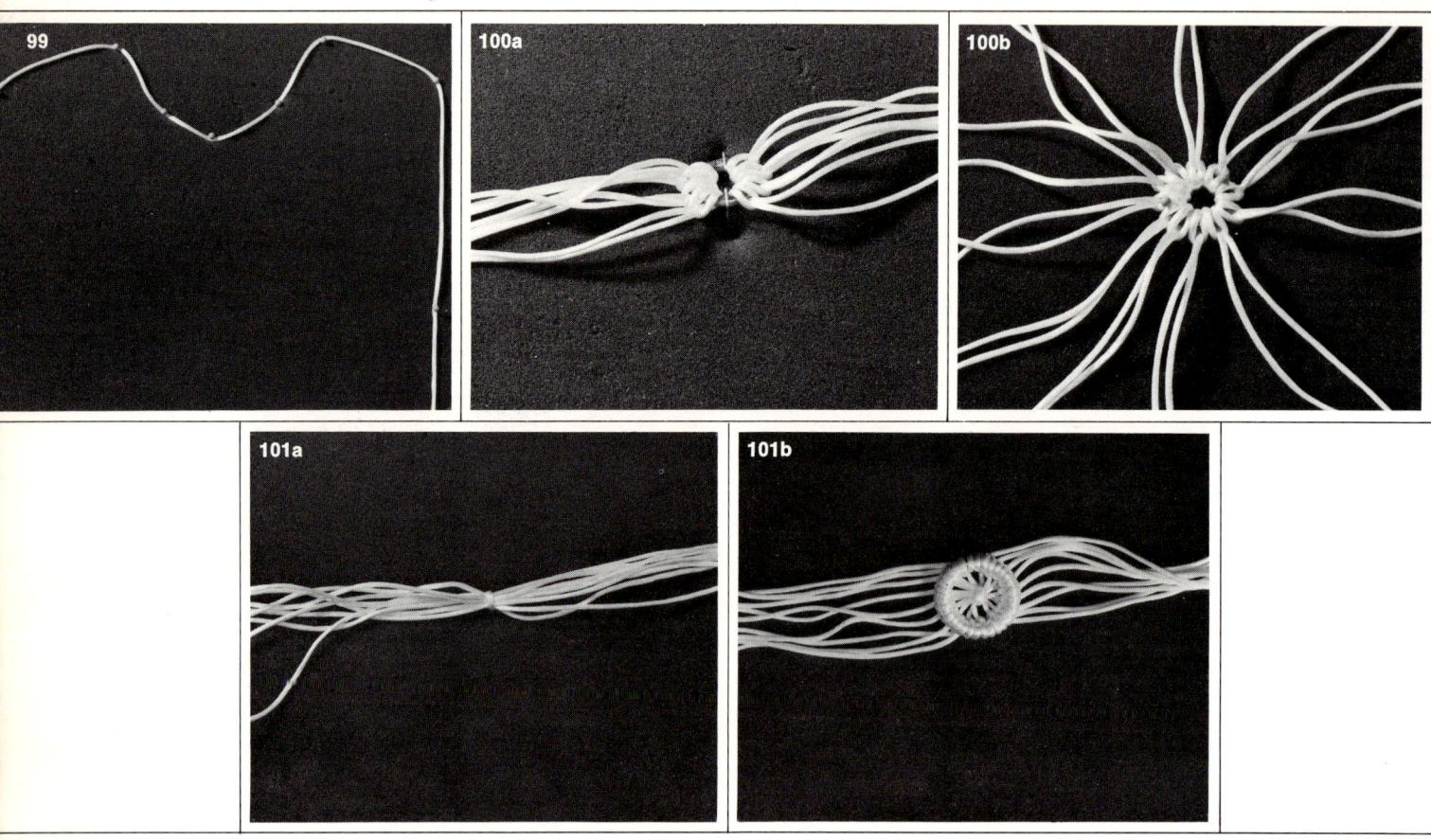

100. Mounting on a Ring with the Reverse Lark's Head

Another simple way to start from the center on a ring is just to mount the doubled cords in the usual manner—the Reverse Lark's Head—using the ring as your mounting bar. This ring can form the center of a choker or belt (A) or, by fanning out the cords (B), can be the center of a circular work. Be sure to pin ring firmly to knotting surface after cords are mounted.

101. Mounting on a Ring with the Clove Hitch

A. Another method for starting from the center is shown here. Cut the cords you will need and tie them firmly in the center, either with a short length of cord (to be removed later) or with one of the knotting cords. Pin the group of cords to knotting surface at center.

B. Pin a ring to knotting surface firmly over the center knot. Working from the center, tie a Clove Hitch with each one over the ring until all cords are used. (The ring acts as mounting bar.)

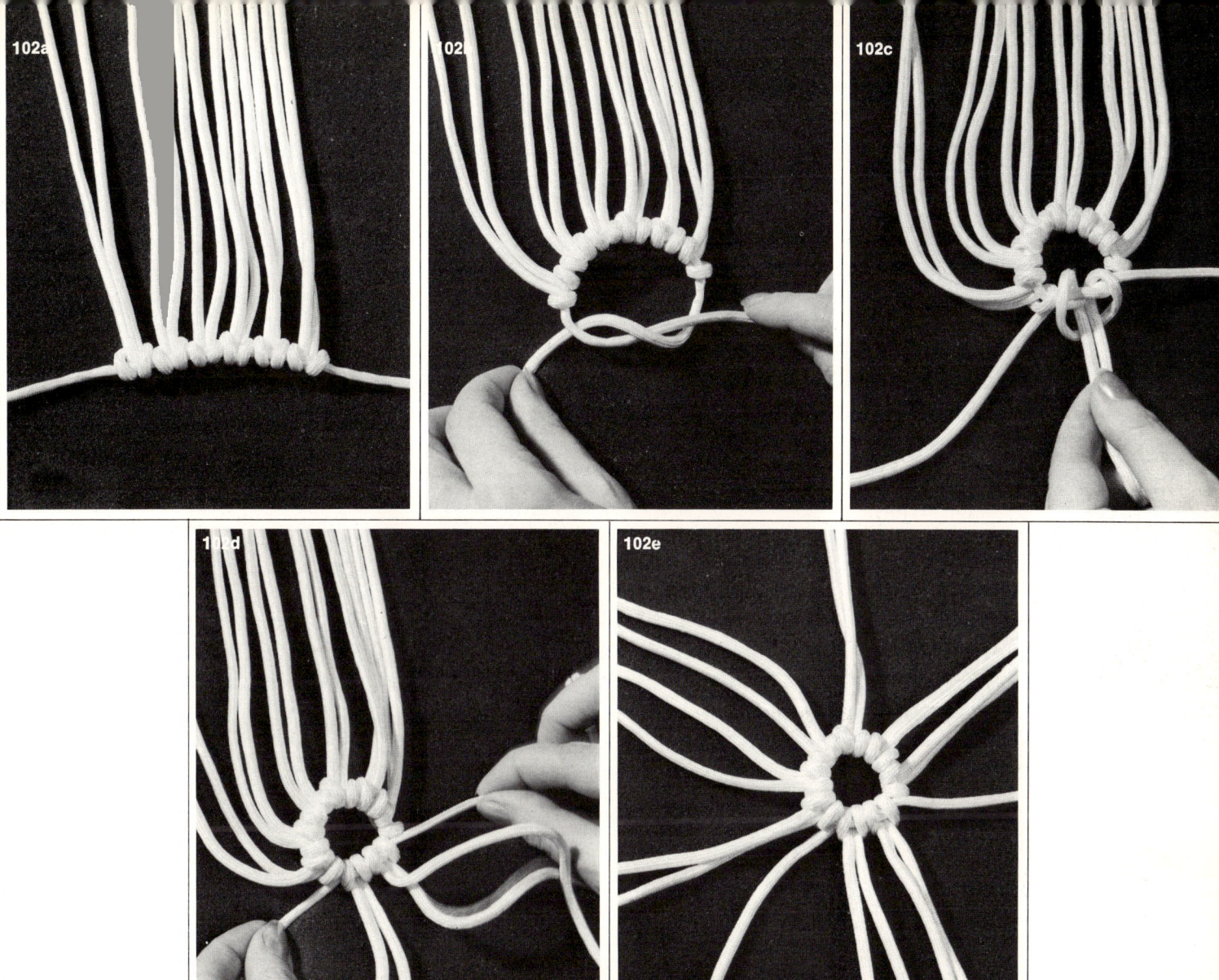

102. Starting from the Center on a Circular Mounting Cord

Here is the procedure for starting from the center on a mounting cord.

A. Mount all but 2 cords in the usual manner.//
B. Tie an Overhand Knot loosely in the mounting cord.
C. Mount the remaining 2 cords over the knot just tied.
D. Pull Overhand Knot tight.
E. Fan out cords and begin knotting. Short ends left from the mounting cord can be turned under the work and glued or knotted when finished.

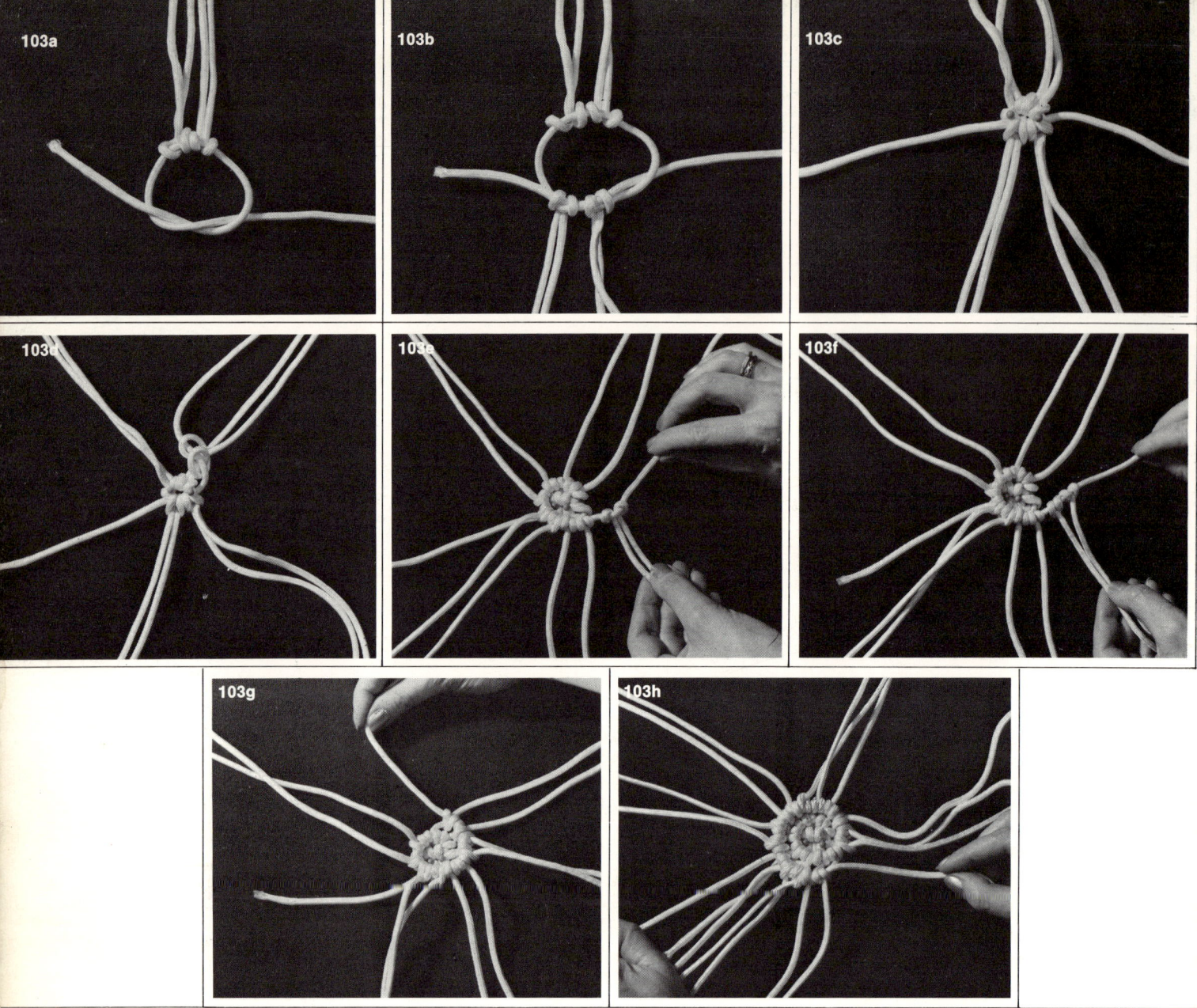

103. Adding Cords from a Central Core to Form Spiral Pattern

- A. Mount 2 cords toward one side of a long mounting cord. Tie an Overhand Knot in mounting bar, leaving one end long to serve as holding cord for added cords.
- B. Mount 2 more cords on the Overhand Knot.
- C. Pull the Overhand Knot taut so that center of spiral is closed. Tuck short end of mounting cord under to avoid confusion; be sure to keep track of mounting bar. (Tying a small Overhand Knot in the end of the cord is one sure way of identification.)
- D. Pin to knotting surface. Continue around spiral by tying a Clove Hitch with first 2 cords after holding cord.
- E. Now add a new cord with Reverse Lark's Head or
- F. Double Lark Head, depending on how tight you want your spiral to be.
- G. Continue around circle, tying a Clove Hitch with 2 of the original cords, then adding a new cord until the circle is completed (H).

You can control the direction and the tautness of the spiral in several ways: by the direction of the holding cord, by adding few or many cords, by knotting the cords with the Clove Hitch or Triple Hitch, or by adding the cords with the Reverse Lark's Head or Double Lark's Head.

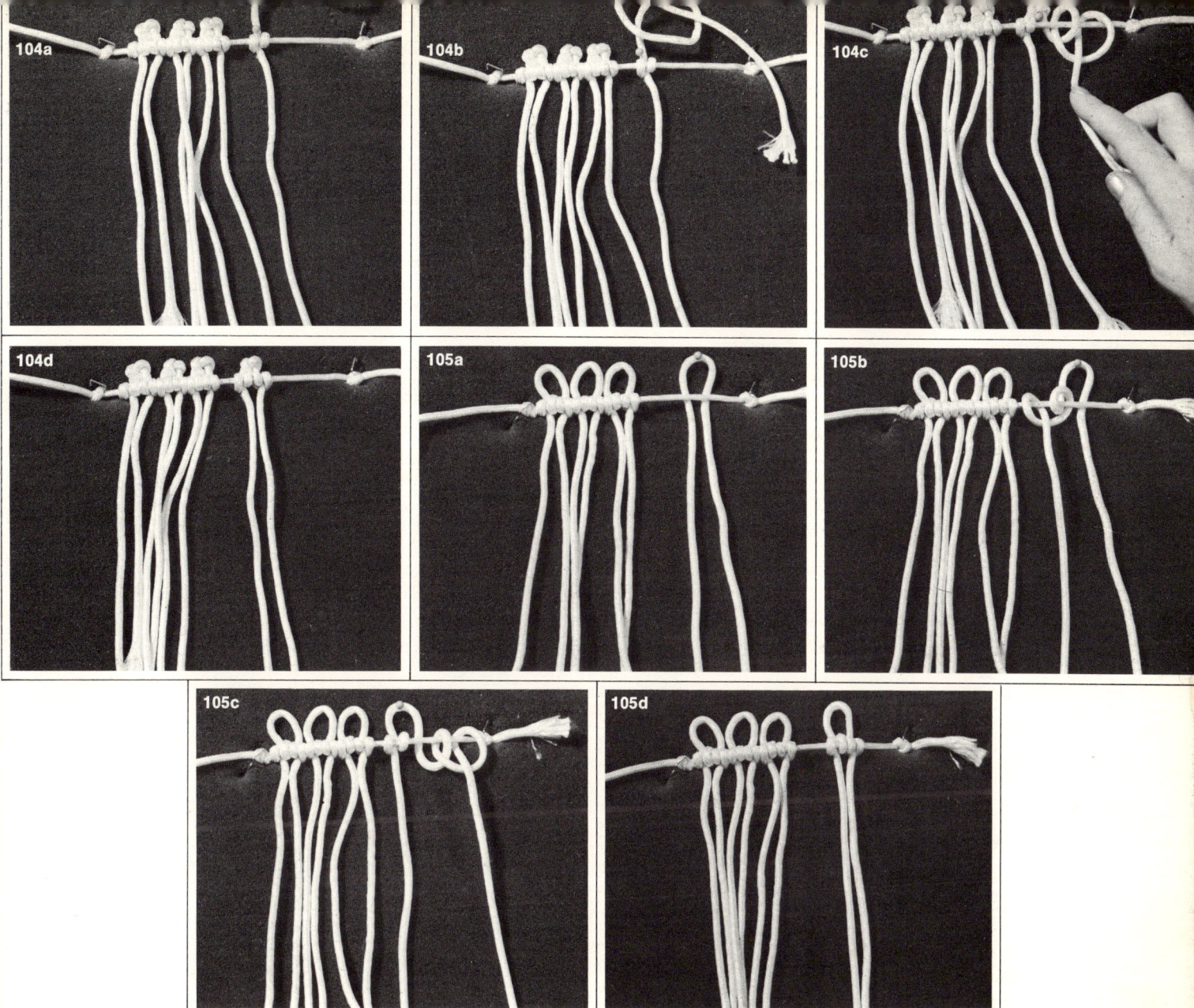

Fancy Mountings and Picots *

There are several ways of adding interest to the beginning of a piece by mounting your cords in different ways. A few of the many possibilities are shown in the following pages.

104. Mount with Overhand Knot

    A. Pin cord and mount left side with Clove Hitch.

    B. Tie an Overhand Knot close to the Clove Hitch.

    C. Tighten Overhand Knot, pin, put right cord under mounting cord and tie Clove Hitch.

    D. Completed knots.

105. Single-Loop Mount

    A. Put loop under mounting cord in usual manner, but pin it in position.

    B. Tie a double Clove Hitch in the left cord with your right hand.

    C. Tie a double Clove Hitch in the right cord with your left hand.

    D. Completed mounting.

Picots—Small ornamental loops forming a border or edging.

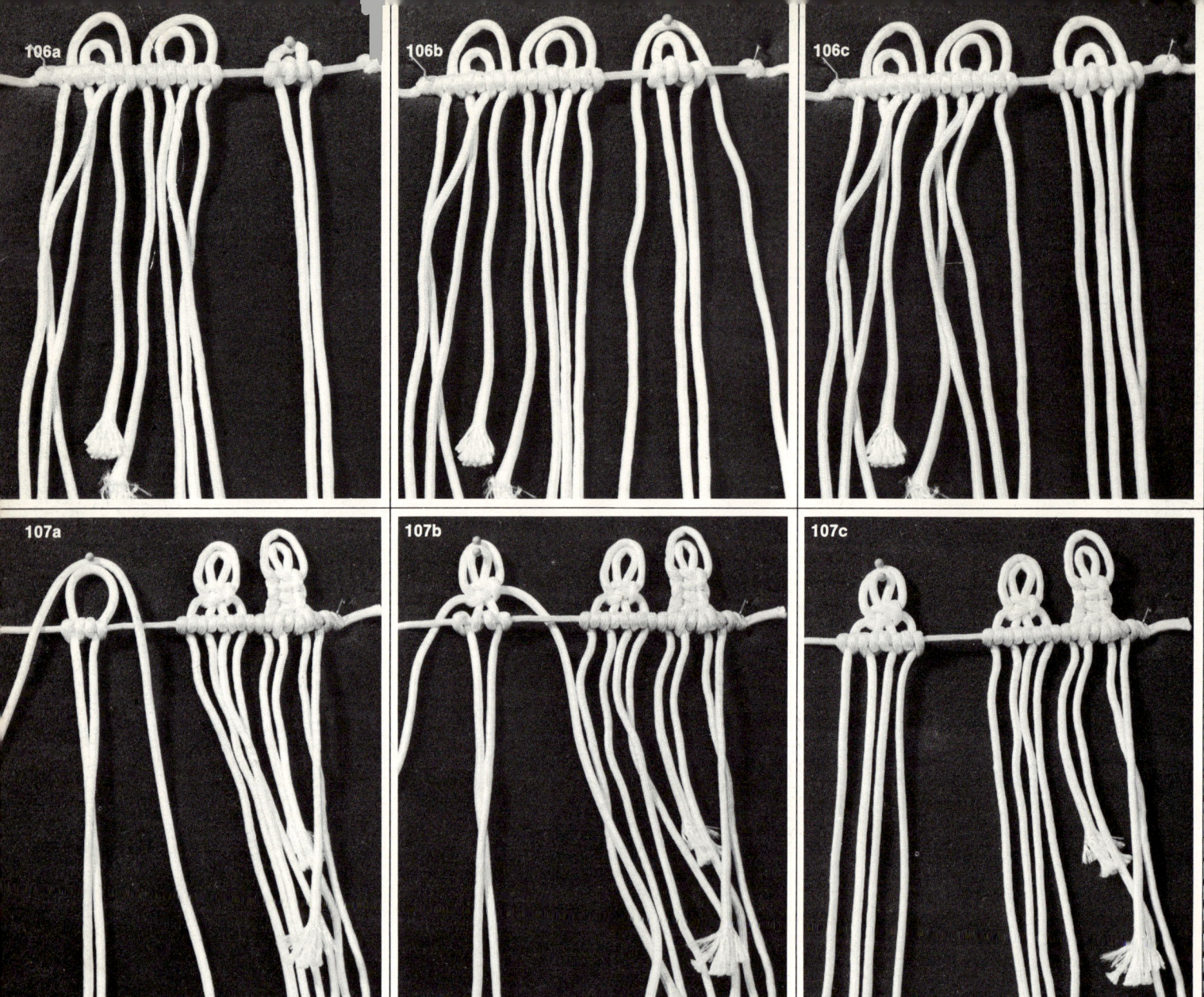

106. Double-Loop Mount

A. Mount half of your cords in the single-loop manner just shown (Ill. 105). Separate the cords.

B. Pin a second loop above the one already mounted and put the ends under the mounting bar.

C. Tie a Clove Hitch with both cords to complete knot.

107. Loop with Square Knot Mount

A. Repeat steps A and B of the double-loop mount previously shown (Ill. 106). Loops should be deeper for this mount.

B. Tie a Square Knot with the cords of the outside loop, using the inside loop as center cords. Put cords under mounting bar.

C. Tie Clove Hitches with the left and right cords.

1. White cotton seine twine is the simplest of materials, yet it makes a pretty special tie. The angling technique is used to bring it to a point.

2. This project is the simplest of all, but versatile enough to wear as a choker or headband.

3. There's more handle and beads and fringe than purse to this project—but it's mostly for show, anyway.

4. You'll spend more time adding the beads to the hem than in tying the knots of this adjustable pinafore.

5. Four hundred cords were used to turn this plain poncho into something spectacular. Using a different color of ribbon for the front and back gives a beautiful effect as you walk along.

6. Any plain dress or sweater is dressed up by this colorful bib.

7. The Clove Hitch is the only knot used for this simple choker. Prewaxed upholsterer's cord ties beautifully and comes in a soft neutral color.

8. This belt makes a fine gift. It's a repeat pattern of several basic macramé motifs, so it's good practice, too.

9. A heavily beaded center section and wide side panels make this belt distinctive.

10. This bikini of polypropylene cord not only looks great at the beach—you can wear it in the water, too. (Photo courtesy of Dick Kreznar.)

11. The nice thing about this pendant is that you can wear it over one hip as well as in the usual center position.

12. Boys and girls can wear this vest of army surplus nylon braid. It adjusts at the sides, so it can "grow" with the child.

13. This bag was adapted from the design of an old purse found in an antique store. Knotting it in two colors adds extra interest.

14. Connie's choker is made with only one knot—the Clove Hitch—and lots of beads and feathers.

15. You can fringe any plain garment with a simple macramé motif and turn it into something special.

16. Suspenders are back in style—especially red ones like firemen use to keep their pants up.

17. Wear this little bag around your neck as a decoration—and carry your cash and keys along.

18. You saw Jann wearing this around her neck on the cover. If you're a bit brave, try wearing it around your waist.

19. Kathy's sash looks almost like silver. It's easy to knot and will adjust to any waist size.

20. Simple marlin twine—and simple knots—make an earthy-looking pin and bracelet.

21. The top of this dress is very tightly knotted and sculptural. But the ends, in contrast, are left raggy and at random lengths.

22. Working with color isn't as hard as it looks, and it adds something extra to the traditional man's tie.

23. Here is a big garment that requires surprisingly little knotting. Lots of crow beads and imitation Indian bone beads are an important part of the design.

24. There are so many beads in this long necklace that you don't have to tie many knots.

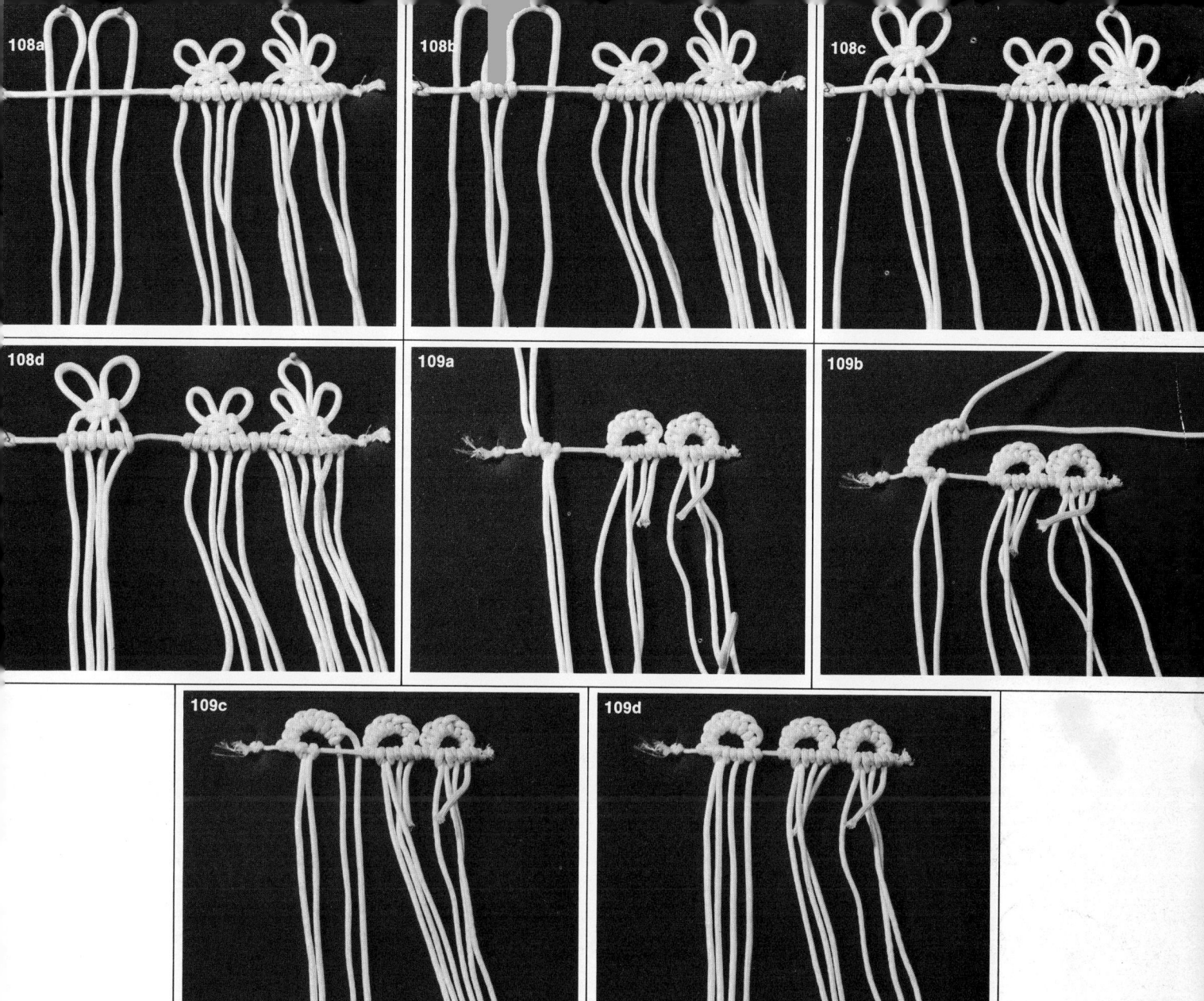

108. Double-Loop Square Knot Mount

A. Pin 2 loops generously above (and behind) mounting bar.

B. Clove Hitch the 2 inside cords.

C. Tie a Square Knot with the 2 outside cords, leaving the loops as decorative elements. (Figure in right of photo is same method with a third cord mounted, with a very high loop in the center. The Square Knot is tied around it also.)

D. Put cords back under mounting bar and tie a Clove Hitch with each.

109. Clove Hitch Mount

A. Mount 1 cord up and 1 cord down on mounting bar.

B. Using the cord mounted above bar, tie 7 to 10 Clove Hitches over right cord with left cord.

C. Pull Clove Hitch sennit around to half-circle shape and put cords under mounting bar.

D. Tie Clove Hitches with 2 cords. (More cords can be mounted inside the semicircle formed if desired, or depending on the size of the circle.)

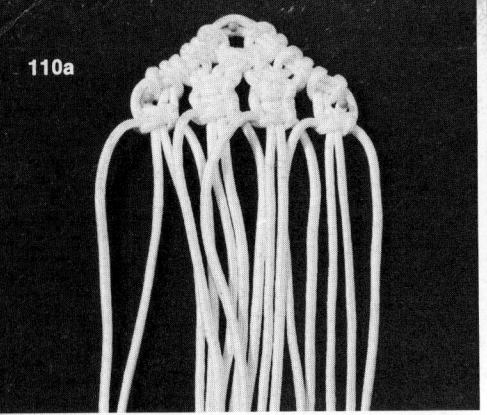 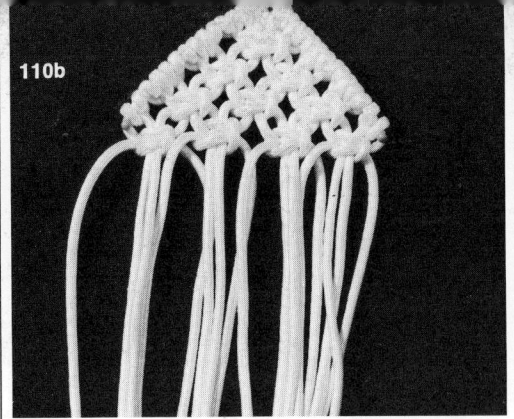 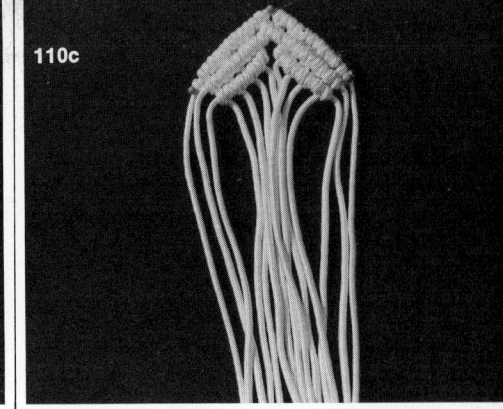

110. Pointed Mountings

A. Two cords are used as mounting cords. Six more cords are mounted on them conventionally, then the holding cords are pinned in pointed pattern at top center and sides before knotting is started. Here is a pattern of 1, 2, and 4 Square Knots.

B. Here 1 cord acts as holding cord for 7 others mounted with Double Lark's Heads, then pinned firmly in point pattern. Knotting starts with increasing Square Knot pattern: 1, 2, 3, then 4.

C. Mounting is the same as in the previous illustration, but rows of Clove Hitches start the knotting.

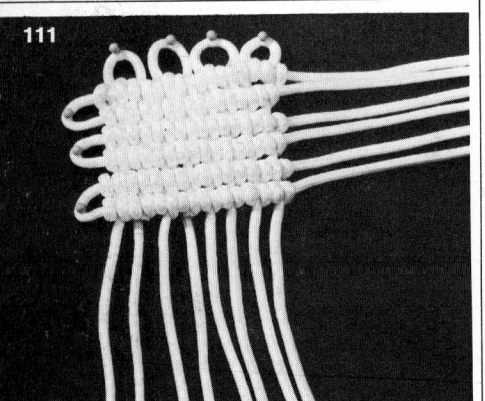 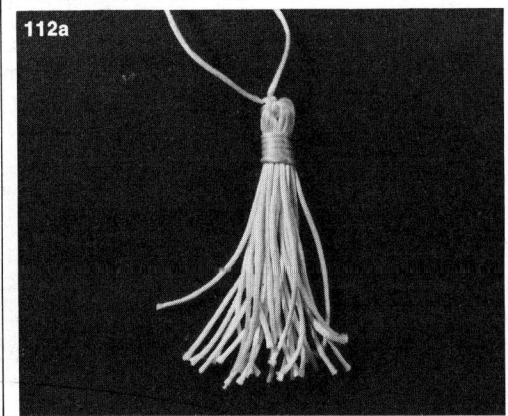 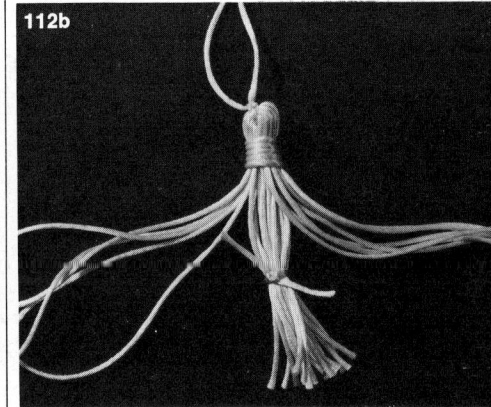

111. Corner Mounting

This is essentially the same method as shown on page 23 for adding separate cords. The vertical cords are pinned firmly in position. The horizontal cords are Clove Hitched on, one at a time. Now the knotting can continue in both directions.

112. Tassels

A. Tassels are simple to make. Cut as many cords as you will need (when doubled) and tie them very tightly at the center with a separate cord (which will later be used to attach the tassel to the work). The wrap which forms the ball can be a separate cord or one of the tassel strands. Tuck the end under with a crochet hook.

B. Tassels can be knotted for an extra fancy effect, if you allow for longer strands. Isolate the outside cords which you will use to tie knots (be sure they are multiples of 4) by tying all the inside cords together temporarily with a separate string until knotting is completed. Then trim off all ends evenly.

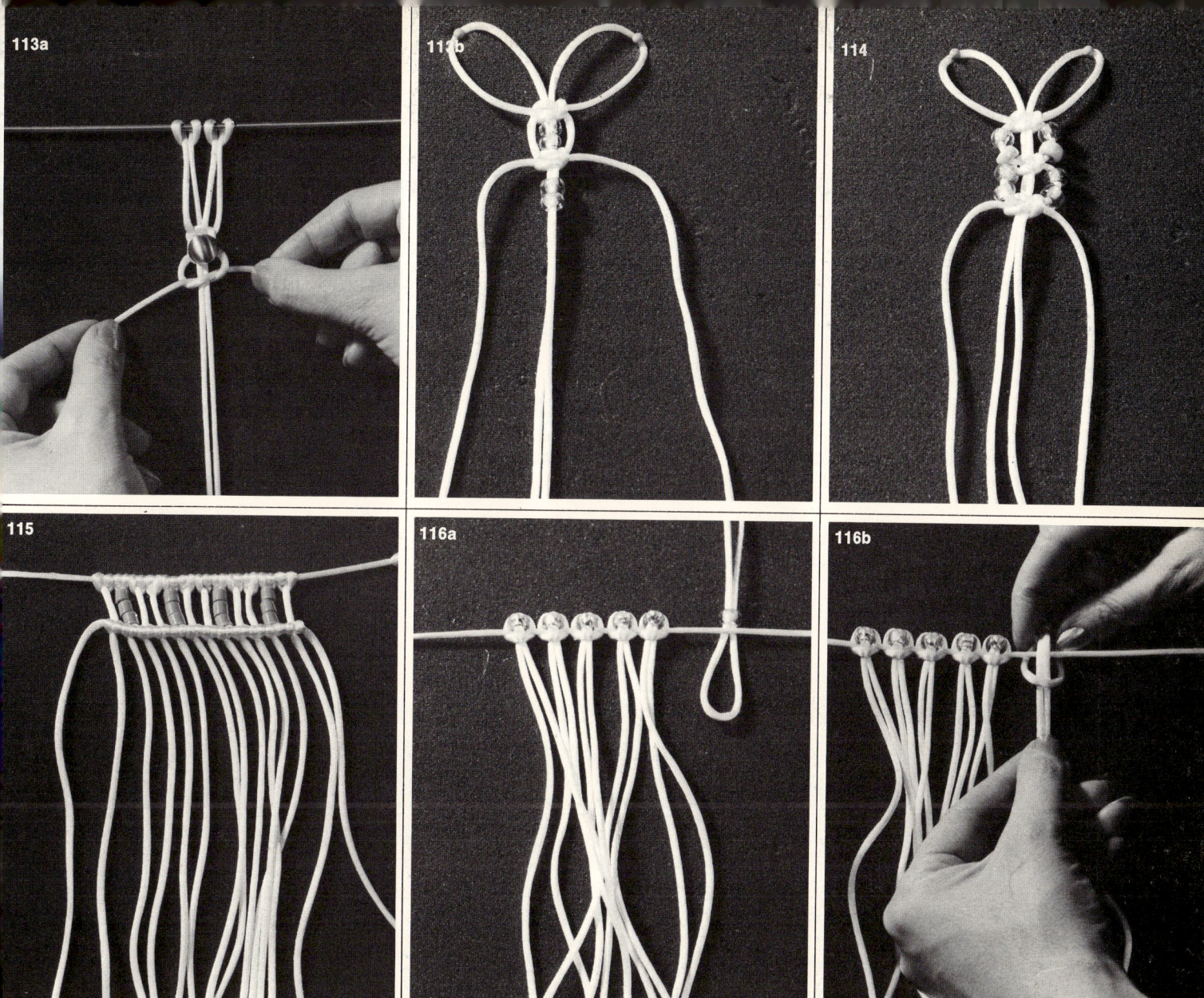

Working with Beads, Rings, and Feathers

Several ways to add beads and other materials to your work are shown in the following pages.

Simple Ways of Adding Beads

113. Beads mounted on center cords between Square Knots.

114. Beads mounted on outside cords between Square Knots.

115. Beads on vertical cords between rows of Clove Hitches.

Adding Beads When Mounting Cords

116. Beads on Mounting with Lark's Head
    A. Put bead on doubled cord and put loop *down* under mounting bar.
    B. Holding bead above mounting cord, pull cords down and through 'til bead is held taut.

55

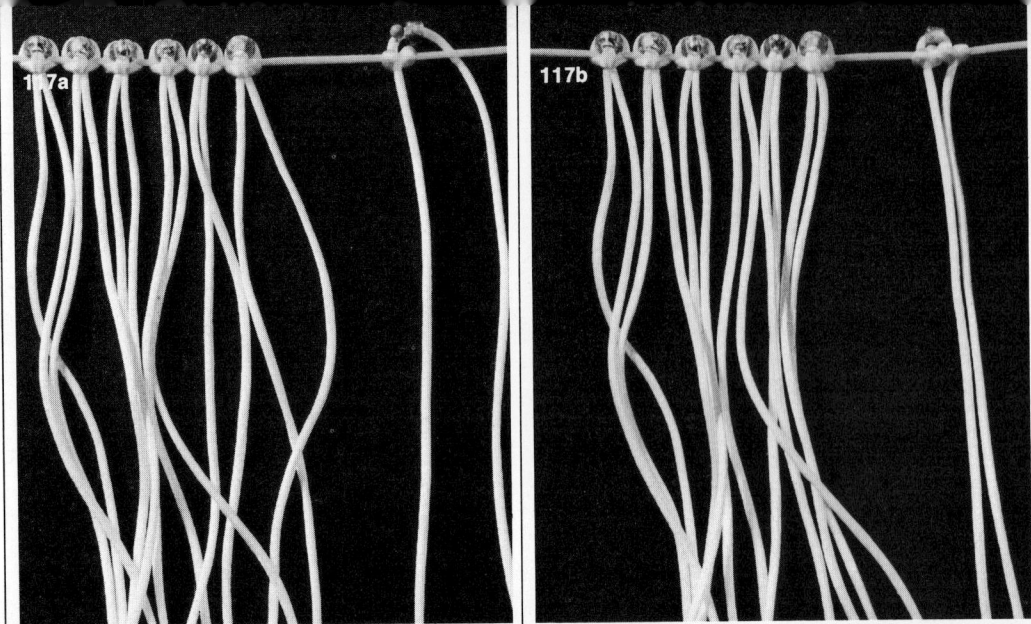
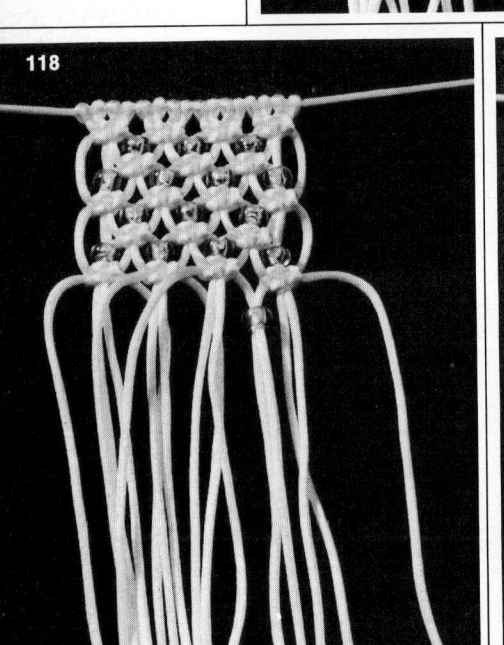
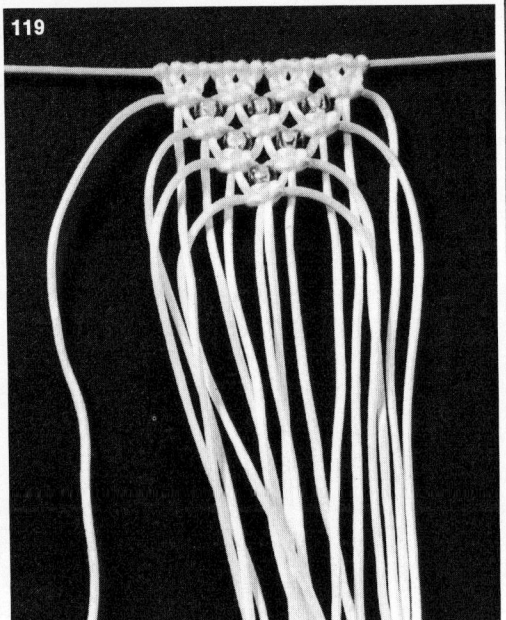
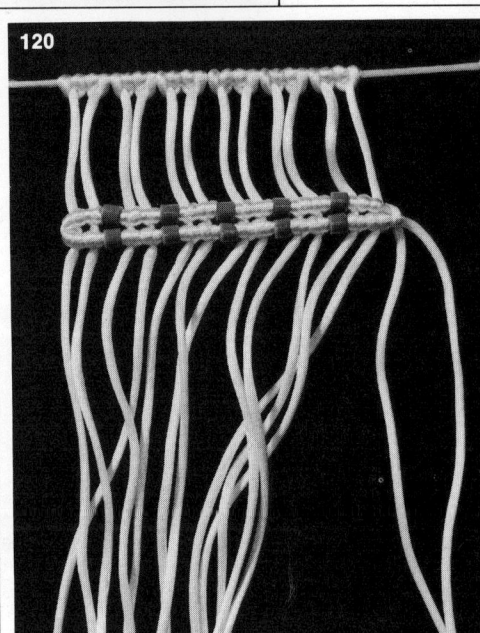

117. Beads on Mounting Cord with Clove Hitch

    A. Pin doubled cord at center behind mounting bar and tie a Clove Hitch in left cord.

    B. Put bead on cord and tie Clove Hitch in right cord.

Beads in Square Knot Patterns

118. Beads Between Alternating Square Knots

119. Beads Between Decreasing Square Knots

120. Beads on the Holding Cord of Clove Hitch Bar

    Be sure to space beads in some logical pattern. This technique is useful for widening a piece of macramé.

121. Adding a Ring with Square Knots

    A. Place ring over center cords and pull center cords through bottom of ring.

    B. Tie a Square Knot where you want the *center* of the ring to fall.

    C. Flip ring over and pull center cords through so they are on top of ring.

    D. Tie another Square Knot under ring to hold it in place.

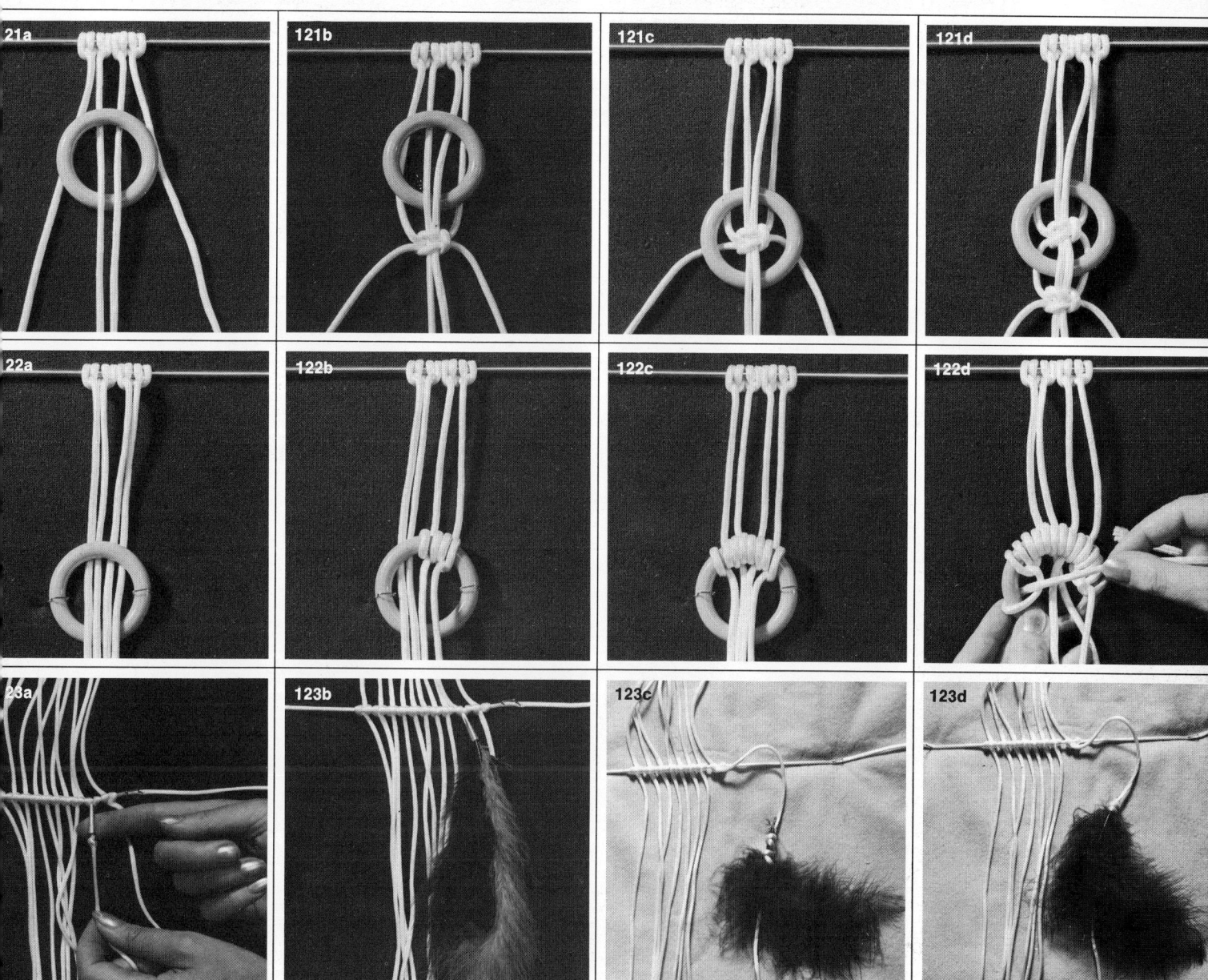

122. Adding or Covering a Ring with Clove Hitches

A. Place ring over cords and pull cords through bottom of ring. Pin or hold ring in place.

B. Clove Hitch each cord toward upper center of ring. Here, right-hand cords are tied with left hand.

C. Left-hand cords are tied with right hand.

D. If you want to cover ring, continue Clove Hitching over ring with right and left cords till covered.

123. Adding Feathers

With a feather cone

A. Slip cone, wide end down, onto strand where feather will go and tie an Overhand Knot close to the cone so it won't slip down.

B. Push a feather quill or two firmly into cone. Cut cord at Overhand Knot. Glue knot and put a dab of glue into opening of cone.

In a coil knot

C. Form Coil Knot loosely. Push quill of feather up through wraps (as though it were a crochet hook).

D. Tighten knot. Cut cord below knot if desired and reinforce with glue.

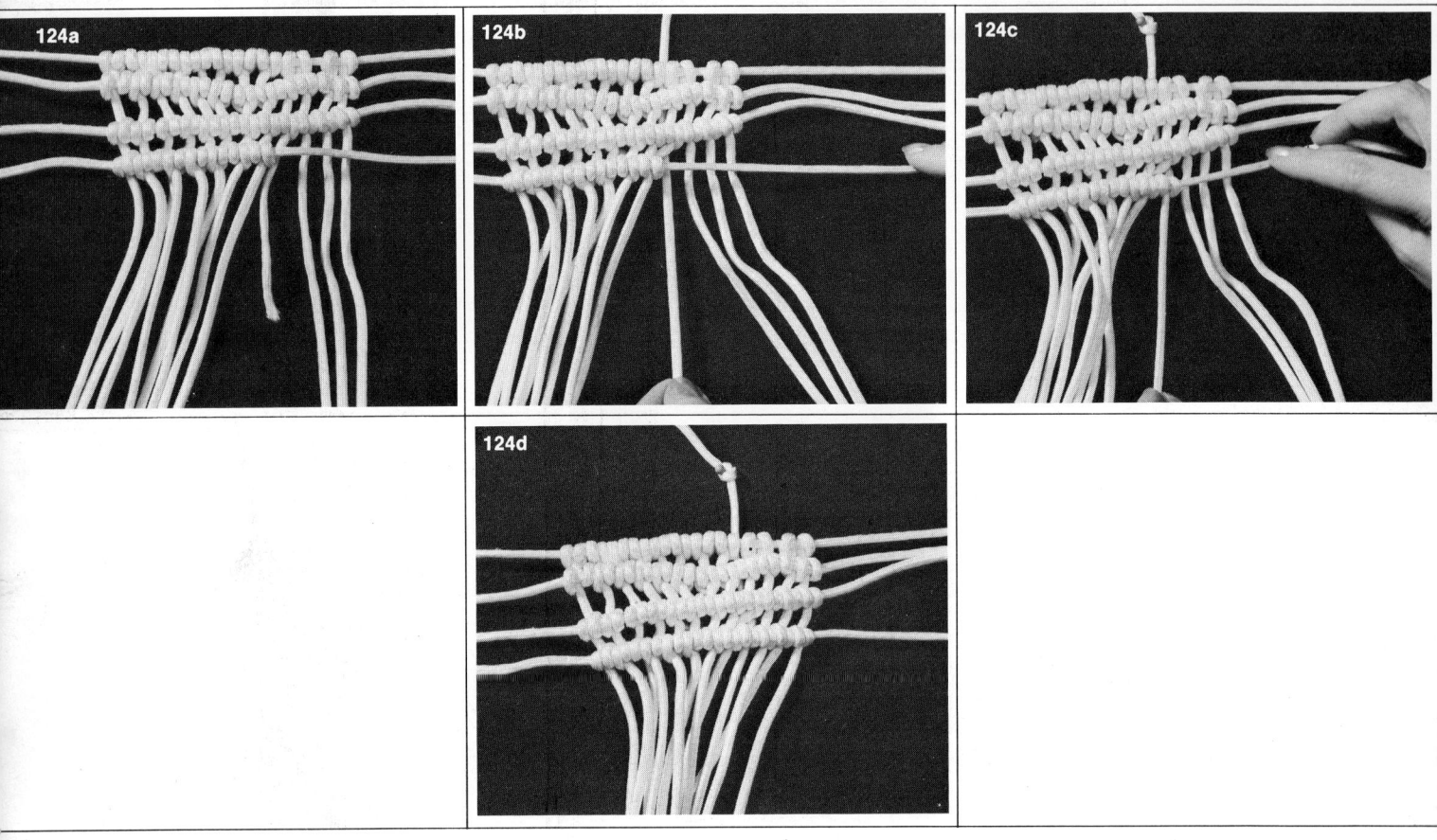

Miscellany

Here is a bunch of miscellaneous notes about working with beads, adding cords, joining pieces, and gluing.

Adding Cords When You Run Short

Several methods of adding cords are now shown. It is not always possible to allow for all the long cords you will need, especially if you are designing as you go. But as you will see, adding in cords is no great problem and the short ends are easily tucked back under the work, cut off, and glued.

124. A. A cord in a Clove Hitch bar has run short.

   B. Tuck short end out of the way. Tie an Overhand Knot in the cord you're adding. Pin it to top of work and bring it down behind bar being Clove Hitched.

   C. Tie Clove Hitch with added cord.

   D. Finish row as usual. Continue using added cord. When piece is completed, cut cord short at top and tuck behind work.

125. Here, the new cord becomes the right-hand tying cord for the bottom Square Knot. Short end has been tucked under.

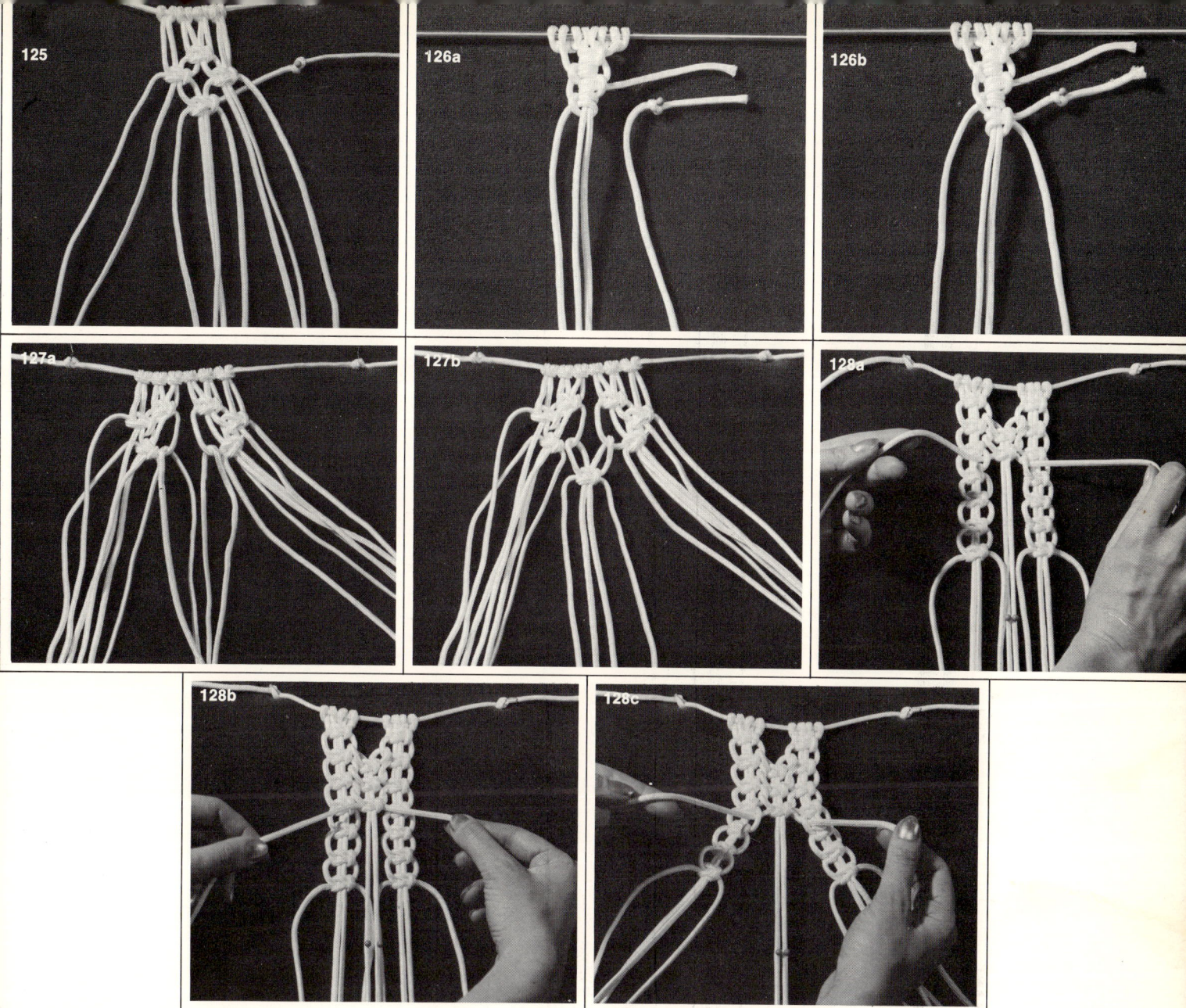

126. Extra cord is added in a Lark's Head sennit. Short cord is shown at upper right.

Adding Extra Cords and Joining Two Pieces

Many times it is desirable to intertwine sennits, for decorative purposes, or to join pieces of macramé to form a larger piece such as the front and back of a handbag, dress, or vest.

Pieces can be joined by intertwining cords as the knotting progresses, adding new cords to join the two pieces and knotting, or by lacing a separate cord through the "openings" formed along the side of a work, by hand or with a crochet hook.

127. A. Two Square Knot sennits are joined by means of new cords. The 2 new cords are looped through openings of the sennits.

    B. Tie a Square Knot with the 2 new cords. As outside sennits are completed, the added cords can be looped through the next knots and tied again, or they can become an integral part of the piece.

128. A. Here 2 new cords are looped between the first "hole" of 2 Square Knot sennits, and a Square Knot is tied.

    B. Continue tying Square Knots, looping the outside cords through the "holes" as you go from back to front.

    C. Cords have just been pulled through next "hole."

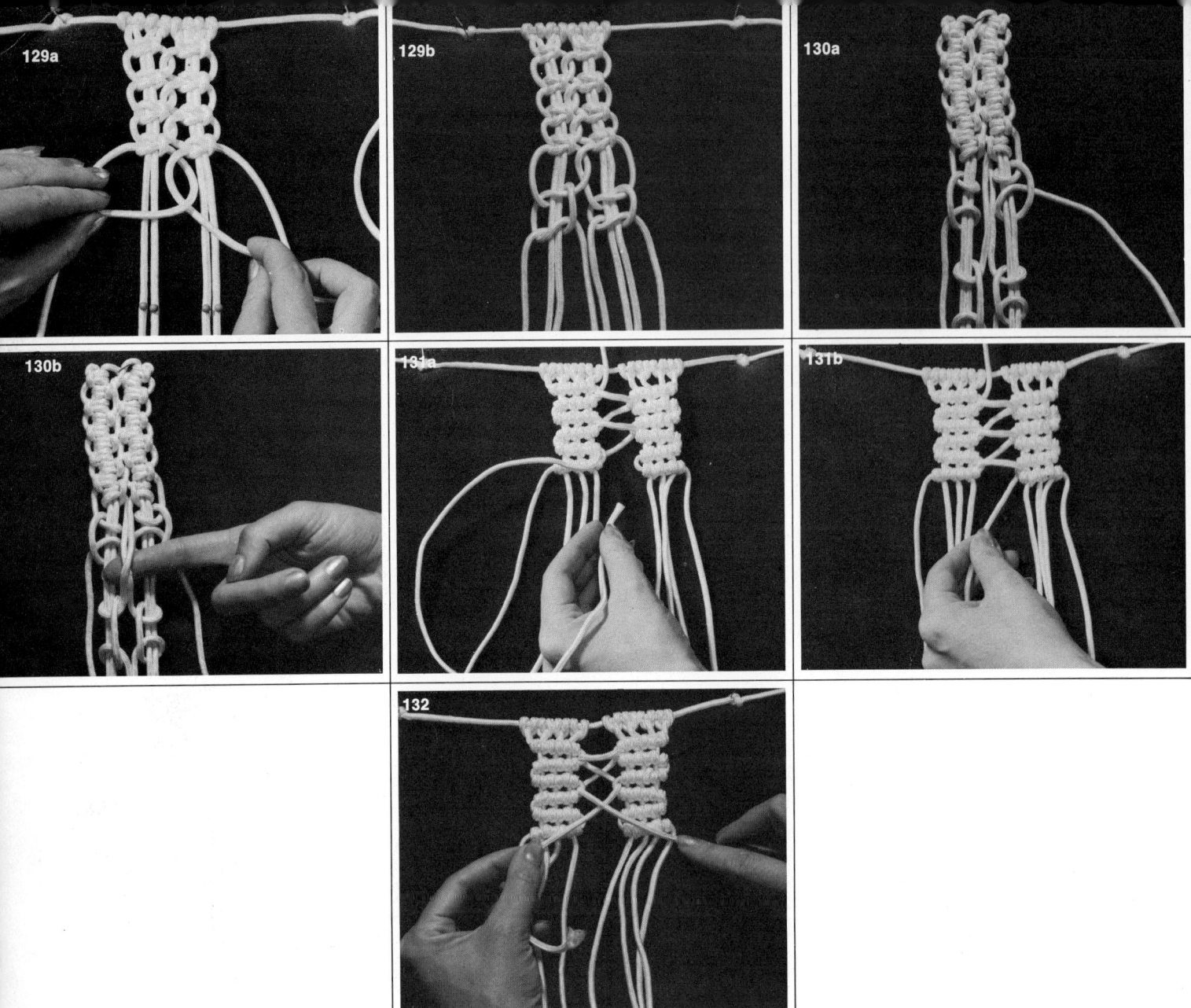

129. A. Two Square Knot sennits are joined merely by looping the inside tying cords around each other before tying each knot.

    B. Series of linked Square Knots.

130. A. An alternating Lark's Head sennit in which the inside tying cords are switched between each sequence of Lark's Heads.

    B. You can see where cords overlap.

Lacing

131. A separate cord is pinned at top and "laced" back and forth through the ends of Clove Hitch bars from back to front. If knots were very tight a crochet hook could be used. I have left a good distance between the pieces being joined for easy visualization, but if you were joining the front and back of a handbag, for example, you would pull the laces tight.

132. This lace also uses the holes in the side of 2 finished pieces, but is mounted and laced in an X pattern just as you would thread a shoelace. It can be pulled as taut as needed.

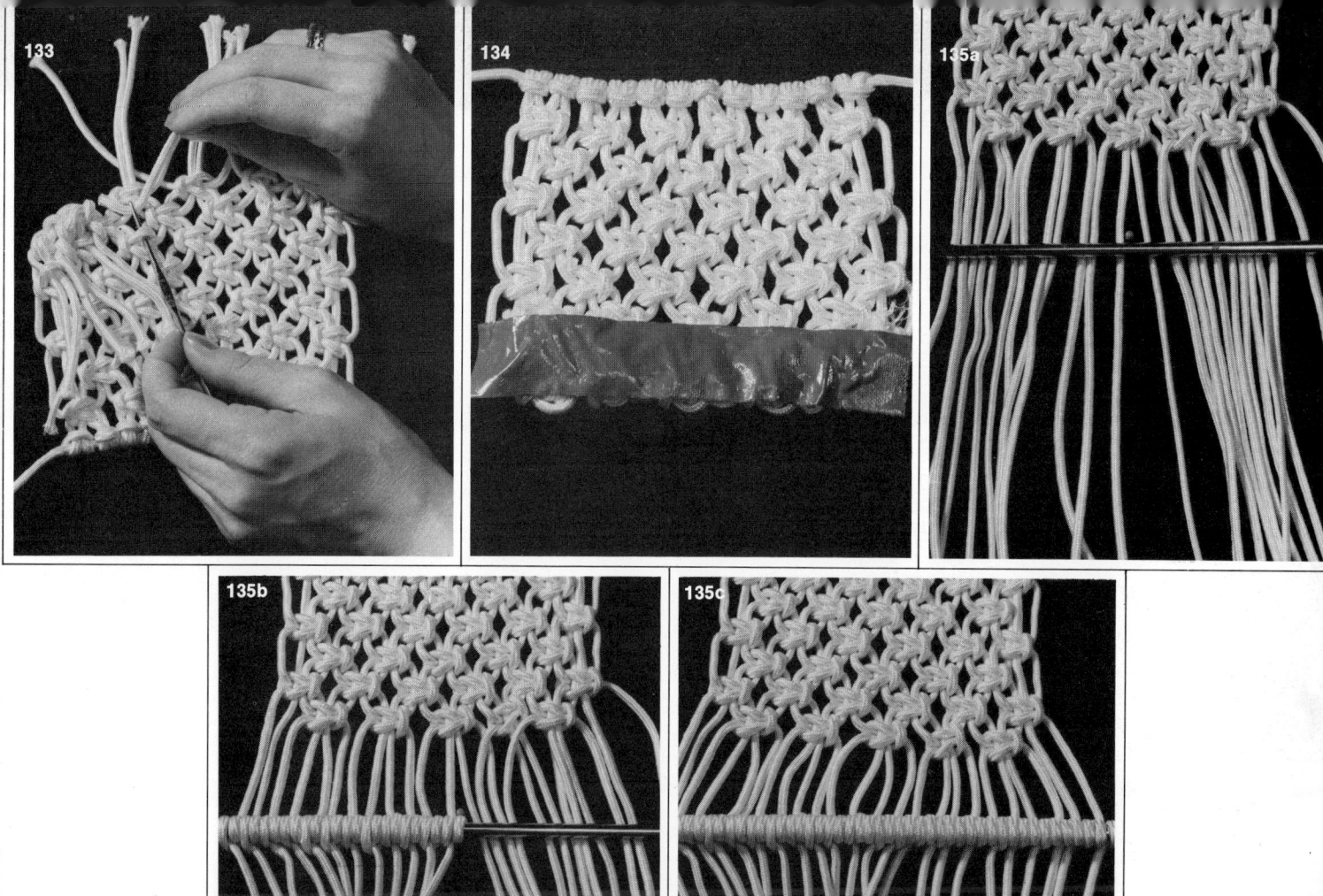

Other Ways to Finish Work

133. Work can be turned over and ends cut short and pulled through back of work with crochet hook. Gluing will insure their staying in place.

134. Another method is to cut ends short and tape them to back of work with facing tape; or sew them with a fabric lining (especially good in the case of handbags or place mats, which will get a lot of wear).

135. Ends can be finished off in a row of Clove Hitches on a cord or dowel pinned to the knotting surface. I find it easiest to Clove Hitch from the center to the sides. Ends can be left long and cut, tied in Overhand Knots, fringed, frayed, or cut short and glued.

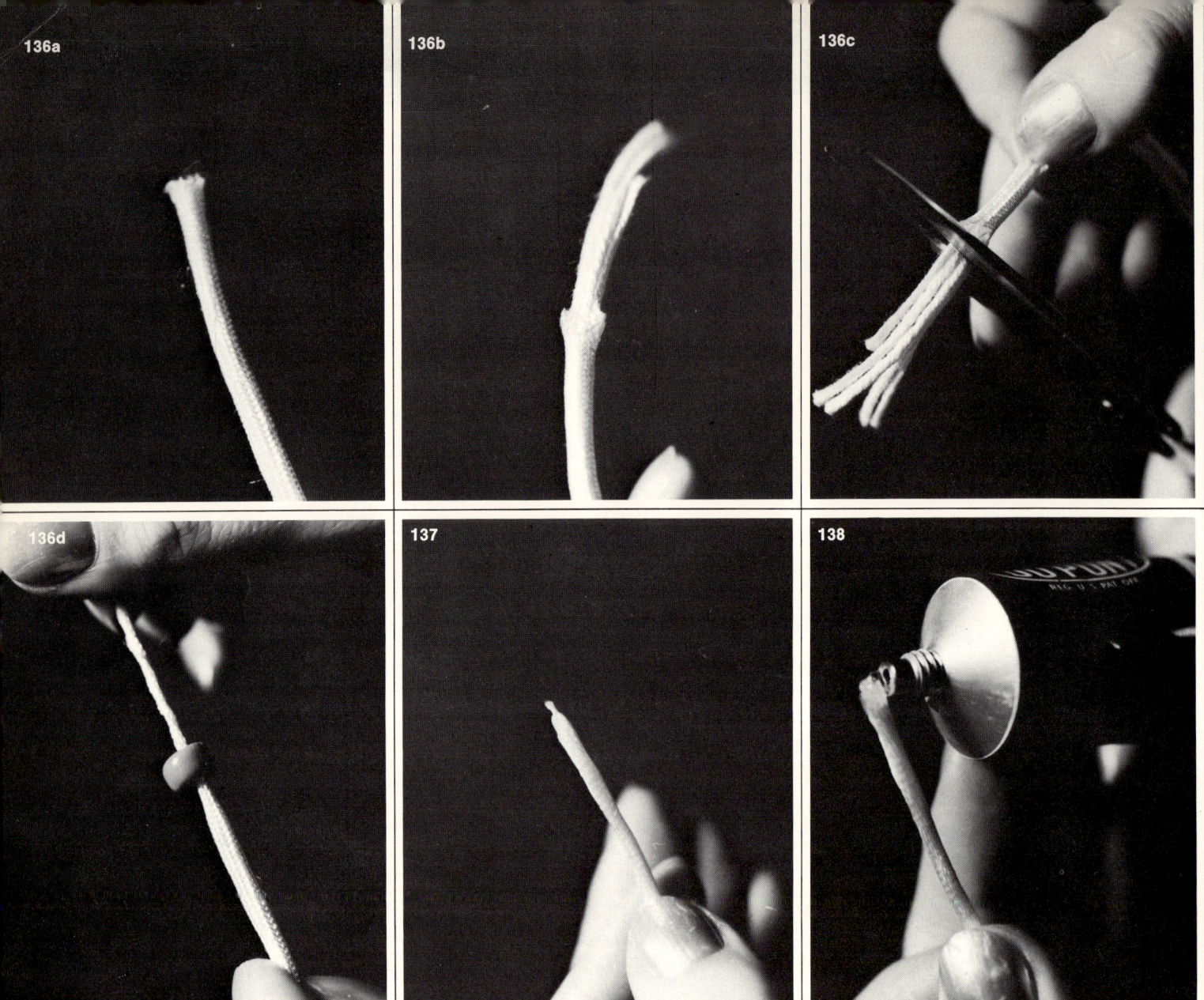

Working with Beads

136. A. Blunt end of heavy braid—too thick to string beads.
      B. Cotton core is pulled out from center of braid.
      C. It is cut.
      D. Now braid will pass through bead.

137. Center cord is pulled out a little way in a piece of rattail to facilitate threading.

138. Gluing

If ends tend to fray, a dab of glue on each end will stop fraying and also make bead threading easier.

Working with Color

Working with color is simpler than it looks and automatically adds interest to a piece. Another variation would be working with 2 or more different kinds of cord; and the method would be the same.

There are several basic ways of working with color, the idea being to change direction, cover certain colors and expose others at different points in the piece.

Basically these are the ways:

- Mount the strands of different colors in some sort of symmetrical pattern in multiples of 4 tying cords, from the left in to the center and out to the right.
- "Bury" a color by using it as holding cords for Clove Hitch bars or as center cords for sennits tied with other colors.
- "Expose" a color by tying rows of vertical Clove Hitches with it, thus covering all the other colors which act as holding cords.
- Change the order of colors by working the center color, for example, out to the edge by using it as holding cords for diagonal rows; the holding cords will end up at the outside of the work.

There are, of course, other ways, but these provide the basic premise of working with color.

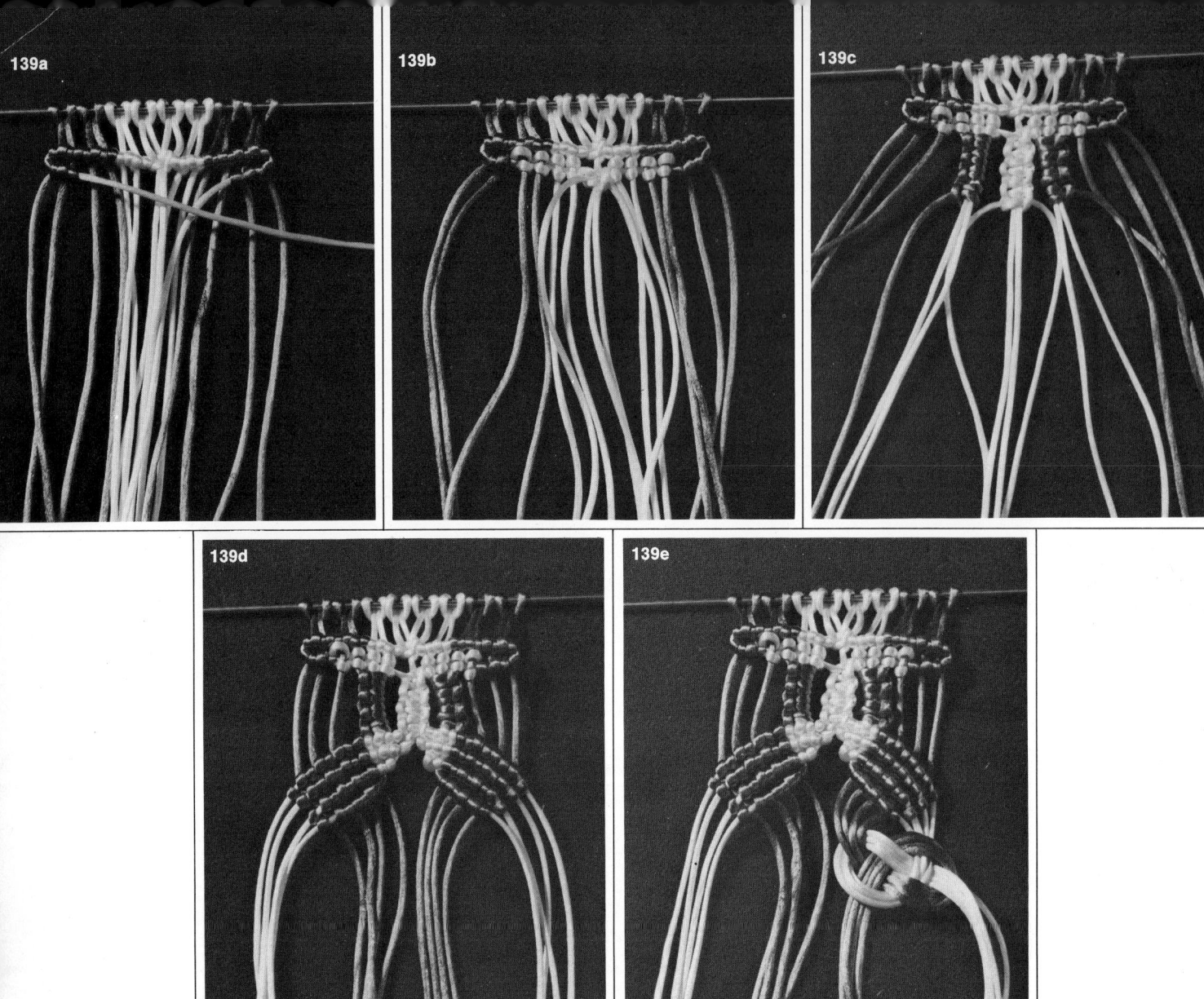

139. A. A Square Knot is tied in the center of work. The tying cords are used as holding cords for a row of Clove Hitches out to each side.

B. On the way back, the first 2 cords are tied in regular Clove Hitches, but then the white holding cord becomes the tying cord and the row is finished with vertical Clove Hitches, thus covering the rest of the darker cords.

C. The white cords are buried by Lark's Head chains tied with the adjoining dark cords.

D. The white cords are brought from the center to the outside by using them as holding cords for rows of diagonal Clove Hitches.

E. The 4 left-hand cords of this Josephine Knot are the dark cord. The 4 right-hand cords are white.

THE PROJECTS

***Very Important Information Which Will Keep You
Out of Trouble When Doing the Projects***

If you've done your homework, you now have a good working knowledge of macramé and are ready to make some things to wear.

The projects are presented in order of difficulty with pictures and instructions which I hope will be easy to follow—but which are based on your having *practiced*.

Now, no matter how dutiful you've been, there will be places where you just don't understand exactly what's to be done. (I have a very hard time with written instructions myself, and learn most from looking at pictures.) What you have to do here is *improvise*. Don't let the word scare you. The ability to improvise as you go is one of the great qualities of this craft. If you do your project a little differently from the way it's presented, it probably won't show—you'll still get the same effect—or it might look even better. In other words, when you run into something you don't understand, do something you *do* understand. Also, learning to improvise a bit will send you on to bigger and better things after this book.

Actually, there are several instances in the projects where I *make* you improvise—in some cases because it's easier than explanations, or because the idea is to achieve a random, asymmetrical look. (Remember, you can always copy from the pictures.)

You will not always be able to find the exact cord and beads I've used for a particular project, and you will have to substitute. Or, you may not want to use beads at all; in this case, use knots of your choosing as "filler."

At the beginning of each project, I've noted any tricky knots or sections that merit special attention, and have suggested alternative types of cord. But trust your own judgment, too, in choice of materials and color. For specific knot patterns, the page reference is given where detailed instructions can be found in the preceding sections of the book.

Note: In giving requirements for materials, "cord" refers to the cut ends. In the instructions, "cords" refers to the working strands (double the number of cut ends).

Project 1: Ring Choker

Here's a very simple project for a start which uses just basic motifs of the Square Knot and Clove Hitch. If you leave the ends long, you can also wear it as a headband.

Pertinent Information

Size: 12" (plus tying ends)
Materials: Soutache 8 cords 40"
          12 crow beads
          20 tile beads
          1 plastic ring (⅞" diam.)
          Rattail #1 (as shown in color plates) or marlin twine might be used instead.

Directions are given for 1 side of choker. Repeat for other side.

To begin: Mount 4 cords on ring with Reverse Lark's Head and pin ring to knotting surface.

1. Tie a row of 2 Square Knots. Tie a Square Knot with the 4 center cords.
2. Add a crow bead to the 2 center cords (together).
3. Tie a Square Knot with the 4 center cords. Tie a row of 2 Square Knots, then another Square Knot with the 4 center cords.
4. Repeat steps 2 and 3.
5. Using the outside cord on each side as holding cords, tie an X pattern (page 12).
6. Add 3 tile beads to the 2 center cords.
7. Repeat steps 5 and 6.
8. Using the outside cords as holding cords, tie a row of diagonal Clove Hitches in a V pattern in toward center, making the crossover (page 12).

To finish: Add a couple of beads (I've used 1 crow and 1 tile bead) to each pair of cords in order and secure them with an Overhand Knot about 7" from the end of the work. (Use these cords to tie the choker.) Cut and glue cords.

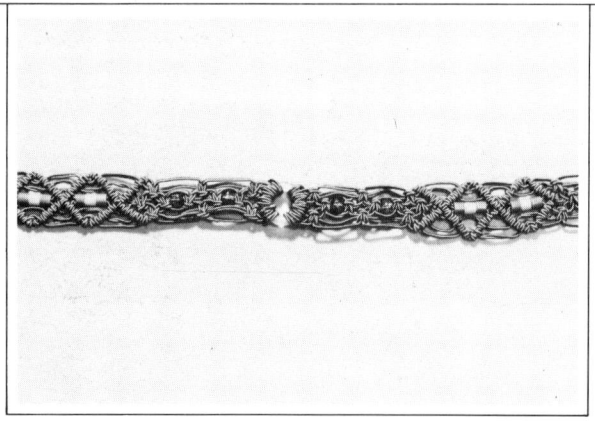

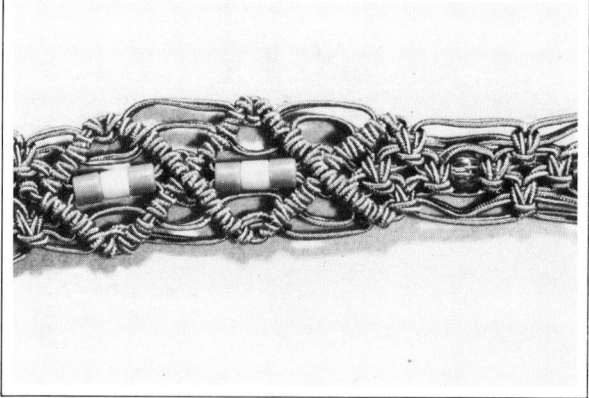

Project 2: Feather Choker

This is the simplest project imaginable: only the Clove Hitch is used to form a wide neckband, double-thick holding cords being added with each row to form ties for the choker. The rest just involves stringing beads and feathers.

Pertinent Information

Size: 7" (plus ties) x 11"
Materials: #1 Rattail 16 cords 50", 14 cords 30"
  592 tile beads
  180 crow beads
  16 small metal beads
  8 feather cones
  16 plume feathers
  Soutache, polypropylene cord, or packaging twine would also look good.

To start: Pin 2 30" cords to the knotting surface as a double-thick mounting cord. Mount the 16 50" cords in the middle with the Double Lark's Head (page 47).

1. Add 2 more groups of 2 30" cords with rows of Clove Hitches, working from the center, by the method shown on page 23.
2. Add 3 tile beads to each vertical cord (32 cords).
3. Add another 2 30" cords with a row of Clove Hitches as in step 1.
4. Repeat step 2.
5. Add the last 3 pairs of 30" cords as in step 1.
6. Add a long row of beads to the 8 cords on each side. I've used the following pattern: 19 tile beads, 3 crow beads, 3 tile beads, 3 crow beads, 3 tile beads, 3 crow beads, 1 small metal bead. Secure each row with Overhand Knots, pushing beads tightly up against neckband.
7. Slip 1 feather cone and 2 feathers onto every other one of the 16 center cords by the method shown on page 57. Tie an Overhand Knot tight against neckband in all the remaining cords. (If you cannot obtain feather cones, use the Coil Knot method also shown on page 57 to secure the feathers.)

To finish: Tight against the end of the Clove Hitch rows, tie an Overhand Knot on each side with each 2 cords used to form the neckband. Slip 3 crow beads (optional) onto each pair of cords except the center pair and secure with another Overhand Knot about 8" from end of neckband (to use as ties for the choker). Cut and glue all cords (neckband, beaded cords, feather cords, etc.).

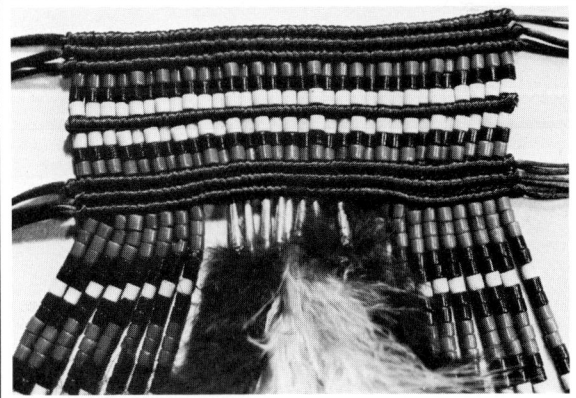

Project 3: Pin

This piece is mounted on a pin back, so it can be worn on a pocket or at the waist as well as on a collar. Tile beads on separate holding cords widen the piece without adding new cords, and create open areas.

Pertinent Information

Size: 3" x 8"

Materials: Marlin twine #18 8 cords 60"
                                        3 cords 8"
       66 tile beads
       16 crow beads
       1 pin back 1¼" wide
       Cotton or nylon seine twine would be suitable substitutes; also rattail or soutache.

To begin: Double 8 60" cords and mount them on pin back with Reverse Lark's Head. Pin the pin back firmly to knotting surface.

1. Tie a pattern of decreasing Square Knots: 4, 3, 2, and 1 (page 20). Make these knots tight to secure mounting on pin back.
2. Using the outside cord on each side as holding cords, do a row of diagonal Clove Hitches in toward center and make crossover (page 12).
3. Add 2 tile beads to each holding cord at this point and complete the X. Beads will widen pattern.
4. Divide the cords into 2 groups. Take the next inside cord on each side of the X as holding cord, and do another row of Clove Hitches out to the sides, leaving out the holding cord from the previous row. Do 2 more rows on each side; the number of Clove Hitches will decrease by one with each row (page 30).
5. Now you have 4 rows of Clove Hitches on each side and 4 cords coming from each side of the two patterns. Cross over the 4 inside cords on each side and weave them (page 29).
6. Tie an Overhand Knot near the end of one of the 8" cords and pin the knot at left side of work just below the weave pattern. Use this as the holding cord for a row of Clove Hitches. Add 2 tile beads to the holding cord after 4 cords, 1 tile bead after 4 more cords (the center), and 2 tile beads after 4 more cords. Tie the last 4 Clove Hitches and finish the row with another Overhand Knot tied tightly against right side of work.
7. Repeat step 6, about ½" below the previous row.
8. Divide the work into 2 groups of 8 cords and tie a lacy sennit of 3 Square Knots over the center cords of each group in order (page 19). Using the 3 inside cords from each group, tie another lacy sennit of 2 Square Knots using the top cord from each group as center cords.
9. Repeat step 6.
10. Tie random Overhand Knots in the cords in a somewhat V-shaped pattern: i.e., more Overhand Knots in the center cords than on the sides.

To finish: Fringe the ends with tile and crow beads as you wish, ending with a tile bead so that the Overhand Knots will not go through hole. Tie Overhand Knots in V shape. Cut and glue ends.

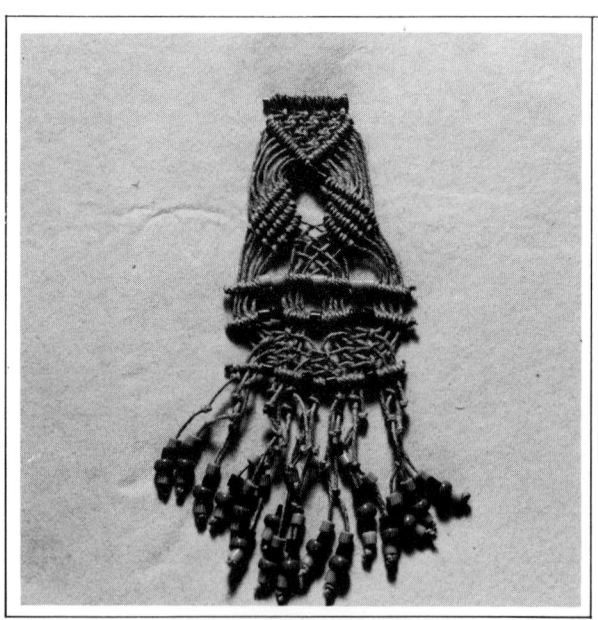

Project 4: Bracelet

The bracelet starts with a buttonhole and ends with a button, combining tightly knotted and beaded areas with areas of open cords.

Pertinent Information

Size: 2" x 7½" (without fringe)
Materials: Marlin twine #18 8 cords 80"
48 tile beads
6 crow beads
1 small button with toggle back
Cotton or nylon seine twine, #1 rattail or soutache are also suitable.

To begin: Use 2 cords as a double-thick mounting bar and mount the other 6 cords with the Reverse Lark's Head. Pin to knotting surface in pointed formation, as shown on page 54.

Note: cords are numbered in some cases to indicate where beads are to be strung.

1. Tie 1 Square Knot with 4 center cords. Tie a row of 2 Square Knots with the 8 center cords, then a row of 4.
2. Tie 1 Square Knot with the 4 center cords. Using the tying cords as holding cords, do a row of Clove Hitches out to the sides and back to the center, securing with a Square Knot tied with the holding cords over the 2 center cords (page 22).
3. Tie a sennit of 3 Square Knots with the 4 center cords. Add 3 tile beads to cords 2, 4, 6, 11, 13, and 15.
4. Repeat step 2.
5. Tie 3 Square Knots with the 4 center cords.
6. Using the outside cords as holding cords, tie an X pattern (page 12), holding the cords at an angle so that at bottom of X bracelet will measure 3½–3¾".
7. Add 1 tile bead to cords 3 and 14, and 2 tile beads to cords 5 and 12. Add 3 crow beads to cords 7 and 10. This is the center of the bracelet. Now we'll repeat the same steps in reverse order.
8. Repeat the X pattern as in step 6.
9. Repeat step 5.
10. Repeat step 2.
11. Repeat step 3.
12. Repeat step 2.
13. Tie a row of 4 Square Knots; then tie a row of 2 Square Knots with the 8 center cords. Slip the button on the 2 center cords of the piece and tie a Square Knot with the 4 center cords to secure it.
14. Using the outside cord on each side as holding cords, tie a row of diagonal Clove Hitches in toward the center and make the crossover.

To finish: Tie an Overhand Knot in each cord tight against work. Add 3 tile beads to the 2 center cords, leave about 3", and secure with Overhand Knots. Cut and glue cords. To wear bracelet, pull the 2 holding cords out at the point at the beginning of the piece to form buttonhole.

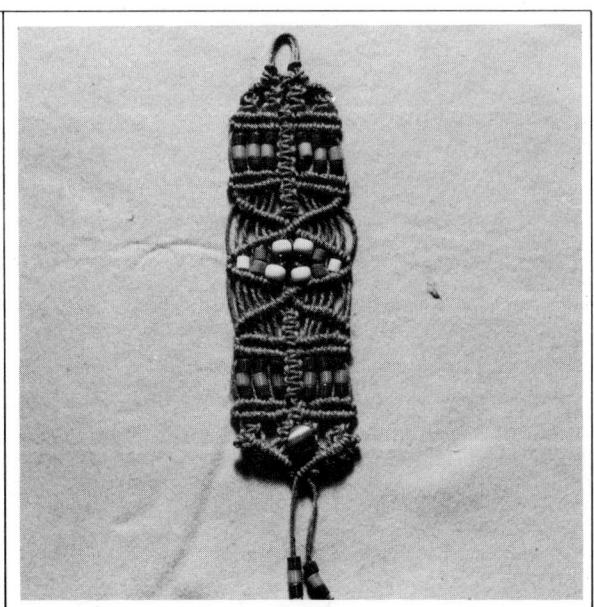

Project 5: Three-Color Fringed Shorts

Fringe and borders are a natural for macramé and a great way to spruce up a plain garment. This fringe pattern (which of course could be made in a single color) can be adapted to anything: a skirt, dress, shorts, shawl, or handbag. Directions are given for just one section, since the garment you fringe will not be exactly like these shorts. I assure you that if you complete one section, it will be easy to see how the rest progresses.

Pertinent Information

Size: 3" deep (to Coil Knots; let ends hang to desired length).

Materials: 4-Line Braid (rayon or cotton) in 3 colors (you will need twice as much of color 1 as of colors 2 and 3) in cords of 36". Rayon ribbon, grosgrain ribbon, soutache, or cotton seine twine will also be attractive.

To begin: Mark off the hem of your garment at 3/8" intervals (on the inside), hopefully ending up with a multiple of 4 cords. If you end up with an uneven number, you can always improvise, but do it in an unobtrusive place (in this case, between the legs of the shorts). If you have a grommeting tool (available in the sewing department of five and dime stores), punch grommets at these intervals and mount cords with the Reverse Lark's Head. Otherwise pull cords through with a crochet hook, as shown on page 46.

Colors are referred to as colors 1, 2, and 3. Mount the doubled cords in this order for 1 section (16 cords) of pattern: color 2, 2, 1, 1, 3, 3, 1, 1, 2, 2, 1, 1, 3, 3, 1, 1.

1. Using the cords of color 1 as holding cords (in order from left to right), tie diagonal Clove Hitch rows from right to left using colors 2 and 3 as tying cords. The first 4 cords of color 1 will tie 4 rows of Clove Hitches with color 2; the second 4 cords of color 1 will tie 4 rows of Clove Hitches with color 3; then the sequence will repeat. You will end up with 4 sections of 4 rows of Clove Hitches, 2 each of colors 2 and 3.
2. Using colors 2 and 3 as holding cords (in order from right to left), tie rows of diagonal Clove Hitches from left to right using color 1 as tying cords. You will get 3 sections of 4 rows of Clove Hitches of color 1.
3. Now the cords of color 1 (which just did all the tying) will be angled from right to left. The cords of colors 2 and 3 will be angled from left to right. Make sure the cords of colors 2 and 3 lie on top of the color 1 cords. You will see that the first 4 cords of color 2 on the left meet the last 4 cords of color 1 on the right. Take these 8 cords and, using 1 cord of color 1, tie a Coil Knot of 6 wraps around the other 7 cords (page 45). Tighten Coil Knot at right angle between groups of cords.

To finish: Continue pattern—it is easiest to do step 1 all the way across, then step 2, and step 3. You will readily see which groups of cords join for Coil Knots—always 4 cords of color 1 and 4 of colors 2 and 3 alternately. Always use color 1 to tie the Coil Knot. Cut ends at desired length.

Note: You may want to add a drop of glue to each Coil Knot to keep it from slipping.

Project 6: Choker

The prewaxed thread used for this choker ties beautiful, even knots. One cord started at the center acts as the holding cord for the entire piece, tracing a somewhat asymmetrical pattern for an "earthy" look. Here is a chance to use beads with small holes.

Pertinent Information

Size: 12" long (plus tying cords)
Materials: Prewaxed thread 16 cords 36"
                             1 cord 48"
    56 small round beads
    55 ½" tubular beads
    Belfast cord or fine nylon seine twine are possible substitutes.

To start: Bunch or tie all 16 36" cords at one end and pin to knotting surface. Double the 48" holding cord, pin it at the middle of the 28" strands at one side and Clove Hitch an inverted V (Λ) with the 16 cords to start work (page 47). Directions are given for one side of choker. Repeat for other side.

1. Turn the work so that you are doing the right side of the choker. A row of diagonal Clove Hitches from *right to left* has just been completed to start the piece. Do another diagonal row of Clove Hitches from left to right. Remember the same cord is used as the holding cord for the entire choker. Also, watch the pictures as you work: you'll see that most of the diagonals are not very sharp angles.
2. Starting with the left cord, slip a small round bead on every other tying cord. Tie another row of diagonal Clove Hitches from right to left.
3. Starting with the left cord, slip a tubular bead on every other tying cord. Pin the holding cord at the height of the first tube bead and do a row of diagonal Clove Hitches from left to right.
4. Do a horizontal row of Clove Hitches from right to left.
5. Take the 8 left cords and curve them to the left, holding them at a right angle by Clove Hitching them over the holding cord. The curved cords will form a quarter circle.
6. Pin the holding cord and add a tube bead to it. Clove Hitch the remaining 8 cords in a horizontal row left to right.
7. Add a tubular bead to every other one of the 8 remaining cords, starting with the second cord from the left. Bring holding cord down and pin it at depth of the tubular bead. Clove Hitch a straight row from right to left.

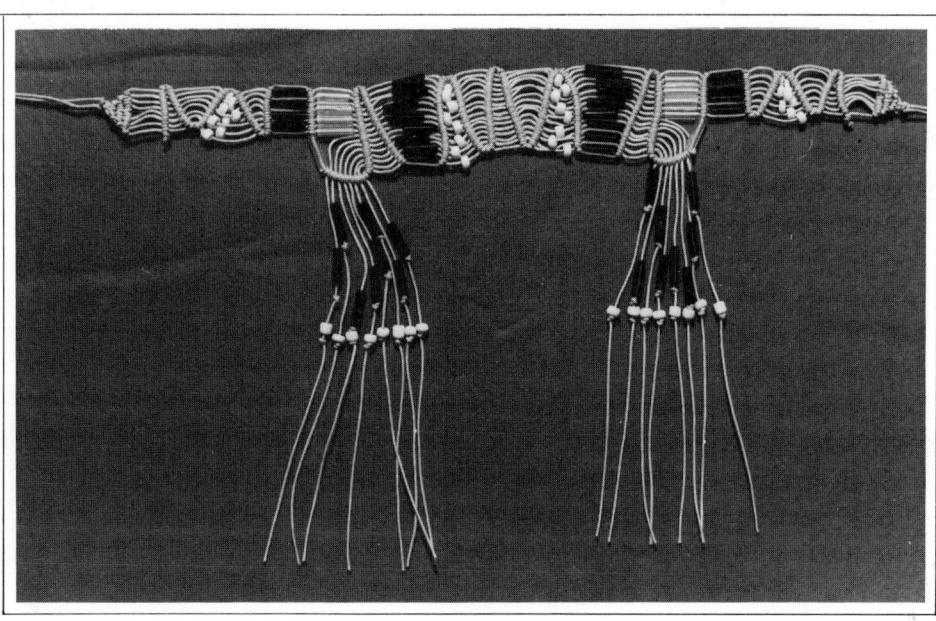

8. Do a row of diagonal Clove Hitches from left to right. Add a small round bead to each tying cord, and Clove Hitch another diagonal row from right to left. Repeat a diagonal row left to right, and another right to left. Here the holding cord ends: tie an Overhand Knot in the cord tight against the work. Cut and glue.
9. The choker ends with a pattern of Clove Hitches angled into the center. Use the outside 2 cords as holding cords and tie a row of horizontal Clove Hitches in toward center. Push leftover cords to back of work. Do this for three more rows—taking the outside 2 cords as holding cords each time—until there is only 1 knot.

To finish: Turn the end over and tie a double Overhand Knot with each pair of holding cords. Leave about 6" in the 2 center cords to tie the choker with, adding a few beads to the cords if desired, securing them with an Overhand Knot. Cut and glue cords.

When both sides of the choker are completed, turn the work so that the 8 curved cords on each side hang down. Knot and bead them in whatever length and pattern you desire. (I chose to add a tubular bead to each cord at random lengths and then finish with a straight line of small round beads.)

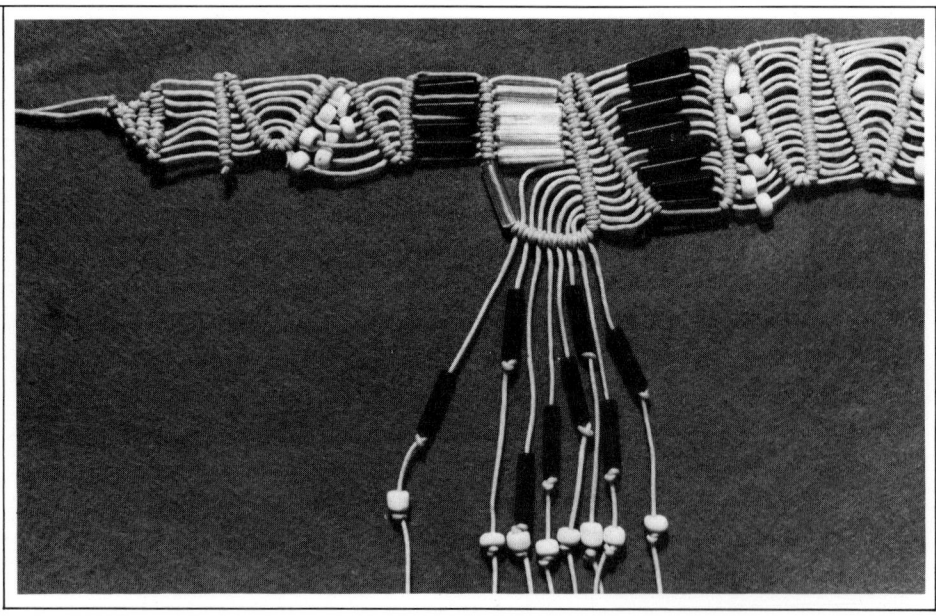

Project 7: Child's Dress

Here is a pinafore for a little girl, made on a flat surface, almost the same front and back. It ties at the sides, so it can be adjusted as the child grows.

While knotting the dress, it can be adjusted to the height of the child at the waistband and in the length of the hanging cords.

Pertinent Information

Size: 10½" wide x 18" long
Materials: Rayon Tubular #837 32 cords 150"
        8 cords 30", 240 crow beads
        2 brass rings (2" diameter)
        Heavy cotton seine twine or clothesline rope could be used instead.

Directions are given for the front of the dress. Repeat for the back, eliminating step 5 if you like.

To begin: Mount 8 150" cords with the Reverse Lark's Head on each ring and pin rings side by side to knotting surface at the distance between the "shoulder straps" of the dress. (Amy is two and a half years old and the rings are 5½" apart, center to center.)
Note: Don't forget—you don't have to start the dress on rings; I just have a preference for a firm hardware foundation, especially on big pieces. Another way of starting would be to just pin the cords at the center and begin (page 47).

1. Tie a pattern of decreasing Square Knots on each side: a row of 4, 3, 2, and 1 (page 20).
2. Tie a lacy sennit of 6 more Square Knots over the 2 center cords with the 6 adjacent cords on each side in succession (page 19). Do this on both rings.
3. Using the 7 inside cords from the sennit just tied on the right ring as holding cords, tie 7 rows of diagonal Clove Hitches using the 7 cords on the inside of the left sennit as tying cords. This will form a diamond pattern in the center of the dress. Be sure to keep the pattern "centered" by pinning it in strategic places as you go; it tends to pull to one side as you tie.
4. Hold the dress up to the child to determine where the waistband (the 4 rows of Clove Hitches) should start. Repin work to knotting surface.

   Add 4 30" cords, starting from the middle, by the method described on page 23. Put 3 beads on the center of the added cord and 3 more after 9 Clove Hitches on each side. (See page 62 for hints on threading beads with heavy cord.) Tie an Overhand Knot against the last Clove Hitch in the row on each side. Leave about 10" in cords 1 and 4 to act as ties. Leave the 2 middle cords short; cut and glue all 4 cords.
5. Do a pattern of decreasing Square Knots with all the cords: a row of 8, then 7, 6, 5, 4, 3, 2, 1.

To finish: Measure the child again to decide the length of the dress. Add beads to each cord (I used 2 and 3 beads on alternating cords) and tie Overhand Knots to secure at length desired. Cut and glue cords.

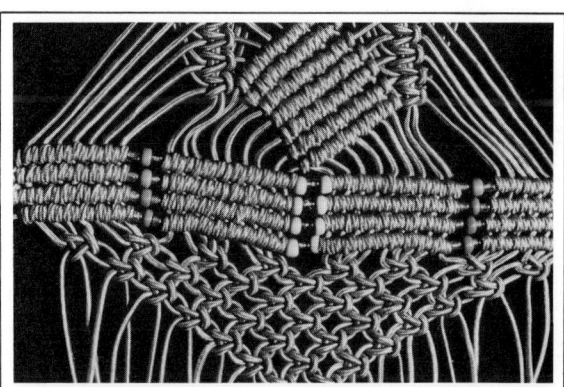

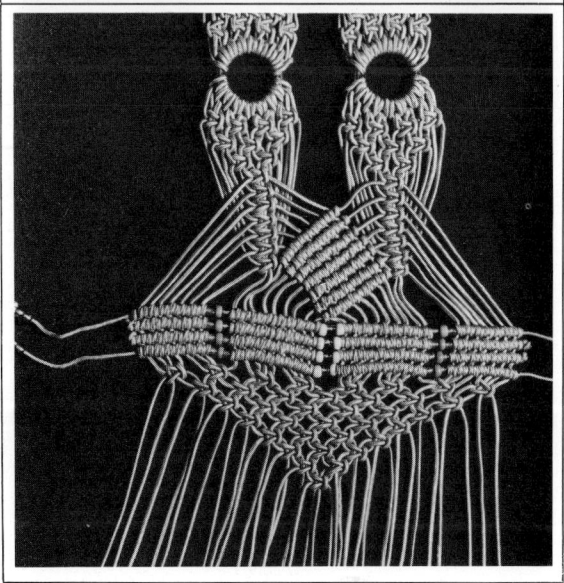

Project 8: Suspenders

Suspenders are back in style. This pair is a repeat pattern of diagonal Clove Hitches and Square Knot bobbles, mounted on the front "clips" of a pair of suspenders and finished at the back where the suspenders cross. The elastic of the remaining part of the suspenders and a small amount of "give" in the nylon braid give them some elasticity, but measure them on your man before tying off the ends. (The macramé section of this pair is 29" long and should fit a man 5'9" to 6' tall.) Unfortunately, this is one of those bothersome long cord projects, but the nylon braid ties easily and doesn't seem to tangle.

Pertinent Information

Size: 29" on each side (plus elastic back) x 1¾" wide
Materials: Nylon braided cord (200-lb. test line from Army surplus store) 12 cords 280"
1 pair wide store-bought *elastic* suspenders. Heavy cotton seine twine or packaging cord might be substituted.

To start: Cut off the suspenders at the *top* of the angle where they cross in back, leaving an inverted V (Λ) shape. If you have a grommeting tool, punch 5 holes in each side of the Λ and one at the top, thereby having 6 holes on each side. (Don't forget you can just pull the ends through with a crochet hook to finish the project, as shown on page 61.) Cut the "hardware" off the unused part of the suspenders and discard the piece used to adjust their length. Mount 6 doubled cords on each of the front "clips." Pin the mounted clips right side up on the knotting surface side by side (to assure an even pattern). Directions are given for one side.

1. Using the right-hand cord as holding cord, tie a row of diagonal Clove Hitches with the next 5 cords, leaving the 6 left-hand cords free. Tie 2 more "half rows" with the next 2 right-hand cords, Clove Hitching in the holding cord from the previous row each time (page 29). Tie a fourth row which continues all the way across from right to left.
2. Leaving the 6 cords free on the right take cord 6 from the left as holding cord for a row of diagonal Clove Hitches from the center to the left side, hitching in the holding cord from above. Do 2 more rows like this.
3. With the center 4 of the 6 *right-hand* cords, tie a bobble of 5 Square Knots at the point where the last row of Clove Hitches on the left *ends*, fastening it with 1 more Square Knot (page 21).
4. Tie 3 "half rows" of diagonal Clove Hitches from left to right with the 3 left-side cords in the same manner described above. The fourth row continues all the way across.

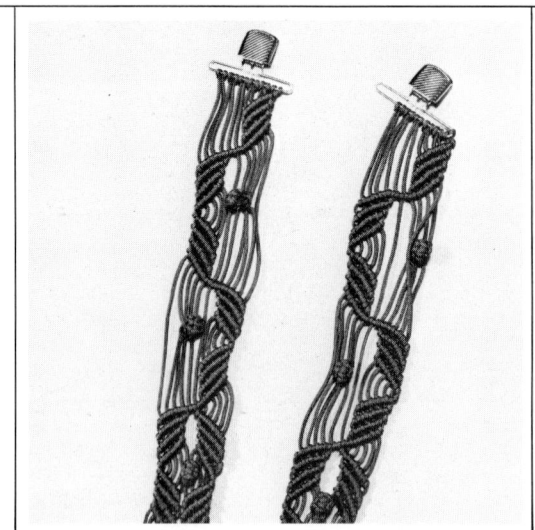

5. Leaving 6 cords free on the left, tie 3 more "half rows" directly under the previous row from the center to the right side.
6. Repeat step 3, with the center 4 of the 6 *left-hand cords*.
7. Repeat steps 1 and 2.
8. Tie 4 diagonal "half rows" of Clove Hitches with the 6 right-side cords from left to right.
9. Tie a bobble of 5 Square Knots with the 4 center cords (of the 12) at the point where the last row of Clove Hitches *ends*.
10. Tie 4 diagonal "half rows" of Clove Hitches with the 6 left-side cords from left to right.

You've now completed the entire pattern once. It's just a matter of repeating this sequence until you reach the desired length. I found that repeating the pattern 3 times, then ending with 4 diagonal "half rows" of Clove Hitches with the 6 right-side cords worked out perfectly. (Each section of the pattern measures about 10½".)

To finish: Pin the elastic back of the suspenders face down to the knotting surface. Pin the 2 sides of the suspenders in position, face down on the knotting surface. Pull 2 cords (in order) through each grommet from the front to the back of the work. (The grommet at the top will have 4 cords pulled through it.) Tie each cord to a cord from the adjoining grommet with a double Overhand Knot. You'll end up with 12 knots. Cut cords. If you are using nylon cord, burn the ends to melt them together. Otherwise, glue.

Note: Be sure to connect the macramé section at the same X angle as the design of the suspenders.

Project 9: Silver Sash

This flashy belt looks almost like real metal—though any heavy, stiff cord could be substituted. It's a very quick project with an interesting random pattern on each side of the center section—your first chance to improvise.

Pertinent Information

Size: 4″ x 24″ (plus ties)
Materials: Silver Metallic Tubular #2401
                             10 cords 150″
                             3 cords 50″
       42 crow beads
       Rayon tubular or lightweight clothesline could also be used.

To begin: Find the center of one of the 150″ cords and pin it to knotting surface to use as the mounting cord. Mount the 3 50″ cords over this mounting cord in the triple-loop pattern, such as shown on page 53. (I've added 9 crow beads to the top loop—refer to page 55.)

1. Add the other 9 150″ cords at the center, Clove Hitching them on with the 6 mounted strands (page 23). You'll get a very solid Clove Hitched pattern with the 6 tying cords hanging down from the belt.

   From this point, directions are given for one side of belt. Repeat for other side.

2. Turn the work on the knotting surface so that you are doing the right side of the belt. The cords from the center section will be to your left.
3. The 3 hanging cords closest to the left side will be used as holding cords to Clove Hitch a random pattern back through the 10 long cords. Starting with the closest one, Clove Hitch it in a curving pattern, pinning it as necessary to change direction (page 24), from left to right through the 10 cords; turn it and bring it part way back if you like. Pull the end through to the back of the work when finished and leave it for now. You can also add crow beads at random intervals for variety. Repeat this process with the other 2 cords, leaving a loop before you start Clove Hitching for decoration. I looped the last holding cord on each side through the previous one for an added touch.

   This step *seems* very complicated in the written instructions, but look at the pictures and it will be simple to follow.

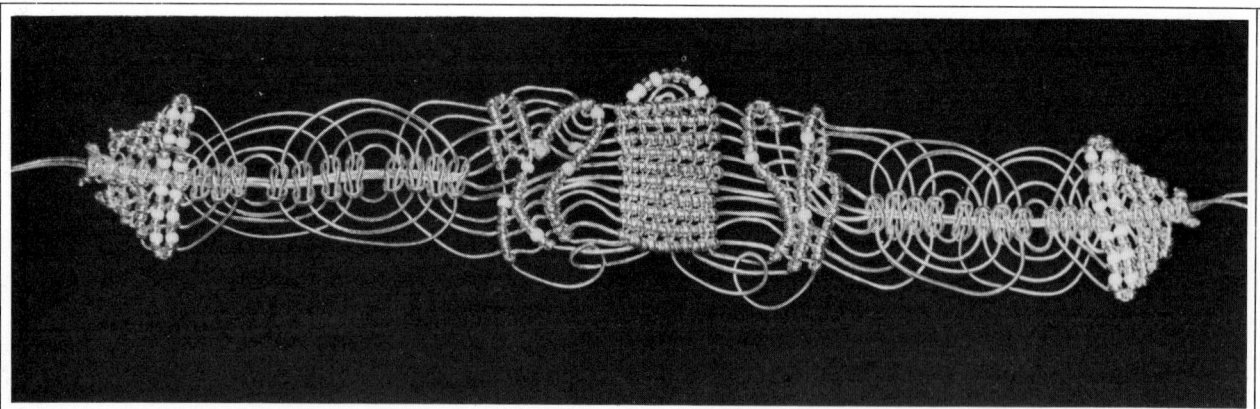

Note: When the belt is completed, anchor the ends of these 3 cords by pulling them through one of the knots on the back and secure them with an Overhand Knot. Cut and glue.

4. Now you are working with just the 10 long cords. Pin the 2 center cords, as they will be doing no tying for the rest of the belt.
   Now tie lacy Square Knot sennits over these center cords with each cord in succession (page 19) until you have 12 Square Knots, leaving very generous "loops." You'll have 3 patterns of 4 Square Knots.

5. Use the tying cords from the last Square Knot as holding cords for a row of Clove Hitches out to the sides and back to the center (page 22). Add a bead to the holding cords before the first knot and between each succeeding cord for extra width. Finish with a Square Knot over the center cords.

6. Now angle in the cords. Use the outside cords as holding cords for a row of Clove Hitches inward the center. Finish with a Square Knot over the 2 center cords and push ends to back of work. Continue this process until there is only 1 Square Knot in the center. Tie an Overhand Knot in the outside cords of this last knot tight against work. Leave the 2 center cords about 16" long for tying and end with an Overhand Knot.

To finish: Turn the belt over and tie an Overhand Knot tight against the work in all the cords pushed to the back in step 6. Cut and glue all cords.

Note: Since the entire side of the belt was tied over the center cords, the Square Knots will slip back and forth along these cords to adjust the belt to just about any waist size.

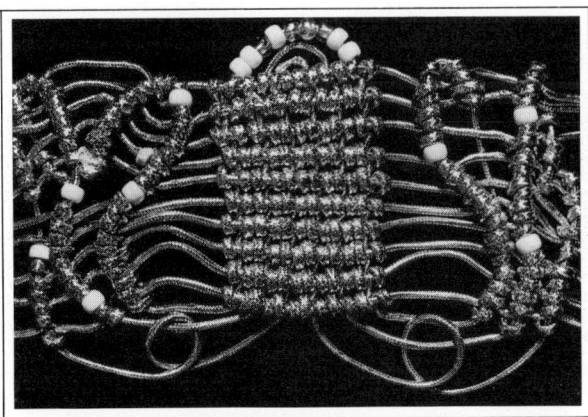 

Project 10: Long Necklace

This waist-length tie is easy to make and will give you practice with the Josephine Knot. I've mounted it on a wire bent with a loop on each end to hold the neck braid. (A pair of snout-nosed pliers did the trick.) You can mount it on a sennit of Square Knots (as shown in Project 18) or on a wire circlet (as in Project 19). Don't forget about substituting other beads or knots for the ones suggested if they're not available to you locally.

Pertinent Information

Size: 2″ x 18″
Materials: Polypropylene Mason Line #18 (from a marine supply store) 8 cords 150″
4 cords 50″
32 crow beads
89 tile beads
7 wood tubular beads (1¾″ long)
14 large round wood beads (⅝″ diam.)
10 small round wood beads (½″ diam.)
2 plastic rings (⅞″ diam.)
1 mounting wire 2″ wide plus loop on each side (or substitute)
Marlin twine, soutache, or #1 rattail might be substituted.

To make neck braid: Mount 2 of the 50″ cords on each loop so that inside cords are approximately 15″ long (outside cords about 35″) (page 9). Pin center cords to knotting surface. Tie a sennit of Square Knots to a length of 6″ on each side. Tie an Overhand Knot in the outside cords of each sennit tight against work. Leave about 6″ in the center cords to tie necklace. Put a couple of beads on the end of the cords and secure with an Overhand Knot. Cut all ends. If you use polypropylene cord, burn the ends to melt them. Otherwise glue knots.

To start: Mount the 8 150″ cords on the wire with the Reverse Lark's Head and pin to knotting surface.

Note: For this project, it seemed easiest to number the cords in some cases to indicate where beads should be strung.

1. Tie 1 row of 4 Square Knots.
2. To the 2 outside cords (together) on each side add 1 crow bead, 1 tubular wood bead, and 1 crow bead.

To cords 4–5 (together) in from each side add 7 tile beads.

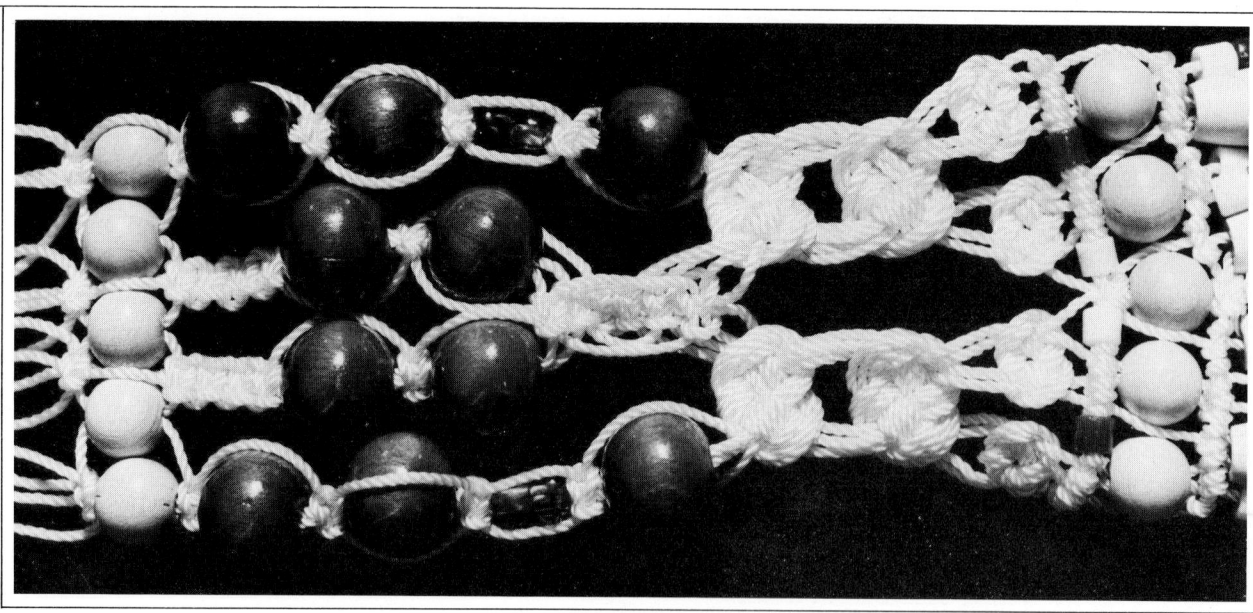

Put a tubular wood bead on the 2 center cords (together).

3. Tie 2 Square Knots with the 4 center cords (cords 7–10). Using the tying cords from the second Square Knot as holding cords, tie a row of Clove Hitches out to sides of work.
4. Add a ring (by the method shown on page 57) to cords 3–6 and 11–14, but add 2 Square Knots to each group of cords to hold ring. With the center 4 cords, tie a Square Knot just under the bar of Clove Hitches and 2 more at the same level as the 2 tied to secure the rings.
5. Tie a third Square Knot with the center 4 cords and use the tying cords as holding cords for another row of Clove Hitches out to the sides.
6. Put 2 crow beads on each 2 cords (together).
7. Now a small pattern of alternate Square Knots: rows of 4, 3, and 4.
8. Divide the 16 cords into 4 groups. Slip a large wood bead on the 2 center cords of each group and secure each with a Square Knot. Add a tubular wood bead to each of these same groups of center cords (cords 2–3, 6–7, 10–11, 14–15).
9. Add 7 tile beads to the 2 center cords together (8–9) of the piece. Add 4 tile beads to each of the remaining cords (1, 4, 5, 12, 13, 16).
10. Tie a Square Knot with the 4 center cords. Use the tying cords as holding cords for a row of Clove Hitches out to the sides.
11. Add a small wood bead to cords 2–3, 5–6, 8–9, 11–12, 14–15.
12. Repeat step 10, but add a tile bead to the holding cord before tying the first Clove Hitch and after the third cord on each side.
13. Divide the cords into 4 groups. Tie a Josephine Knot (page 36) with each group (2 cords for each side of the knot).
14. Divide the cords into 2 groups. Tie 2 Josephine Knots with each group. (It doesn't matter here about alternating the direction of the knots.) Each knot will use 4 cords for each side of the knot.
15. Take the 4 inside cords from the Josephine Knots just tied. Using the top cord coming from each knot as center cords, tie a lacy sennit of 6 Square Knots by the method shown on page 19.
16. Divide the cords into 4 groups again. With the outside group of cords on each side: add a large wood bead to the center cords, tie a Square Knot, add 2 crow beads to the center cords, tie a Square Knot, add another large wood bead, a Square Knot, a third large wood bead, and a Square Knot.

With the center 2 groups: add a large wood bead to the center cords, a Square Knot, another large wood bead, and 4 more Square Knots.
17. Repeat step 11.
18. Tie a Square Knot with each group of 4 cords.

To finish: Add 2 tile beads to each cord, secure with Overhand Knots. Cut and burn ends, if using polypropylene cord. Otherwise glue.

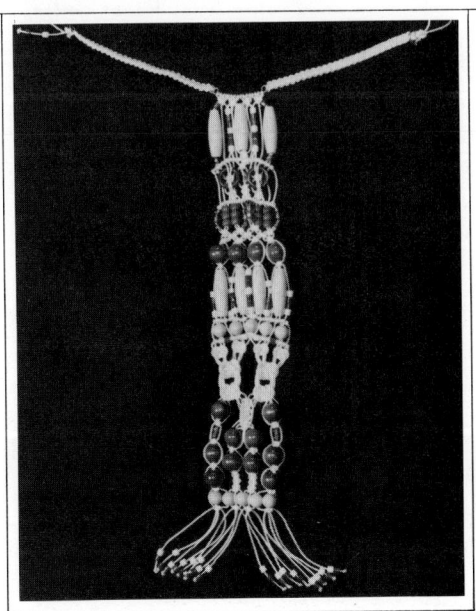

Project 11: Beaded Belt

Dress up a plain outfit with this heavily beaded sash which widens at the sides. It's easy to make and will give you practice with several basic macramé motifs.

Pertinent Information

Size: 3" x 22" (plus ties)
Materials: #1 Rattail   24 cords 160"
           180 crow beads
           240 tile beads
           Soutache, marlin twine, or polypropylene cord would also work.

Directions are given for one side of belt. Repeat for other side.

To begin: Line up the 24 cords and pin them at the center in a straight line to the knotting surface (page 47).

1. Divide cords in groups of 4. Slip 1 crow bead onto the 2 center cords of each group and tie 1 Square Knot.
2. Leaving the 2 outside cords on each side, divide the remaining cords into groups of 4. Slip 3 crow beads onto the 2 center cords of each group and tie 1 Square Knot.
3. Again divide cords into groups of 4. Slip 3 crow beads onto the 2 center cords of each group and tie 1 Square Knot.
4. Leaving the 2 outside cords on each side, divide the remaining cords into groups of 4, and tie 2 Square Knots with each group.
5. Repeat step 3.
6. Repeat step 4.
7. Divide all cords into groups of 4 and tie 2 Square Knots with each group.
8. Use the right-hand cord as holding cord for a row of Clove Hitches from right to left. Pin and do another row from left to right. Close bar with crochet hook (page 12).
9. Slip 4 tile beads onto cords 1, 7, 13, and 19. Using cords 6, 12, 18, and 24 as holding cords, tie a row of 5 diagonal Clove Hitches from right to left, ending each row by securing a beaded cord (1, 7, 13, and 19 respectively). Add 4 tile beads to the right-hand cord.
10. Repeat step 8, but use the left-hand cord as holding cord.
11. Tie 1 Square Knot with the 4 outside cords on each side and with the 4 center cords. Slip 1 crow bead onto the 2 center cords of these 3 knots and tie 1 more Square Knot with each group.
12. Tie a Square Knot with the 4 center cords. Use the outside cords as holding cords for a row of

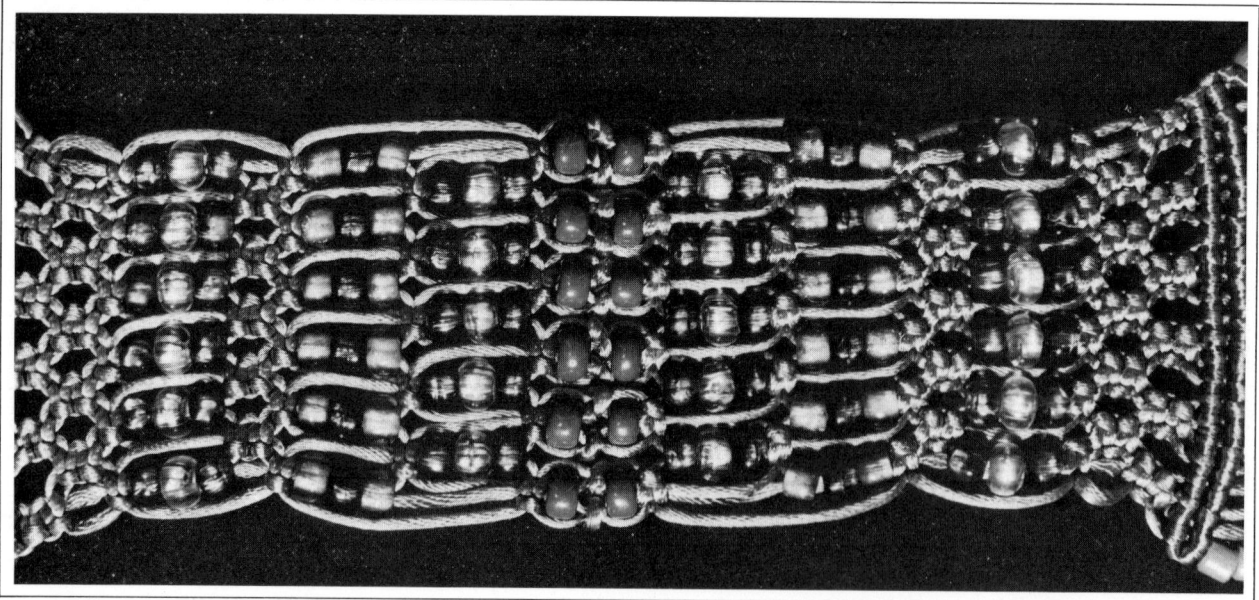

Clove Hitches out to the sides and back to the center, ending with another Square Knot (page 22). Add 1 tile bead to the holding cords on each side before the first cord, after 2 cords, and after 4 cords, then in the same position in the row back to the center.

13. Slip 2 crow beads onto the 2 center cords. Tie a lacy sennit of 4 Square Knots using the 4 pairs of adjacent cords in succession (page 19). Add 2 more crow beads to the center cords and do another sennit of 4 Square Knots in the same manner. Add 2 more crow beads to the center cords. Slip 14 tile beads onto the sixth cord in from each side.
14. Repeat step 12.
15. A. Tie a Square Knot with the 10 outside cords on each side; use 4 cords on each side to tie over 2 center cords.
    B. Take the 4 inside cords from these 2 Square Knots and tie a Square Knot around the 4 center cords of the belt.
    C. Repeat 15A.

To finish: Add beads to each cord in any combination (I've used 1 tile, 1 crow, and 1 tile bead on each cord), and secure with Overhand Knots far enough back from end of work to tie around waist or hips. Cut and glue cords.

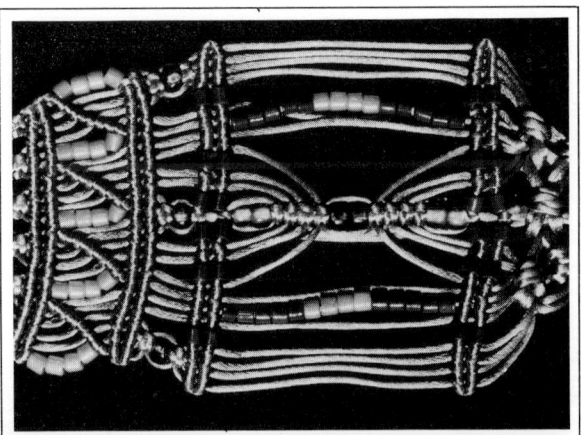

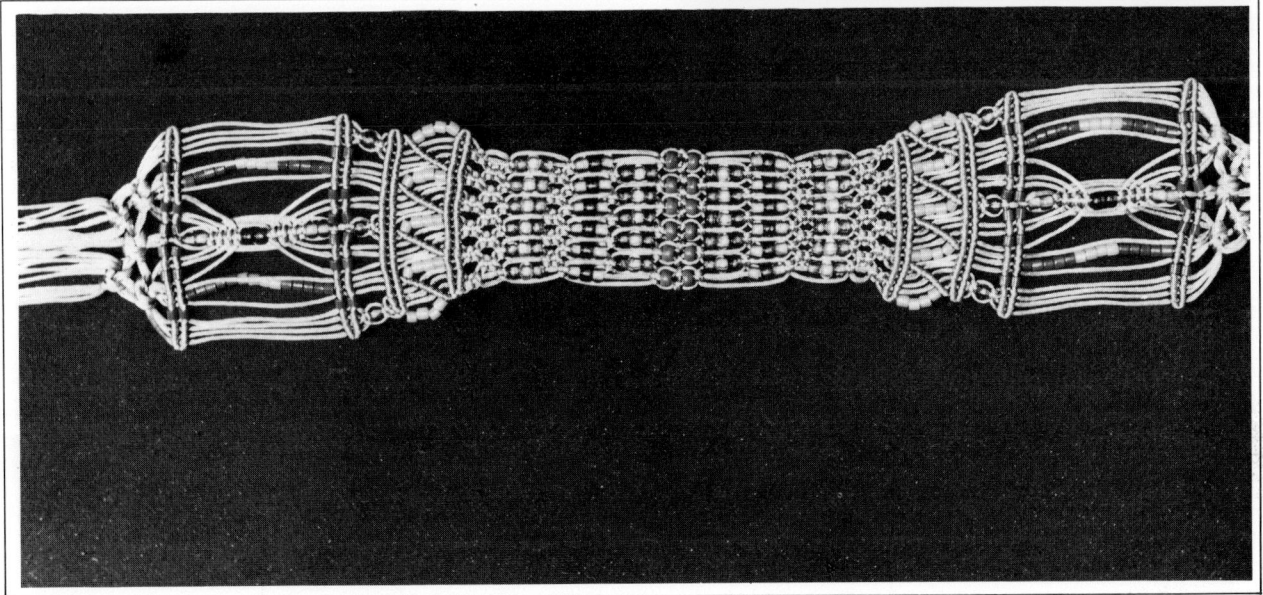

Project 12: Child's Vest

Army surplus nylon braid comes in several colors and is great to tie with. This vest is the same front and back and ties at the sides. A couple of places where it can be adjusted for the child's height are noted in the directions. Better bone up on your Coil Knots.

Pertinent Information

Size: 9″ x 18″ (including fringe)
Materials: Braided nylon line (200-lb. test)
  32 cords 180″
  16 cords 150″
  6 cords 30″
2 chain links or rings (2″ wide)
Cotton seine twine or #2 rattail are suitable substitutes.

Directions are given for one side of the vest.

To begin: Mount 8 150″ cords on each ring with the Reverse Lark's Head. Pin the rings about 7″ apart, center to center, on the knotting surface. (Measure your child for this distance. Alexander is six years old and this vest was made to his measure.)

1. Using the inside cord on each ring as holding cord, tie a diagonal row of Clove Hitches out to the sides, a straight row in toward the center, another diagonal row, and another straight row.
2. Tie an Overhand Knot about 10″ from the end of one of the 30″ cords and pin it to the left side of the vest just below the last row of Clove Hitches. Clove Hitch in the 16 cords from the left ring, add 8 150″ cords by means of the Double Lark's Head (page 47) and Clove Hitch in the 16 cords from the right ring. Adjust the knots on the holding cord to be sure everything is centered, and tie an Overhand Knot on the right side of the holding cord to secure work (page 23).
3. With the 16 new cords in the center, tie a pattern of 7 rows of alternating Square Knots: 4, 3, 4, 3, 4, 3, 4. (If the child you're making the vest for is bigger than Alexander, add a few more rows of alternating Square Knots.)

On each side, switch the 8 outside cords over the 8 inside cords to form an X pattern.

4. Add another 30″ cord with a Clove Hitch bar, working from left to right, securing each side with an Overhand Knot and leaving about 10″ of cord on each side.
5. Tie an alternating triple hitch braid with the 2 groups of 4 cords nearest the outside on both sides (a variation of the braid shown on page 34). Specifically, the tying cord goes over both center cords, 1 center cord, then both center

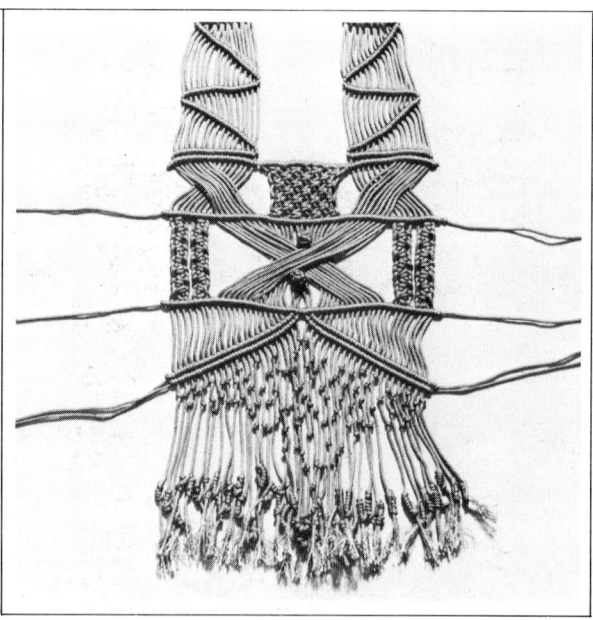

cords each time. (There are 8 triple hitches in each braid.)

With the 4 center cords of the vest, tie a Square Knot bobble (page 21) of 4 knots close to the bar of Clove Hitches above, and secure it with 1 more Square Knot.

Take cords 9–16 in from each side and crisscross them over the center section, so that the cords end up in the same position on the opposite side.

Tie another Square Knot bobble just under the crisscross pattern.

6. Repeat step 4. Be sure to keep the crossed cords in order.
7. Divide the cords into 2 groups. Use the 2 center cords on each side to tie 2 rows of diagonal Clove Hitches out to the sides. Secure the rows with Overhand Knots against the side of the work. Leave about 10" in the holding cords and tie another Overhand Knot to use as a tie.

To finish: Tie random Overhand Knots with all the remaining cords, with a heavier concentration of knots toward the center for a sort of V pattern. Tie all the ends in Coil Knots of about 6 wraps in a somewhat random line across the bottom. Tie Overhand Knots in all the side cords of the Clove Hitch bars about 10" from the side of the work to use as ties. Cut and glue ends.

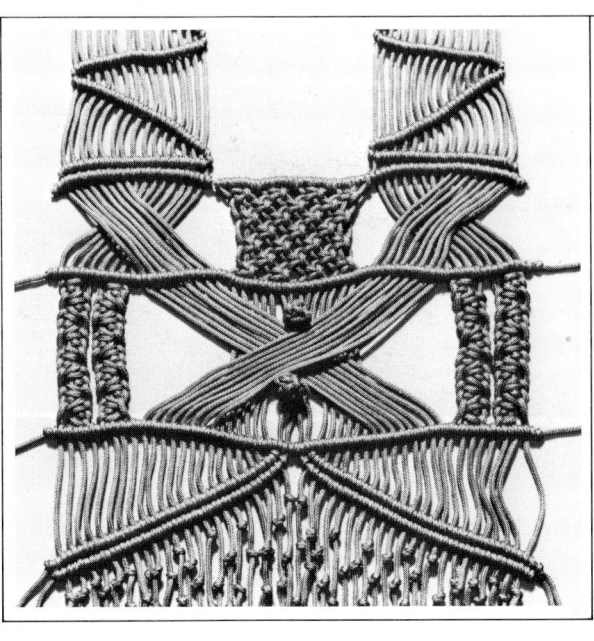

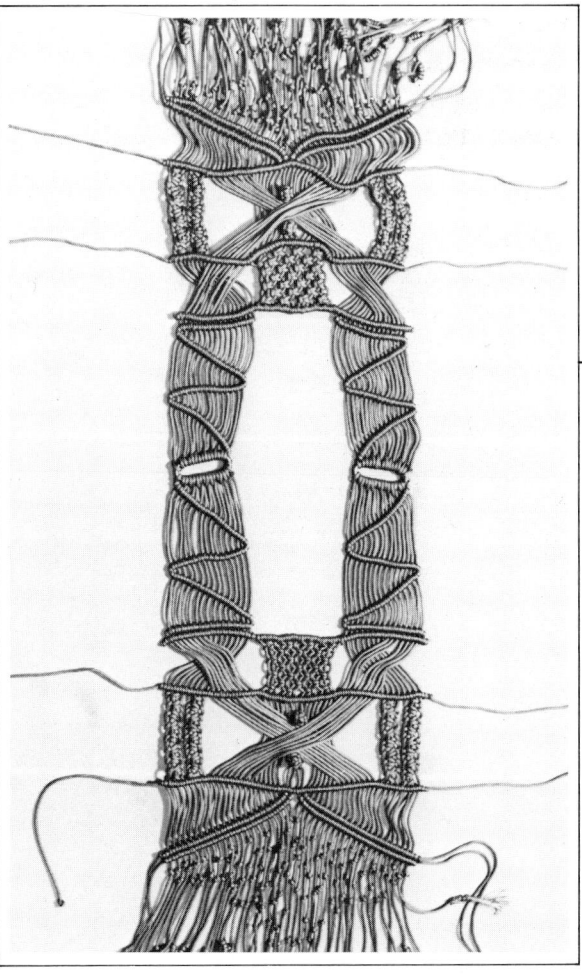

Project 13: Man's Belt

Marlin twine, available at hardware stores and marine supply houses, has a rich natural color and ties very neatly. This belt is a repeat pattern of several basic motifs. Again the cords are inordinately long and your suffering will be great. But such a nice belt.

Pertinent Information

Size: 2½″ x 38″
Materials: Marlin twine #24   8 cords 400″
  1 buckle at least 2″ high with a center bar

Note: This belt is made for a 32″ to 36″ waist. Add or eliminate a section of the pattern as necessary for proper length.

Cotton seine twine, polypropylene cord, or soutache could be substituted.

Each section of the pattern measures about 8″ in Marlin twine.

To begin: Mount 8 cords on the center bar of the buckle, 4 on each side of the prong with the Reverse Lark's Head. Pin the buckle to the knotting surface with the prong facing up—away from the knotting.

1. Tie a sennit of 6 Square Knots with each 4 cords.
2. Tie a Square Knot with the center 4 cords. Leaving the 2 center cords hanging, tie 6 rows of decreasing diagonal Clove Hitches from the center out to each side, as shown on page 20. Finish with a Square Knot over the 2 center cords.
3. Now a double diamond pattern (page 26). Using the outside cords of the above Square Knot as holding cords, tie a row of diagonal Clove Hitches out to the sides. Tie a second row using the center cords of the Square Knot as holding cords, Clove Hitching in the holding cord from the row above.
Tie a pattern of 1, 2, 3, 2, and 1 Square Knots inside the diamond (page 26).

Close the diamond. Tie a row of Clove Hitches in toward the center with the inside holding cord, making the crossover. Tie the second row, using the outside cord on each side as holding cords. Finish with a Square Knot using the center 4 cords rather than the usual crossover.

4. A. Using the outside cords of the Square Knot just tied as holding cords, tie a row of horizontal Clove Hitches out to the sides and back to the center, ending with a Square Knot (page 22).

B. Using the outside cords of the Square Knot just tied as tying cords, tie a row of vertical Clove Hitches (page 13) out to the sides and back to the center, finishing with a Square Knot (page 22). Now take the center cords of the Square Knot just tied (to use up cord evenly) and tie another row of vertical Clove Hitches out to the sides and back to the center, ending with a Square Knot.

C. Repeat 4A.

Note: This is the center section of the pattern. It's just a matter of doing the same steps in reverse order and then starting over. Here is the order of steps for completing a belt for a 32–36" waist.

    Step 3.
    Step 2.
    Step 1.
    Step 2.
    Step 3.
    Step 4.
    Step 3.
    Step 2.
    Step 1.
    Step 2.
    Step 3.
    Step 4.

To make end of belt: Tie a sennit of 15 Square Knots with the 4 center cords. Tie 2 Square Knots with the 4 outside cords on each side in line with knots 9 and 10 of the center sennit. Use the second cord in on each side as holding cord for a row of diagonal Clove Hitches in toward center sennit. Use the outside cord on each side as holding cords for a second row of Clove Hitches. Make the crossover.

The end of the belt has lots of loose cords so that it will pass easily through the buckle. The prong will fasten through the center cords of the Square Knot sennit at any point.

To finish: Tie an Overhand Knot in each cord tightly against work. Cut ends and glue.

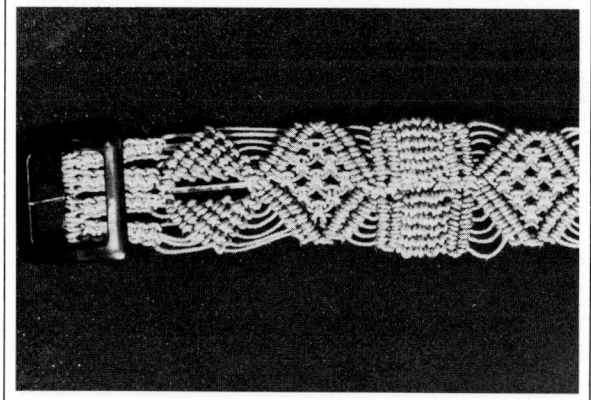

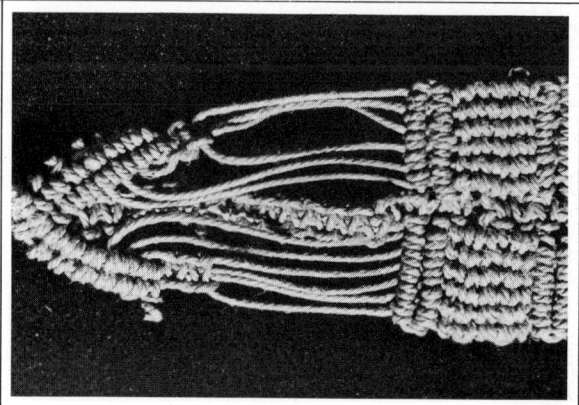

Project 14: Drawstring Bag

This bag is adapted from the design of a smaller antique macramé bag found in a Greenwich Village shop. It is essentially a repeat pattern, the same front and back. I've done it in two colors, reversing their order front and back for variation, but it isn't important to the instructions as the colors don't intermix at all.

Pertinent Information

Size: 9" x 12" (without tassel)
Materials: Slide cord #5 in 2 colors.
  32 cords color 1 120"
  32 cords color 2 120"
  18 cords (of either color) 15"
  4 cords color 1 200"
  60 cords color 2 12"
  Cotton or nylon seine twine, #1 rattail, or soutache would also make a nice bag.

Directions are given for one side of bag. Repeat for other side, reversing the order of colors in mounting the cords.

To begin: Using 2 15" cords as a double-thick mounting bar, mount 32 120" cords with Double Lark's Heads in this order: 8 cords of color 1, 16 of color 2, 8 of color 1.

1. Directly underneath, add 1 15" cord working from the center to the outside (page 23), leaving the ends of the holding cords for now.
2. With each 4 cords, tie a sennit of 4 Square Knots all the way across (16 sennits).
3. Repeat step 1.
4. Tie an X pattern with each group of 16 cords (page 12) all the way across (4 X patterns).
5. Repeat step 1.
6. Repeat step 4.
7. Repeat step 1.
8. Repeat the X pattern with the left and right groups of 16 cords (color 1).
9. With each of the 2 center groups of 16 cords, tie the following pattern: using the outside cord on each side as holding cord, tie a row of diagonal Clove Hitches in to the center. Tie 3 more rows on each side, using the outside cord as holding cord each time and Clove Hitching in the holding cord from the row above (page 29).

Tie a 5 Square Knot bobble with the center 4 cords, fastening with one more Square Knot (page 21).

Now do 4 rows of diagonal Clove Hitches from the center out to the sides, using the inside cords as holding cords each time, and Clove Hitching in the holding cord from the row above.

10. Add another bar as in step 1, just under the X completed in step 8, but run the cord loose *behind* the center 16 cords (since it will fall in the middle of the pattern tied in step 9).
11. Repeat step 8.
12. Repeat step 1.
13. Repeat step 4.
14. Repeat step 1.
15. Counting from the center, use cords 8, 16, 24, and 32 (the outside cord) on each side to tie 4 rows of diagonal Clove Hitches in to the center, curving them as you go, to give the bottom of the bag a rounded look.

Side of bag is complete.

To join bag: Place 2 sides of bag face to face and pin to knotting surface. Tie each matching horizontal holding cord (front and back) with a double Overhand Knot tight against work. Tie each corresponding knot (front and back) along the bottom of the bag in the same way. Cut and glue cords. Turn bag right side out.

To make drawstring: Fold 2 200" cords so that short ends are 30" long. Using short cords as center cords, tie sennit of Square Knots to length of 30" (yes, it's really a long one; you may want to start in the center and work out). Make 2 drawstrings.

To add drawstrings: Thread 1 drawstring in and out every 2 sennits (tied at the top of the bag) from left to right across front of bag and around back in a full circle. Tie the ends of the drawstring together with Overhand Knots. Thread the other drawstring from right to left around bag and join ends.

Tassels: Make 3 tassels of 20 doubled 12" cords each (see page 54). Make 1 over each drawstring at the point where the ends join. Make the third tassel complete according to the instructions and tie it with the center cord to the bottom of the bag.

Project 15: Pendant Money Bag

Many different knots and techniques are involved in this little neck bag (great when you just want to carry cash and keys), so it's good practice in the basics of the craft.

Pertinent Information
Size: 4" x 5" deep
Materials: Polypropylene Mason Line #18
                                      32 cords 80"
                                      4 cords 16"
                                      2 cords 150"
       136 tile beads
       16 jump rings (⅝" diam.)
       #1 rattail, polished cotton twine, or packaging twine might be substituted.

Directions are given for one side of the bag.

To begin: Mount 2 80" cords each with Reverse Lark's Heads on 8 jump rings and pin the rings side by side to the knotting surface.

1. Tie a sennit of 7 half knots (1 full twist) with the 4 cords on each ring (page 9). Make sure the twists lie flat when completed.
2. Take 2 16" cords to act as a double-thick holding cord and Clove Hitch all the cords over them, working from the center to the sides (page 23). Leave the ends for now.
3. Now a pattern of decreasing Square Knots, but decreasing out to the sides instead of in toward the center. First tie a row of 8 Square Knots. Leave out the 4 cords in the middle, and tie 3 Square Knots on each side from the middle out. (The 2 outside cords on each side will be left over.) Continue leaving 4 more cords out in the middle with each row until there is 1 Square Knot tied with the 4 outside cords on each side.
4. Take the left-hand cord from the fifth Square Knot in the top row as holding cord for a diagonal row of Clove Hitches. These will start from the center and go from right to left, following the angle of the decreasing Square Knot pattern.

Use the first tying cord from the previous row as holding cord for a row of diagonal Clove Hitches from left to right along the angle of the decreasing Square Knots.

5. Take cord 11 from the left as holding cord and tie another row of diagonal Clove Hitches from right to left just under the row above. Use cords 10, 9, and 8 as holding cords for 3 more rows.

Take cord 11 from the right and repeat the above steps on the right side.

6. Do a series of 1, 2, and 3 bobbles (page 21) in the center of the piece as though doing alternate Square Knots. Use 4 Square Knots for each

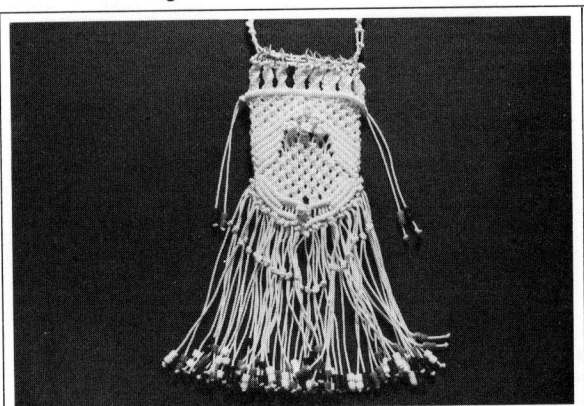

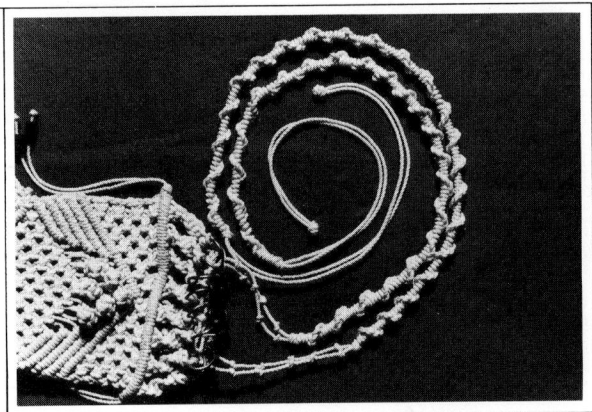

bobble, then 1 more to hold it in place.
7. Starting just below the center bobble in the row of 3, do a pattern of increasing Square Knots from 1 to 7 in a row (2 cords will be left on each side), then decreasing to 4 in the last row.
8. Using the outside cord from the Square Knot in the row of 7 on each side as tying cord, tie 1 Lark's Head (page 35) over the 2 cords left hanging on the outside. Use the same cord as holding cord for a row of Clove Hitches in toward the center from each side, curving it under the decreasing Square Knots as you go.
9. Tie 1 more 4-knot bobble in the center, using the 2 holding cords from the row above and the 2 adjoining cords.
10. Use the inside cord of the 2 left hanging on each side as holding cord and tie a row of Clove Hitches toward the center with the first 8 cords only.
11. Use the outside cords as holding cords for a row of Clove Hitches which curves and ends under the bobble in the center. Make the crossover.

The side is complete.

To join sides: Make sure sides are face to face (right side out). Take 1 cord each from the front and back of bag from the 2 used for the horizontal bar near the top and lace down the sides (using a crochet hook) through the "holes" in the Square Knots and in the ends of Clove Hitch bars (page 60). Finish with an Overhand Knot with the 2 cords pushed tightly against the work at the bottom of the sides. Tie an Overhand Knot with the 2 cords left at the top tightly against side of the bag.

At the bottom, take each pair of corresponding cords front and back and tie them in an Overhand Knot pushed tightly against work.

To finish: I've tied a pattern of alternating Overhand Knots, using cords from adjacent knots in the row above, in a semicircular pattern. Then there are 2 tile beads on each of the cords secured in a straight line with Overhand Knots. Also, add 2 tile beads to each of the cords from the horizontal bar at the top, securing with Overhand Knots. Cut and burn ends if using polypropylene cords. Otherwise glue cords.

To make drawstrings: Fold 150" cord so that one end is 30" long (and the other 120") and tie an Overhand Knot close to the place where the cord folds. Tie a second Overhand Knot 6" down. Pin this knot to knotting surface. Tie a continuous chain of Clove Hitches with the long cord over the short cord to a length of 12". The chain will automatically spiral as you tie (page 33). Tie another Overhand Knot with both cords. Now, using each cord separately, tie Overhand Knots at about ½" intervals to a length of 5". Repeat for other drawstring.

To attach drawstrings: Take 1 drawstring and thread 1 cord through the back 8 jump rings from left to right, and the other cord through the front 8 jump rings from left to right. Join the 2 cords at right side just beyond last Overhand Knot with another Overhand Knot using both cords. Do the same with the other cord from right to left. Cut and burn ends, or glue.

Project 16: Beaded Shoulder Bag

This fancy little dress bag won't hold much, but it looks terrific. It's not hard to make, but you'll have to improvise a little in joining the sides of the bag with the cords used to knot the shoulder strap.

Note: This bag will need a lining. (I made a simple suede pouch, 4" x 4½" deep, sewn on 3 sides, which just slips into the bag.)

Pertinent Information

Size: 4½" wide x 5" (plus beaded fringe)
      Handle 12" on each side of center ring.
Materials: #1 Rattail 24 cords 70"
                       16 cords 100"
                       8 cords 15"

118 tile beads
175 crow beads
27 1" plastic tube beads
1 brass ring (1¼" diam.)
Soutache, polypropylene cords, or marlin twine would also be suitable.

Directions are given for one side of bag.

To begin: Pin 4 15" cords to knotting surface as a thick mounting bar. Mount 12 70" cords in middle of mounting bar with Double Lark's Head (page 47).

1. Divide the cords into groups of 4 and add 2 crow beads to the center cords of each group, securing with a Square Knot. This is the first row of a pattern of alternating Square Knots.
2. Leaving the 2 outside cords on each side, add 1 crow bead to the center cords of each remaining group of 4, securing with Square Knots.

Continue the pattern of alternating Square Knots with a row of 6, then 5 Square Knots. Add a crow bead to the center cords of these 5 groups, then tie another row of 6 Square Knots. Add 2 crow beads to the center cords of these 6 groups of cords.

3. Using the left-hand cord as holding cord, tie a row of Clove Hitches from left to right, pin and tie a second row from right to left, closing the double bar with a crochet hook (page 12). Add a tile bead to the holding cord after each 4 cords in both rows (between each Square Knot above).
4. Add 1 crow bead, 1 tile bead, 1 plastic tube, 1 tile bead, and 1 crow bead to the center cords of each group of 4 cords.
5. Repeat step 3, using the right-hand cord as holding cord.

Side of bag is complete.

Directions are given for one side of shoulder strap.

To make shoulder strap: mount 8 100" cords on brass ring with the Lark's Head. Pin ring to knotting surface.

1. As you can see, the shoulder strap is a series of single diamonds with alternating inside motifs. Tie a pattern of decreasing Square Knots (page 20): a row of 4, then 3, 2, and 1.
2. Using the outside cords as holding cords, tie an X pattern (page 12).
3. Slip 1 tile, 1 crow, 1 tile, 1 crow, 1 tile, 1 crow, and 1 tile bead onto the 2 center cords.
4. Repeat step 2.
5. Do a pattern of increasing, then decreasing Square Knots (page 20): rows of 1, 2, 3, 4, 3, 2, and 1.
6. Repeat step 2.
7. Repeat step 3.
8. Repeat step 2.
9. Tie a pattern of increasing Square Knots: rows of 1, 2, 3, and 4.
10. Slip 1 crow bead, 1 tile bead, 1 plastic tube, 1 tile bead, and 1 crow bead onto the center cords of the 4 Square Knots just tied. Secure with another Square Knot.

Handle is complete. Repeat for other side.

To finish bag: Pin the sides right sides out, one on top of the other (inner sides together), on the knotting surface. Tie an Overhand Knot with each 2 corresponding knots, front and back, tight against bottom of bag. Tie a second row of alternating Overhand Knots—1 each from adjacent knots in the row above—about 1" below the previous row. Fringe the bag as you wish. I've beaded the cords pretty elaborately with a combination of crow beads, tile beads, and plastic tubes, as you can see in the pictures.

To add handle: Pin the finished bag to the knotting surface and pin the handle roughly in position. Use the 4 cords on each side of the bag which served as the mounting bar to tie Clove Hitches over each group of 4 cords in the handle. Clove Hitch 2 bars with the front 2 groups of 4 cords and 2 bars with the back 2 groups of 4 cords on each side. Tie the 8 cords from the mounting bar in 1 big Overhand Knot on each side, and cut ends at desired length. Then divide the cords of the handle into 3 groups—4 on each side and 6 in the center. Use the 2 side groups of cords to lace through "holes" in the sides of the bag, tying big Square Knots over the 6 center cords after you lace through each hole (page 59). At the bottom of the bag, join the 4 outside cords in a big Overhand Knot and cut at the length you want. I know these instructions seem difficult to follow but you can find your own way; and since the bag is lined anyway, it isn't important to close up every gap.

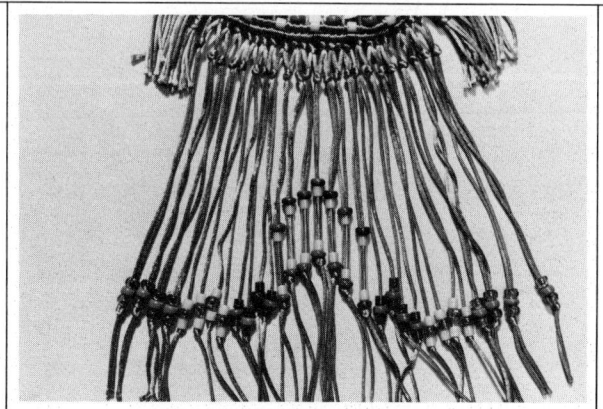

Project 17: Three-Color Man's Tie

Working with color is fun and not as hard as it looks: if you follow the instructions, the colors will automatically come out in the right place. This variation on the traditional man's tie gives good practice in vertical Clove Hitching and Lark's Head chains. This may also be worn as a necklace.

Pertinent Information

Size: 4" x 15½"
Materials: Soutache in 3 colors
          12 cords 120" (six color 1, four color 2, two color 3)
          4 cords 50" (of any color)
          24 tile beads

1 chain link or similar link 2" wide (Not necessary, of course; you can make the tie on the same kind of braid shown in Project 18 or 22.)

To make braid: Follow the instructions given for the braid in Project 10 on page 78. Use the 4 50" cords.

To start: Colors are referred to as 1, 2, and 3. Mount the 120" cords on the chain link in the following order left to right: 1, 1, 1, 2, 2, 3, 3, 2, 2, 1, 1, 1.

1. Tie a sennit of 6 Square Knots with the 4 center cords (color 3). Tie a sennit of 2 Square Knots with the inside 4 cords of color 1 on each side.
2. Using the 2 outside cords on each side as a double-thick holding cord, Clove Hitch a V into the center and make the crossover (page 12).
3. Tie a Lark's Head chain (page 35) of 7 knots using cords 4 and 5 in from each side as holding cords. Cord 3 in on each side ties the first and seventh Lark's Head (color 1). Cord 6 in ties the second through sixth Lark's Heads (color 2).
4. Finish the X pattern started in step 2.
5. Cover color 3 by tying 2 Lark's Heads chains. Use the closest cord of color 2 on each side of the center to tie 4 Lark's Heads over the adjacent 2 cords of color 3.
6. Using the left-hand cord to tie, do a row of vertical Clove Hitches from left to right, pin, and do a row from right to left (page 13). This will create a solid band of color 1.
7. Tie a Square Knot with the 4 center cords (color 3), and use the tying cords as holding cords for a row of Clove Hitches out to the side and back to the center, fastening with another Square Knot (page 22).
8. Repeat step 5, this time making each chain 10 Knots long.

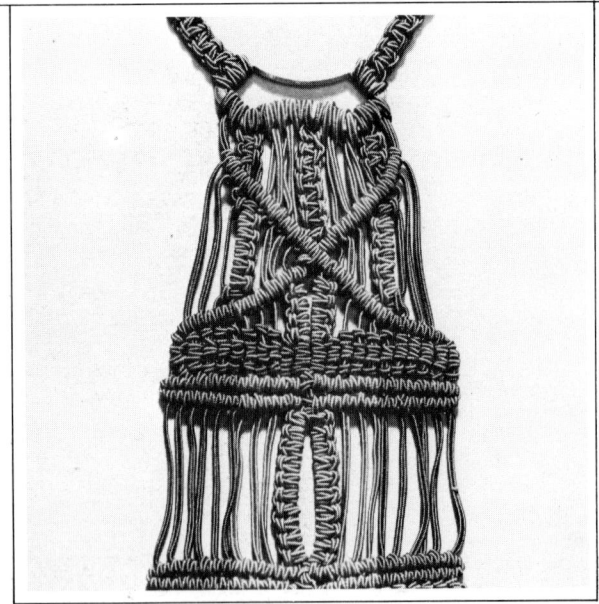

9. Repeat step 7.
10. Using the outside cords of the Square Knot just tied as tying cords, do a row of vertical Clove Hitches out to each side and back to the center. Now use the center cords of the Square Knot as holding cords and do the same. You now have a double band of color 3.
11. Repeat step 7.
12. Using the 4 cords of color 2 on each side as holding cords, tie 4 rows of diagonal Clove Hitches toward the outside of the work with the cords of color 1. This will bury color 2 and also bring it to the outside of the work.
13. Using the inside tying cord of color 1 on each side to tie, cover color 3 again with a Lark's Head chain of 9 knots as described in step 5.
14. To widen the tie, use the same cords used in step 13 as holding cords for a row of Triple Hitches (page 24) out to the side and back to the center, securing the row with another Lark's Head over the same 2 groups of center cords.
15. Use the 4 cords of color 3 as center cords for a lacy sennit of 6 Square Knots tied in succession with the cords of color 1 (page 29).
16. Repeat step 7, but again use the Triple Hitch.
17. Leaving the 4 outside cords on each side (color 2), use the rest of the cords for a pattern of decreasing Square Knots in groups of 2: i.e., 2 rows each of 4, 3, 2, and then just 1 Square Knot. (Colors 1 and 3 will mix amicably.)
18. Using the cords of color 2 as holding cords, tie consecutive rows of diagonal Clove Hitches in toward the center in a chevron pattern (page 27) to bring the tie to a point. Tie Overhand Knots in the 2 center cords tight against work.

To finish: Slip a tile bead on each cord and tie an Overhand Knot in a straight line at desired length. Cut and glue cords.

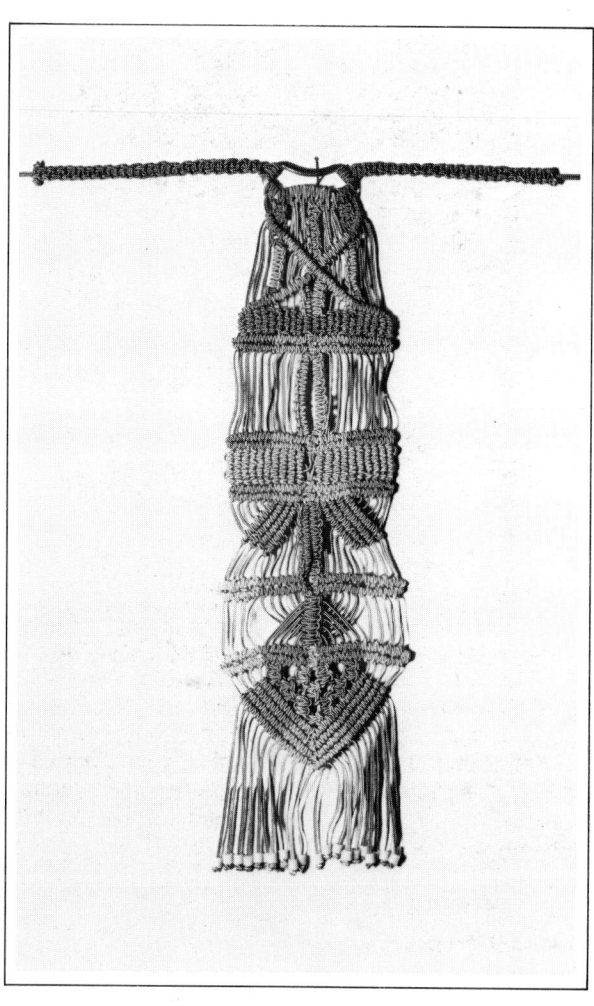

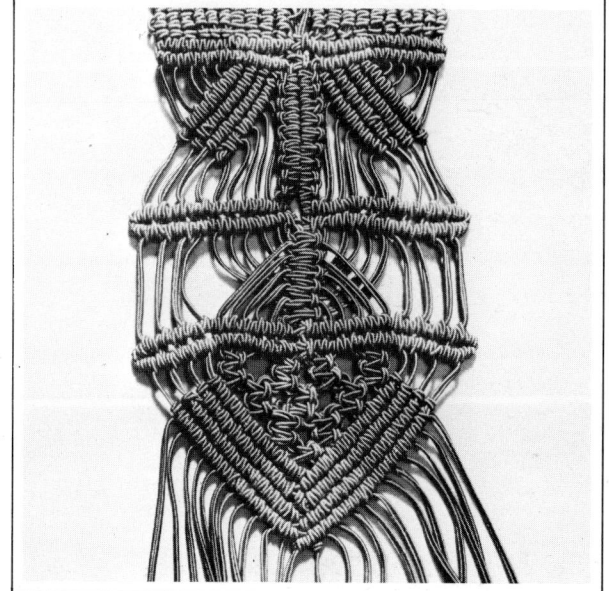

Project 18: Bib

This necklace gives a high-fashion look to a simple dress or sweater and requires surprisingly little knotting. Take care with the double V of Clove Hitches to be sure they're symmetrical and that the cords are in order. Other than that, most of the bib is wide-open spaces.

Pertinent Information

Size: 6½" (plus ties) x 9" (plus fringe)
Materials: #1 Rattail 20 cords 90"
                    2 cords 60"
                    2 cords 30"
          116 tile beads
          52 crow beads
          6 1" plastic tube beads
          1 1½" wood tubular bead
          1 small wood tubular bead
          Soutache, slide cord, or polypropylene cord would make good substitutes.

To make neck braid: Pin the 2 60" cords and the 2 30" cords at the center to the knotting surface so that the 30" cords are in the middle (page 47). Tie a sennit of Square Knots to a length of 6" on each side of the center pins. Leave about 10" in the cords to serve as ties for the necklace and tie them together with one Overhand Knot on each side.

To begin: Pin the neck braid to the knotting surface and mount the 20 90" cords in the middle with the Reverse Lark's Head.

1. Divide the cords into 2 groups. Slip 1 crow bead, 1 plastic tube, and 1 crow bead onto the inside pair of cords on each side.

   Leaving the 2 outside cords on each side, tie a pattern of decreasing Square Knots on each side —a row of 4, then 3, 2, and 1—with a crow bead between each knot (page 20).
2. Using the 4 middle cords of the necklace as center cords, tie a sennit of 7 Square Knots with each pair of cords (in order) coming from the pattern of decreasing Square Knots on each side.
3. Take the second cord in on each side of the bib as holding cord and tie a V pattern of diagonal Clove Hitches in toward the center along the angle of the decreasing Square Knot patterns and ending under the last Square Knot in the center sennit. Be sure to Clove Hitch in the cords from the center sennit in order from the top. Add 3 tile beads to the holding cord after 9 Clove Hitches (the end of the decreasing Square Knot pattern), and finish the row with a Square Knot tied with the 2 holding cords around the 4 center cords.

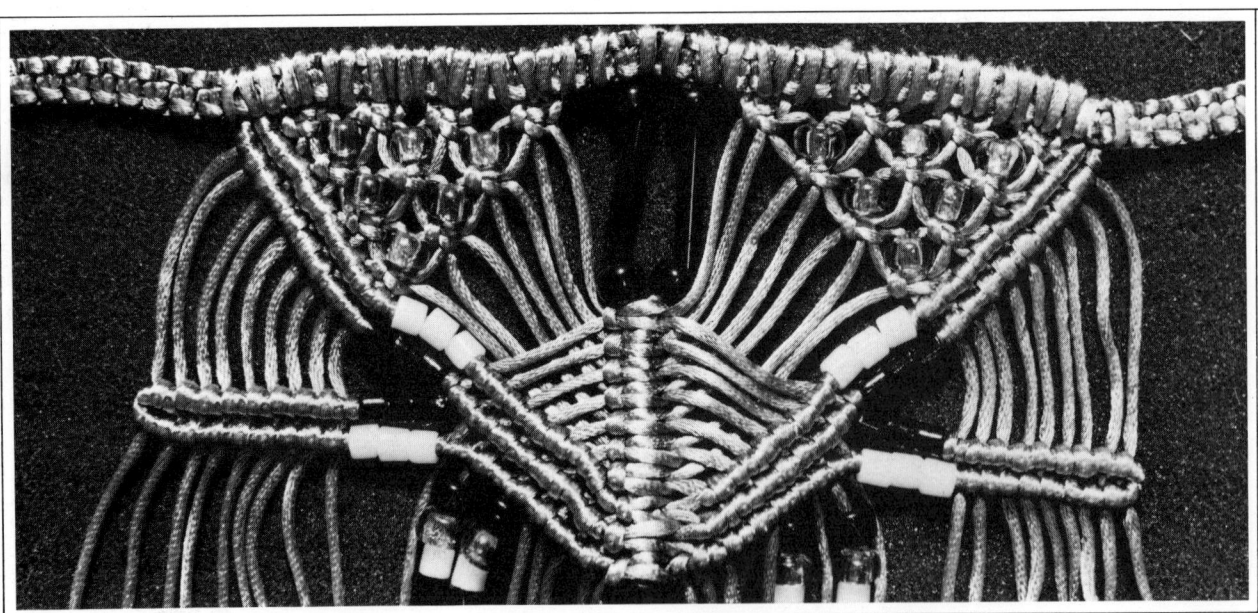

Do a second diagonal row in the same manner, using the outside cords as holding cords.

4. Use the tenth cord in from each side (this will be the first cord after the beads on the row of diagonal Clove Hitches) as holding cord for a row of Clove Hitches out to each side and back to the center, then angling down along the line of the V and ending with a Square Knot over the 4 center cords. Add 3 tile beads to each holding cord *before* you start the row out to the sides and *after* the first 9 Clove Hitches in the row back to the center.
5. Slip 3 tile beads onto each of the 8 outside cords on each side and secure them with Overhand Knots 2½" below the double Clove Hitch bar. Cut fringe at length desired.
6. There are 24 cords left. Slip 1 tile and 2 crow beads on each outside cord. Slip 2 crow beads, 1 tile bead, 1 plastic tube, 1 tile bead, and 2 crow beads onto the third and fifth cord in from each side.

Slip the long wood tubular bead onto the 4 center cords. Tie a Josephine Knot (page 36) using the 4 cords on each side of the tubular bead and pull the 4 center cords through the middle of the knot (page 39).

7. Pin the Josephine Knot securely. Take one of the cords from each side of the Josephine Knot as holding cords, slip 2 tile beads on each cord, and tie a row of Clove Hitches out to the sides and back to the center, Clove Hitching in the other cords from the Josephine Knot in the bottom row. Secure with a Square Knot over the 4 center cords.
8. Slip 1 crow bead, the small wood tube bead, and 1 crow bead on the 4 center cords. (It can be done; use a crochet hook to pull the cords through the crow beads.) Secure with a Square Knot using the adjacent cords.

To finish: Now you're on your own. Knot and bead the remaining cords as you choose. (I've tied a few more Square Knots and added tile and crow beads to single and double cords to finish the piece.)

Project 19: Bolero

This bolero, which is adjustable at the front and sides, is made on a wire circlet such as used for making necklaces. If you can't find one in a jewelry or hobby store, bend a piece of wire yourself; it really helps to knot on a firm base when working from a circle. The instructions should fit a size 5 to 9.

Note: This bolero is meant to be worn open—Spanish-style—it is small and fitted and does not close in front. The wire circlet on which it is made is left open, though you can tie it across the front as shown.

Pertinent Information

Size: 14" wide x 20"
Materials: #2 Rattail 52 cords 180", 1 cord 50"
12 cords 30"
104 1" plastic tube beads (These are imitation Indian bone beads available by mail from Plume Trading Co. or Del Trading Post—see list of suppliers.)
468 crow beads, 1 wire neck circlet
Heavy cotton seine twine, packaging cord, or nylon braid could be used instead.

To begin: Pin wire neck circlet, in closed position, to knotting surface. Mount 52 180" cords around circlet with Reverse Lark's Heads.

1. Tie 2 Square Knots with each 4 cords. Leaving the 2 outside cords on each side (the cord closest to the point where the circlet latches), tie 1 Square Knot with each remaining group of 4 cords. Leave about ½" between this and the previous row of Square Knots.
2. Tie a knot about 8" from the end of the 50" cord. Pin this knot just below the row of Square Knots just tied at the point where the wire circlet latches. (This is the center front of the bolero.) Use this cord as holding cord for a row of Clove Hitches circling the vest about ½" below the row of Square Knots. You might want to pin the cord at intervals to be sure to get a nice even circle. Tie another Overhand Knot against the last Clove Hitch to secure row.

Directions are now given for right front of vest. Repeat for left side, reversing the direction where necessary.

3. Take the first 24 cords to the left of the opening of the wire circlet for the front of the bolero. Pin the wire to the top of the knotting surface and isolate these 24 cords.
4. Tie a knot about 8" from the end of a 30" cord and pin it to the right of the 24 cords about ½" below the circle of Clove Hitches just completed. Use this as holding cord for a straight row of

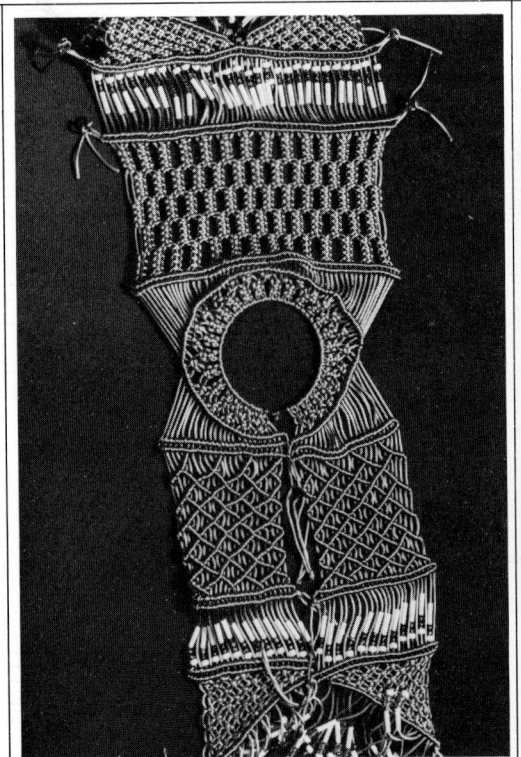
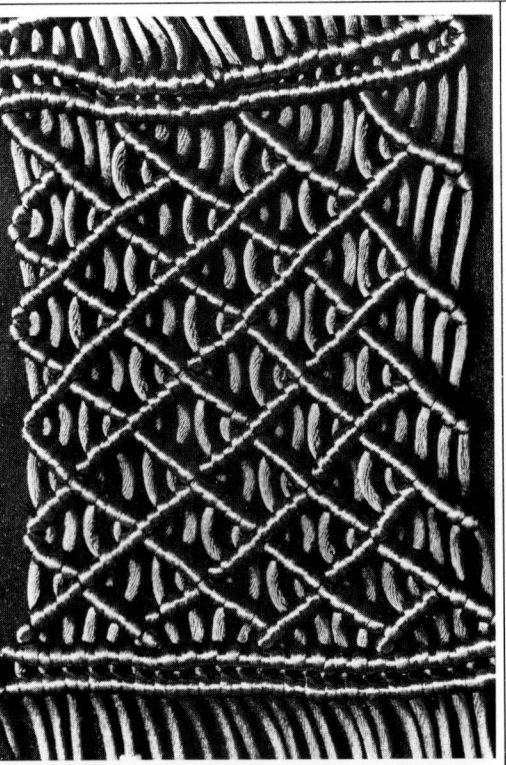

Clove Hitches from right to left, and then back, from left to right. Secure with another Overhand Knot tight against work. Leave ends for now.

5. Now to tie a crisscross pattern of Clove Hitches with multiples of 6 cords.

   A. Use cords 6, 12, 18, and 24 as holding cords for diagonal rows of 5 Clove Hitches each from right to left.

   B. Now use cords 4, 10, 16, and 22 as holding cords for diagonal rows of 5 Clove Hitches from left to right. You'll note that you can only tie a "half row" with cord 22.

   Repeat pattern in this order: 5A, 5B, 5A, 5B, 5A, 5B, 5A, and a "half row" of 5B.

6. Repeat step 4.
7. Starting with cord 2 (the second cord from the *outside* of the vest), add 1 tube bead and 3 crow beads to every other cord.
8. Repeat step 4 about 3″ below step 6.
9. Tie a pattern of decreasing Square Knots (page 20) out to the side from the center front of the vest to the side. Do a row of 6 Square Knots; leave 2 cords off on the right side each time (toward the center front of the vest) until you have just 1 Square Knot tied with the 4 left cords. (You will have a pattern of 6, 5, 5, 4, 4, 3, 3, 2, 2, 1, 1.)
10. Using the right-hand cord as holding cord, tie a row of diagonal Clove Hitches along the angle of the decreasing Square Knot pattern from right to left. Secure the row with an Overhand Knot in the holding cord.

To finish side: Repeat step 7; also add 3 crow beads to all the other cords. Secure beads with an Overhand Knot 3½″ from diagonal Clove Hitch bar (so fringe will also fall at the same angle). Cut and glue cords. Tie an Overhand Knot about 6″ from side of work with each group of cords used for the Clove Hitch bars. These will act as ties for front of vest. Cut and glue cords.

Now for the back of the bolero.

11. If you've completed both sides of the vest, there are 56 cords left for the back. Turn the work and repin it so that these cords are isolated.
12. Add 2 30″ cords with Clove Hitch rows by the method shown on page 23, working from the center to the sides, securing each side with an Overhand Knot. Leave the ends for now.
13. Now do a pattern of alternating sennits of 4 Square Knots (page 21). There will be 14 groups of 4 Square Knots alternating with 13 groups of 4 Square Knots in this order: 14, 13, 14, 13, 14.
14. Repeat step 12.
15. Starting with cord 2, add 1 tube bead and 3 crow beads to every other cord.
16. Divide the cords into 2 groups. Repeat step 9 for the left side, and reverse the order for the right side. The only difference is that the first row of this pattern will have 7 knots, not 6.
17. With the cords still in 2 groups, repeat step 10 for the left side, and reverse it for the right side.

To finish: Start with second cord in on each side, add 1 tube bead and 3 crow beads to every other cord in to the center. Add 3 crow beads to every remaining cord. Secure beads with Overhand Knots 3½″ from diagonal Clove Hitch bars. Cut, glue cords.

Leave about 6″ on the holding cords (except for those in step 12) for the Clove Hitch bars and cut the ends (*no* Overhand Knots). The front and back of the vest can be joined and adjusted by tying these cords through the "holes" in the ends of the corresponding double Clove Hitch bars on the front of the bolero. The holding cords from steps 10 and 17 can be joined with Overhand Knots.

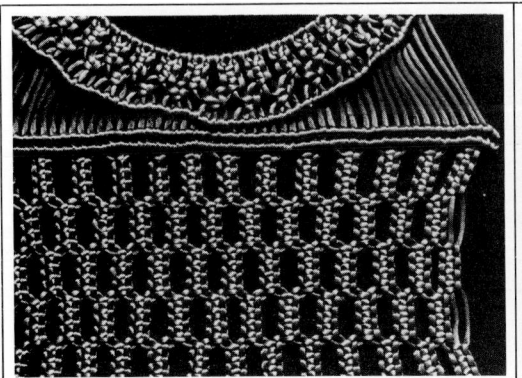
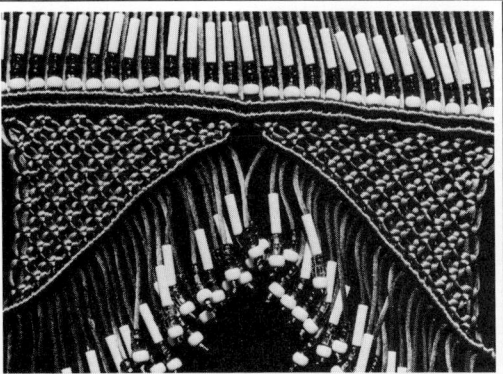
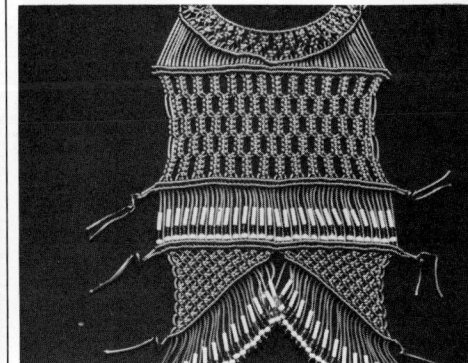
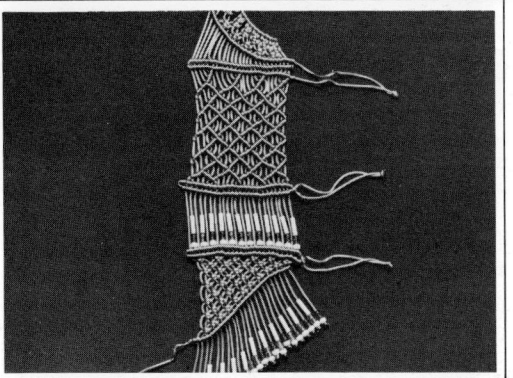

Project 20: Fringed Poncho

This deep, swinging fringe will make a knockout of any plain garment. The front and back of this poncho are fringed in different colors so that one shows through the other as you walk. I've chosen to fringe a poncho, but it would work as well on a long narrow scarf or just on a plain square of fabric which could be worn as a shawl. Directions are given for one section of the fringe. Once you've completed the section, you'll be able to figure out how to repeat and interconnect the pattern. A complete section involves 32 doubled cords (64 working cords). If you can't work your garment out to an even multiple of 32 cords on a side, you'll have to improvise by modifying the full pattern a bit. (The fabric section of this poncho is 36" on each side.)

Pertinent Information

Size: 9" deep (to last Collecting Knot; plus fringe)
Materials: ¼" rayon ribbon 80" cords (384 cords for the poncho shown here). Any kind of ribbon or soft cord could be substituted. (I prefer ribbon for fringes; it knots rather strangely, but it hangs well.)

To begin: Mark off the back of the hem on your garment at ⅜" intervals and mount 32 cords with the Lark's Head, pulling the cords through with a crochet hook, as shown on page 46.

1. Divide the cords into 4 groups of 16 and do the following with each group: using the eighth cord in from each side as holding cords, tie a row of diagonal Clove Hitches from the center to the outside.

   Twist the tying cords from the left and right sides of the inverted V (Λ) pattern just tied and bring them back to their original position, as shown on page 26. Pin the twist in place.

2. Now close the diamonds, but in the following manner: close the *right* side of the first and third diamonds first, and the *left* side of the second and fourth diamonds first. (There's a reason for this, as you'll see.)

3. Divide the cords into 2 groups of 32 and do the following with each group: take the tying cords from the bottom of the right-hand diamond and cross them over the tying cords from the bottom of the left-hand diamond (page 26).

   Close the left side of the left-hand diamond, make the crossover, and continue the row at the same diagonal, Clove Hitching in the 7 tying cords from the bottom of the right-hand diamond.

   Close the right side of the right-hand diamond, make the crossover, and continue to Clove Hitch in the 7 cords and the holding cord from the bottom of the left diamond.

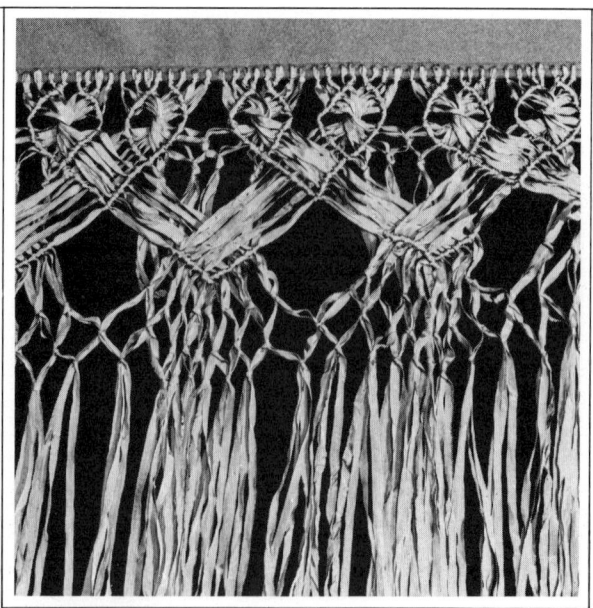

4. Now work with the cords as 1 group. (The 16 cords on each side of the group will interknot with adjoining groups, so leave them for now.)
5. Use the 8 inside cords from the 2 center diamonds to tie a pattern of Overhand Knots using multiple cords: 1 knot with the 4 center cords, then a row of 4 Overhand Knots of 4 cords. The 2 center knots in this row use 2 cords each from the knot above.
6. Take the 7 tying cords from inside of the bottom diamond on the left and cross them over the 7 tying cords from the inside of the right-hand diamond.

   Use the left and right side holding cords to continue a large V shape by Clove Hitching in the 7 cords on each side at the same angle as the diamond above. There will be a big gap in the holding cords before the Clove Hitches begin, in order to maintain the angle.
7. Make sure the cords from step 5 hang behind the cords of the V in step 6.
   To finish: Tie a row of 4-cord Overhand Knots using 2 from the V pattern of step 6 and 2 cords in back of them from step 5. You'll find it easy to match up the corresponding cords. Now do two more alternating rows of Overhand Knots: 2 cords each from adjacent knots, then a row with the original 4 cords.

This sounds much more complicated than it actually is; the pictures are much better than the instructions in this case.

When you fringe your garment, do all of step 1, all of step 2, 3, etc. It's easier to work that way and you'll more readily see how the sections interconnect.

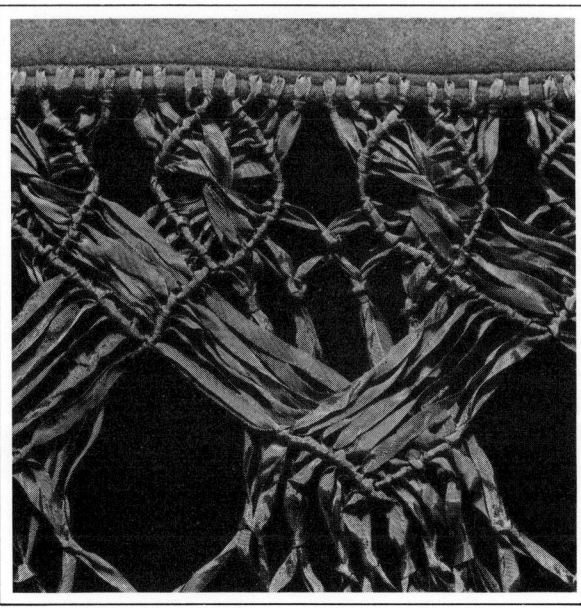

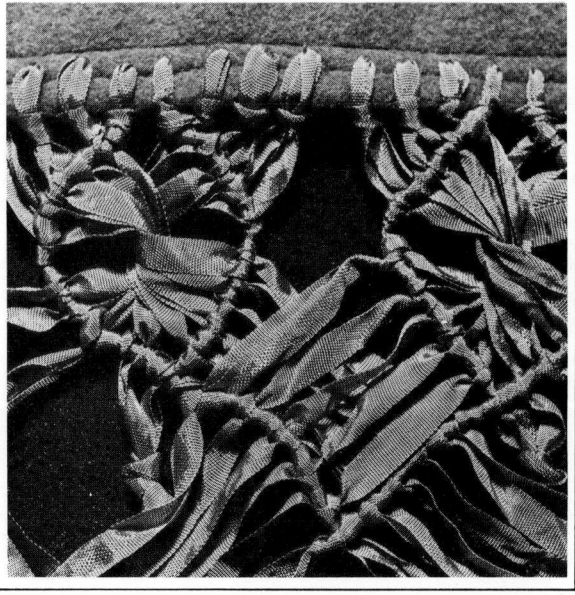

Project 21: Pendant Necklace

A little improvisation is necessary for this project: its beauty is in the randomness of the bottom section. Directions for the neckbands are very specific —after that you're somewhat on your own. This necklace can also be worn over the hip like a bandolier.

Pertinent Information

Size: Neckbands 16″ long
Center section 8″ (plus fringe)
Materials: Guimpe 12 cords 180″
8 cords 80″
60 crow beads
60 tile beads
40 miscellaneous beads
1 toggle-back button
Belfast (or Navy) cord, nylon seine twine, or upholsterers' waxed cord would also be good.

To make neckpieces: Both sides are the same, except one starts with a buttonhole and one with a button. Directions are given for one side, but do them side by side on your knotting surface to assure evenness. Also, there are a couple of places where the knots of each neckpiece have to be done in the opposite direction for symmetry. (These places are noted in the directions with an asterisk *.)

1. Using 2 more 180″ cords as a double-thick mounting bar, mount 4 cords in the middle with the Reverse Lark's Head and pin to knotting surface in pointed pattern shown on page 54.
2. Tie a Square Knot with the center 4 cords. (Slip the button on the 2 center cords at this point on *one* of the neckbands.) Do a pattern of decreasing Square Knots (page 20); a row of 3, then 2, and 1.
3. Use the tying cords from the last Square Knot as holding cords for a row of diagonal Clove Hitches out to the sides. Use the center cords to tie a second row, Clove Hitching in the holding cord from the first row.

Add 1 tile bead, 1 crow bead, and 1 tile bead to the 2 center cords.

4. Now do a double X pattern (page 30), closing the bottom of the diamond shape with 1 row of Clove Hitches in toward the center, then taking the outside cords again as holding cords for a second row, crossing over and completing the double X, Clove Hitching in the holding cord from the first row.

Again add 1 tile, 1 crow, and 1 tile bead to the 2 center cords.

5. Close the double diamond again, this time using the 4 holding cords to tie a Square Knot at the end (instead of crossing over).
6. With the 4 cords on each side, tie a sennit of double alternating Lark's Head chains (page 35), using the outside cord on each side for the first 2 and the last 2 knots in each chain. (There are 28 Lark's Heads in each sennit.) Try to exaggerate the outside loops a little.

With the center 4 cords: add a crow bead to the 2 center cords and tie 2 Square Knots. Repeat this 7 more times, ending with 1 more crow bead and 1 Square Knot.

7. Repeat the 2 double diamond patterns you did in the beginning (steps 3, 4, and 5) but cross over the cords inside the diamonds (page 26) instead of using beads. Cross the left cords over the right in the top diamond, and the right cords over the left in the bottom diamond. (* Reverse

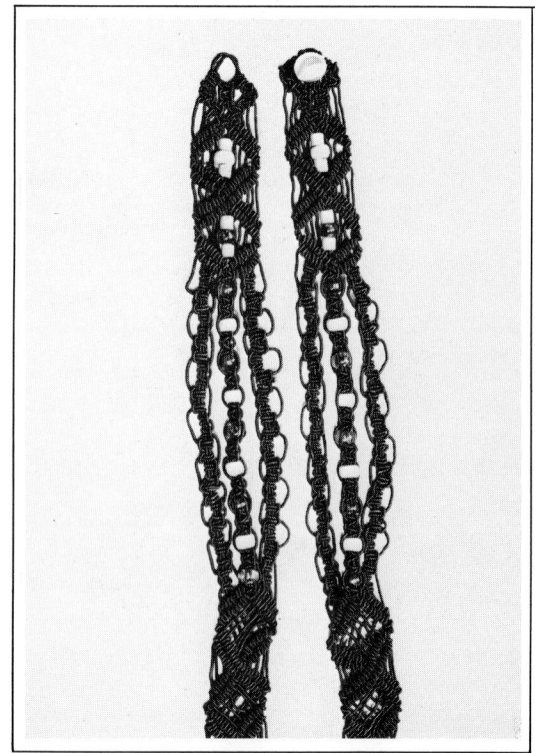

this order for the other side of the neckpiece.)

8. Using the 2 inside cords as a single holding cord, tie a row of diagonal Clove Hitches from right to left (* for the left side; reverse for the right). Tie 2 more rows in the same manner, Clove Hitching in the holding cords from above (page 29) and leaving about ¼" between rows.
9. Using the center 8 cords, tie a Berry Knot, as shown on page 40.

Divide the cords into 2 groups of 6 and tie 2 small Berry Knots just below the large one. (The Square Knots will be tied around just 1 center cord.)

10. Repeat step 8, but slip a bead on cords 3, 5, 8, and 10 between each row.

Neckband is complete. Now for the pendant section.

11. Pin the neckbands to the knotting surface with about 2½" between them. Take the 8 80" cords together and pin them in the middle between the neckbands about 1" above the point where the neckbands end.
12. Using 7 of the 8 cords as holding cords, tie a continuous chain of Clove Hitches over them with the eighth cord from the center toward the neckbands along the angle of the last row of Clove Hitches in the neckbands. When you reach the neckbands, Clove Hitch the cords from the neckbands over all 8 of the 50" cords.
13. Now it's up to you to "shape" these 8 cords, curving them around, using whatever cords you wish to Clove Hitch over them, curving it back toward the center. (I've used beads on some of the cords from the neckbands to hold the curve in place on the bottom, and the cords from the beads strung to Clove Hitch the curve against the beads.)

When the cords meet in the center, cross them over and use 1 cord to tightly wind around and join all 16 cords securely.

To finish: Cords will now be basically in 3 sections: the neckband cords on the left and right, and the 16 added cords in the middle.

The object is to give a nice "raggy" appearance to the piece with a mixed use of Clove Hitches, Collecting Knots, Overhand Knots, Coil Knots, and a mixture of all kinds and sizes of beads—many kinds of beads can be threaded on this thin cord. Leave a variety of lengths and of frayed and finished ends.

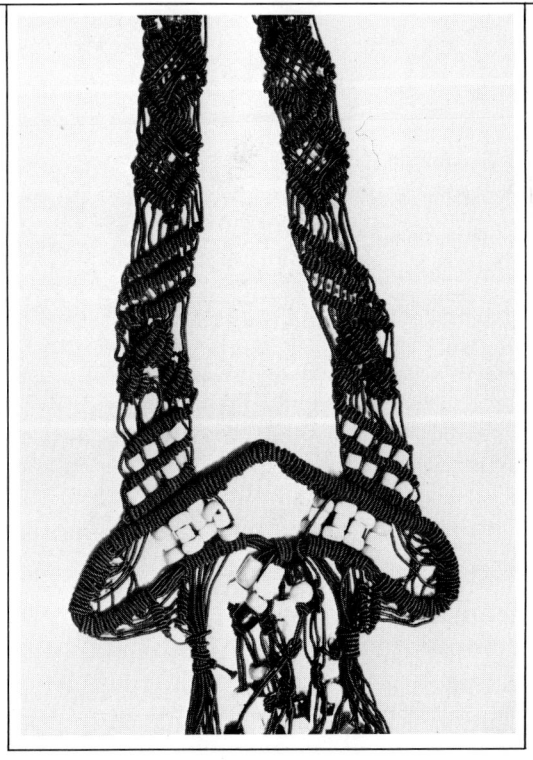

Project 22: Man's Tie

Here is a more traditional tie—it has a "Windsor Knot," after all. A solid angled technique is used to widen it and bring it to a point. Two new cords are added at the beginning of the angled pattern.

Pertinent Information

Size: 6" x 16"
Materials: Cotton seine twine #48 8 cords 200"
                                    2 cords 50"
                                    2 cords 72"
   14 crow beads
   Marlin twine, packaging twine, slide cord, or #2 rattail might be substituted.

To begin: Pin the 2 50" cords, at the middle, to the knotting surface to serve as the mounting cords. Mount the 8 200" cords: mount the 2 outside cords on each side with the Double Lark's Head and the 4 inside cords with the plain Reverse Lark's Head.

1. First we make the "knot" of the tie: the idea is to bring all the cords tightly in to the center to give the "knot" its shape.

   Use the outside cord on each side as holding cord for a row of Clove Hitches in toward the center. Now use these 2 holding cords as center cords for a sennit of alternating Clove Hitches (page 34) tied with the adjacent cord on each side. Tie 3 Clove Hitches with each cord for a sennit of 6.

2. Take the outside cord on each side for a row of 4 Clove Hitches toward the center; repeat this process for a row of 2, and a row of 1 Clove Hitch.

3. Use the 2 cords now closest to the center sennit on each side and tie 1 vertical Clove Hitch in succession with the 4 remaining cords on each side.

4. Take these same 4 cords on each side in the order that they emerge from the sennit in step 3, and tie an alternating single chain (page 33) with each cord in succession—left and then right—over all the center cords. Each succeeding single loop should encompass the previous cord and all the center cords, so that all cords are included in the last knot. Pull these knots very tight to bunch the cords.

   Now the "Windsor Knot" is complete. It sounds more complicated than it is. Any way you can devise to bring everything together in the center will work just as well.

5. To widen the tie gradually, tie a Square Knot

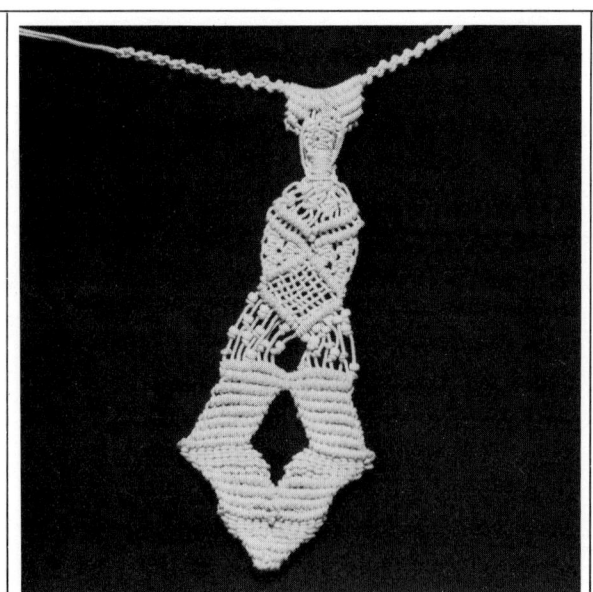
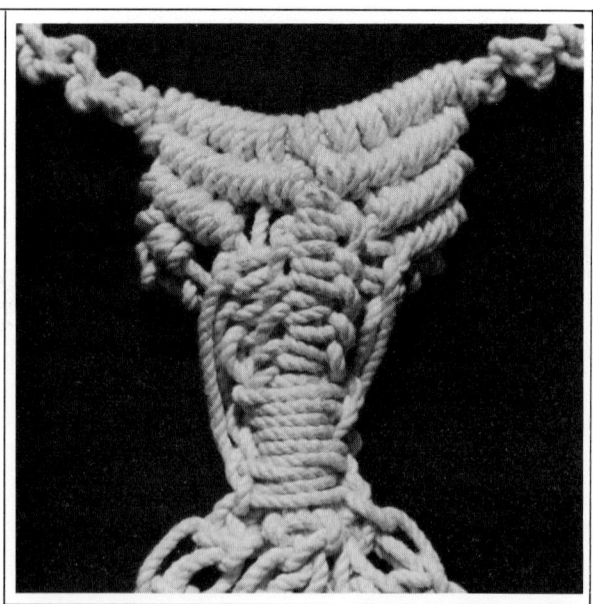

over the 4 center cords tightly with the adjacent cord on each side. Tie a Square Knot with the 4 outside cords on each side.

Do a row of 4 Square Knots.

6. Use the outside cords as holding cords for a V of Clove Hitches in toward center making the crossover (page 12).
7. Repeat step 6, leaving about ¼" between the rows.
8. Now use cords 2–3 and 5–6 in from each side as center cords for intertwining Clove Hitch chains (page 35 shows an intertwining Lark's Head chain. It's the same principle). Cord 4 on each side is the alternating cord for *both* chains.

To be more specific: tie a Clove Hitch with cord 1 over cords 2–3, then a Clove Hitch with cord 4 over cords 2–3. Tie a Clove Hitch with cord 7 over cords 5–6, then a Clove Hitch with cord 4 over cords 5–6, and another Clove Hitch with cord 7 over cords 5–6. Finally, tie a Clove Hitch with cord 1 over 2–3, with cord 4 over 2–3 and cord 1 over 2–3.

9. Finish the X pattern started in step 7.
10. Weave the cords inside the diamond, as shown on page 27.
11. Complete the bottom of the diamond.
12. Do a random pattern of Overhand Knots and beads ending about ½" below the bottom of the diamond.
13. Using the right-hand cord as holding cord, do a row of Clove Hitches from right to left, adding the 2 72" cords (with the Double Lark's Head method on page 47) after the first 8 Clove Hitches. Pin and do another row of Clove Hitches left to right, hitching in the new cords and closing the double bar with a crochet hook (page 12).
14. Now for the angling pattern (check page 32). Divide the cords into 2 groups of 10. Taking the inside cord in each group as holding cord each time, tie 6 rows of Clove Hitches out to each side, hitching in the holding cords from the row above each time (page 29).
15. Taking the outside cord on each side as tying cord each time, do 3 rows of Vertical Clove Hitches in toward the center, hitching in the cord from the row above each time.
16. Now to close the tie. Continue to angle in, using the outside cords as holding cords for 4 more rows of Clove Hitches in toward the center, pushing the holding cords to the back of the work as each row is completed. (*Don't* hitch in the above holding cord.)
17. Do 3 more rows of vertical Clove Hitches as in step 15, but push the holding cords to the back of the work as each row is completed. (Don't hitch in the cord above.)
18. Finally, 3 more rows of Clove Hitches as in step 16, until there's only 1 row of 2 Clove Hitches.

To finish: Turn work over and tie each pair of cords with a double Overhand Knot or Clove Hitch. Pull the cords near the edge to the back of the work and through other knots with a crochet hook (page 61). Secure with Overhand Knots. Cut and glue. Neckband of tie can be finished with an alternating single chain as shown on page 33. Secure with Overhand Knots and cut to length desired.

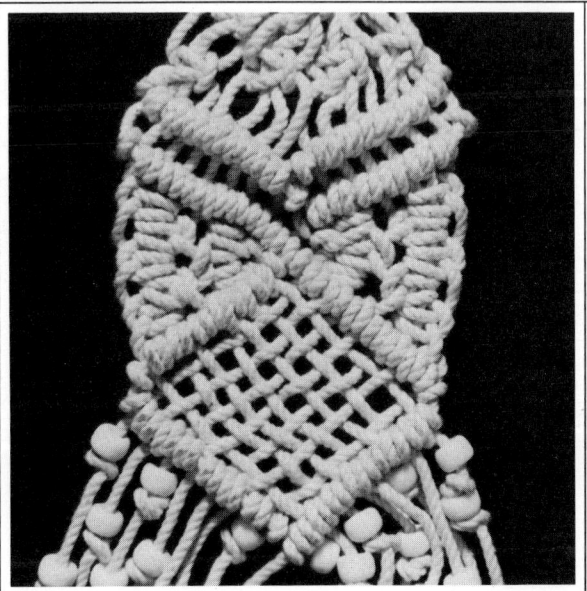
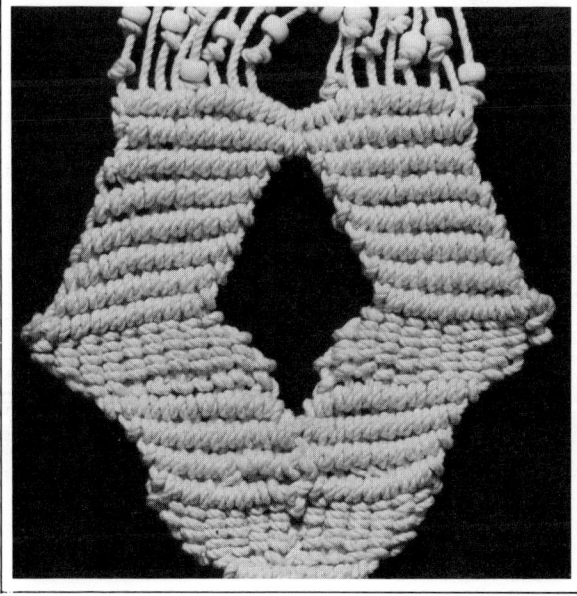

Project 23: Bib/Apron

If you don't have the nerve to wear this piece around your waist, it makes a smashing bib. There's a lot of crossing over of cords here, so check page 19 before you start, and watch the pictures as you work.

Pertinent Information

Size: 8" (plus ties) x 11" (plus fringe)
Materials: #1 Rattail 28 cords 110"
                         2 cords 100"
                         2 cords 60"
    160 tile beads
    40 crow beads
    9 small wood beads
    4 plastic rings (1" diam.)
    Soutache, slide cord, or cotton seine twine might also be used.

To make waistband/neckband: Pin the 2 60" cords and the 2 100" cords to the knotting surface at the center next to each other so that the 60" cords are in the middle (page 47). Tie a sennit of Square Knots to a length of 6" on each side of the center pins. Add a couple of wood beads to each group of 4 cords and secure with an Overhand Knot about 15" back from end of sennit on each side to allow for tying around the waist or neck.

To start: Pin the waistband to the knotting surface as mounting cord and mount the 28 110" cords in the middle of the band with the Reverse Lark's Head.

1. With the outside 2 groups of 4 cords on each side, tie a sennit of 6 Square Knots, leaving about ¼" between the 1st and 2nd Square Knots. Using cords 4 and 5 in from each side as center cords, tie a lacy sennit of 6 Square Knots using each pair of adjacent cords in succession, as shown on page 19. Add 2 crow beads to the center cords and tie 2 more Square Knots with the 2 adjacent pairs of cords in the same manner.

2. With all the remaining cords, tie a pattern of decreasing Square Knots; a row of 10 decreasing to 1.

3. With the 2 groups of 4 cords closest to the outside of the decreasing Square Knot pattern on each side, tie a sennit of 5 Square Knots. Join each 2 sennits by adding 2 crow beads to the adjoining cords (cords 12 and 13 in from each side). Then tie another lacy sennit of 6 Square Knots using each cord in succession (again, see pattern on page 19) and add 1 more crow bead to the center cords.

4. Now there are 3 groups of 8 cords left. Use the center 4 cords of each group to add a ring by the method on page 57. Then tie 5 more Square Knots in the 2 outside sennits, 1 with the first 2 adjacent cords and 4 with the second 2 cords. Tie 3 more Square Knots in the center group, 1 with the first 2 cords and 2 with the other 2.

5. Tie a Square Knot with the 4 center cords and use the outside cords from this Square Knot to tie a row of Clove Hitches out to the sides and back to the center, securing with a Square Knot (page 22). Be sure to keep the cords in their new order.

6. Take the 8 outside cords on each side, add a few tile beads, and secure them with Overhand Knots about 2" below the double bar. Cut the fringe at the length you desire.

7. With the remaining cords, take cords 8, 16, and 20 in from each side and use them (in order) as holding cords to tie a row of diagonal Clove

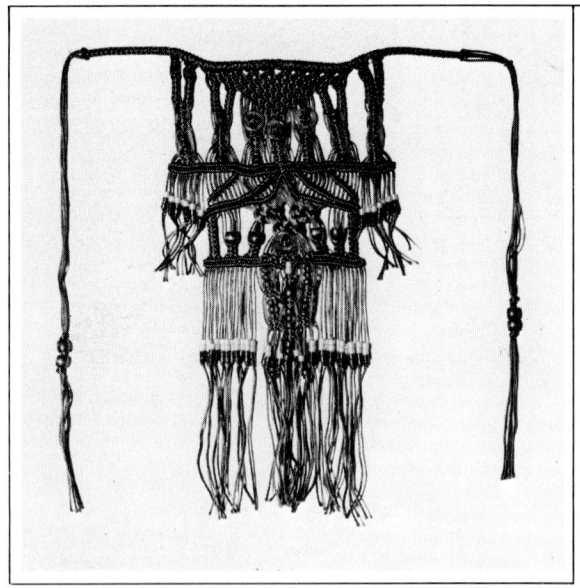

Hitches out to the sides, curving the rows as you go for a nice effect.

8. With the 4 outside cords on each side, tie a sennit of 8 Square Knots.
9. With the next group of 4 cords toward the center on each side, add a wood bead to the center cords and tie 3 Square Knots in line with the last 3 Square Knots of the outside sennits.
10. Now there are 2 groups of 12 cords left. Divide each *group* into 3 groups of 4 cords. Tie a Josephine Knot (page 36) using 4 cords for each side and pull 4 through the center (as on page 39).
11. This part is quite tricky. First take the 4 cords coming out on the left of the first Josephine Knot and the 4 cords coming out on the right of the second Josephine Knot and repeat step 9 with each group.

    Next, take the 4 cords from the center of each Josephine Knot and 2 from the inside of each Josephine Knot and tie another Josephine Knot of 6 cords on each side. Pull the 2 remaining cords from the inside of each previous Josephine Knot through the center.

    Use these 4 cords to add another ring, as on page 57.
12. Repeat step 5 (variation from actual apron), but add 2 tile beads to the center cords before securing with a Square Knot at the end. Tie another Square Knot on the same center cords with the adjacent cord on each side.
13. Take the 11 cords on each side and repeat step 6, leaving 3" before securing the knots.
14. Now there are 18 cords left. Divide them into 3 groups of 6. Add 3 crow beads to the 2 center cords of the left and right groups and a wood bead to the center group. Tie 2 Square Knots under the beads in each group—1 each with the 2 adjacent pairs of cords on each side (page 19).
15. Take the inside 2 cords from the 2 outside groups, cross them over, and tie 1 Square Knot with each pair in succession around the center cords of the center group.

Add 3 more crow beads to the center cords of the left and right group. Cross the cords from the center knots back again and tie 2 more Square Knots on the right and left in the same manner.

Add 3 more crow beads to the center cords of the middle group and cross the tying cords over again, and tie 2 more Square Knots in the middle.

To finish: Finish the 18 cords in any combination of beads desired, securing with Overhand Knots. Cut and fringe at desired length.

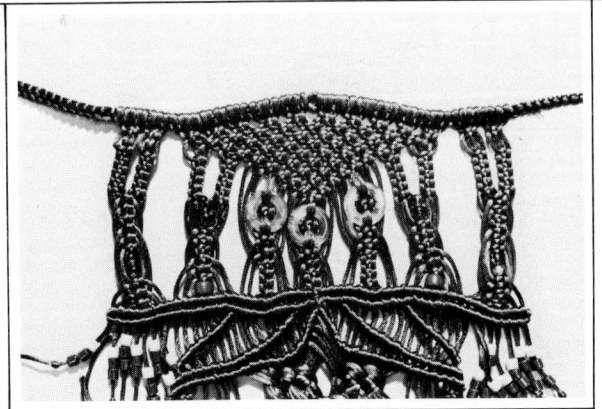

Project 24: Dress

Ain't it amazin' what you can do with cotton string? This dress is a big project and involves working with long cords—all those Clove Hitch bars are a big job—but it's really fun to wear. The dress slips over the head, laces up the center front and sides to adjust, and ties on the sides at the waist. These instructions are for size 7 to 11.

Pertinent Information

Size: 13" wide x 23" to bottom of knotting in front; hem length is up to you.
Materials: Cotton seine twine #48 54 cords 250"
                                    7 cords 40"
  2 chain links or rings (2½" wide)
  Nylon braid, #2 rattail, or a lightweight rayon tubular could be used as well.

Front of Dress

To begin: Mount 8 250" cords on each link or ring with the Reverse Lark's Head and pin side by side to knotting surface about 9" apart, center to center.

1. Add a ninth cord on each side with a row of Clove Hitches by the method shown on page 23.
2. Use the 2 center cords on each side as holding cords to tie a diamond pattern (page 25). Don't forget to include the added cord from step 1. Cross the left tying cords over the right tying cords inside the left-hand diamond (and the right cords over the left cords inside the right-hand diamond).
3. Take another 250" cord and pin it in the middle between the "shoulder straps," just below the diamond patterns just tied.

   Mount 8 more 250" cords in the middle of the new cord with the Double Lark's Head (page 47).

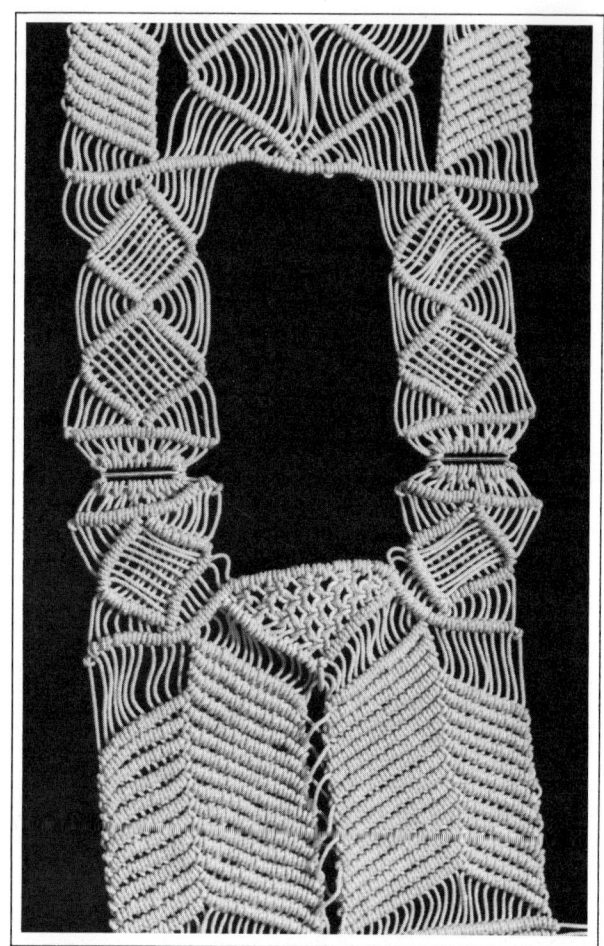

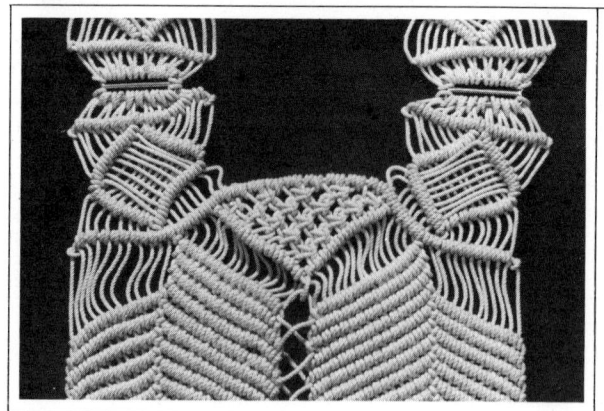

Then Clove Hitch on the cords from the left and right shoulder straps. Let the ends of the holding cord hang down so they'll be incorporated in the knotting.

4. Tie a pattern of decreasing Square Knots (page 20) in the center: a row of 5, then 4, 3, 2, and 1.

Use the adjacent cord on each side as holding cord for a V of Clove Hitches along the angle of the decreasing Square Knot pattern.

5. Divide the cords into 2 groups. Take cord 16 in from the center on each side as holding cord for a row of diagonal Clove Hitches in toward the center on each side.

Taking the first tying cord as holding cord for each succeeding row (page 29), tie 2 more rows of diagonal Clove Hitches in this manner, hitching in the holding cord from the row above each time.

6. Now take the first tying cord from the row just tied as holding cord for a row of diagonal Clove Hitches out to the sides.

Then take the first tying cord from the row above and tie another row in toward the center. This is the chevron pattern shown on page 27, but upside down.

Repeat this sequence—a row toward the center, a row toward the outside—always using the first tying cord as holding cord and always Clove Hitching in the above holding cord, until there are 16 rows of Clove Hitches on the inside and 12 on the outside (on each side of the dress front). End each side with a row in toward the center.

7. Add 2 40" cords with a Clove Hitch bar, working from the center by the method shown on page 23. This is the waistband. Leave ends long to use as ties.

8. Leave out 8 cords on each side and do a pattern of decreasing Square Knots: a row of 9, decreasing to 1. Use the adjacent cord on each side to tie a V pattern along the angle of the decreasing Square Knots, making the crossover.

Continue to tie a diamond pattern (page 25) using the same holding cords and the same tying cords.

Back of Dress

To begin: Turn work and mount 8 cords on other side of each link or ring and re-pin to knotting surface.

9. Repeat step 1.
10. Repeat step 2, but tie 2 diamonds on each side and alternate the direction in crossing over the cords inside each diamond.
11. Repeat step 3, again adding 8 new cords.

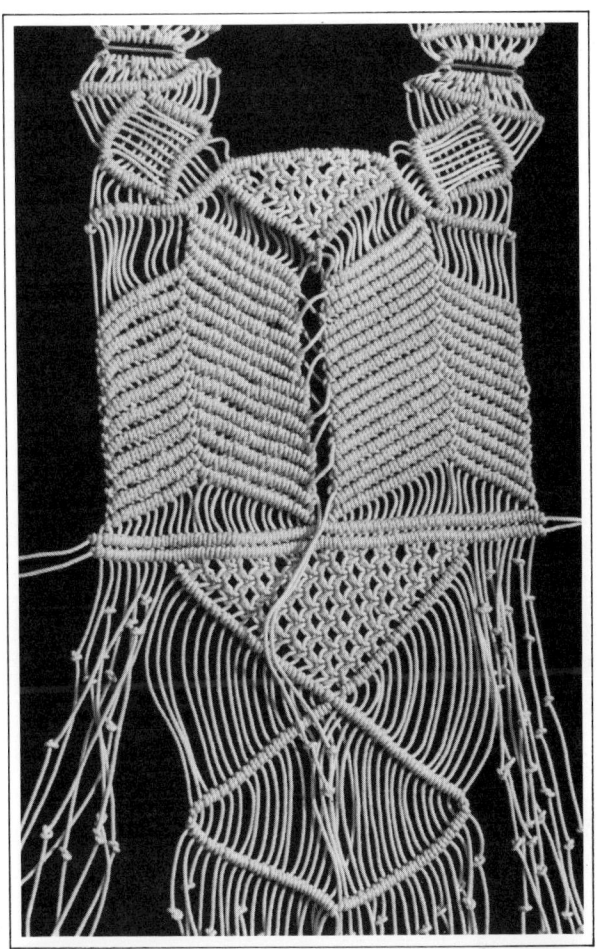

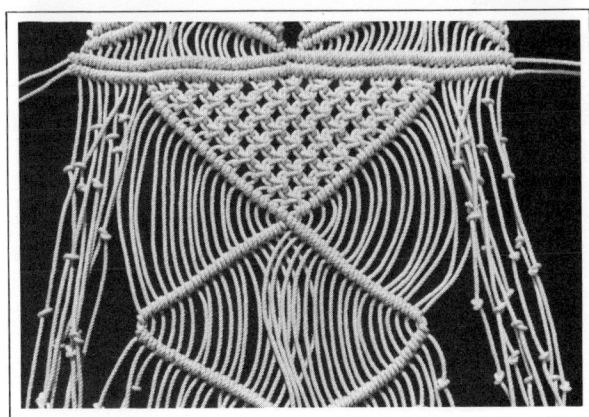

12. Using cord 12 in from each side as holding cords, tie a row of diagonal Clove Hitches out to each side. Taking the first tying cords as holding cord for each succeeding row, tie 7 more rows, Clove Hitching in the previous holding cord each time (page 29).
13. Using the 2 center cords of the dress, tie a diamond pattern with the remaining cords (page 25), making the crossover to finish it. Have the diamond end where the last of the 7 rows of diagonal Clove Hitches ends.
14. Repeat step 7.
15. Using the 2 center cords as holding cords, tie an inverted V (∧) of diagonal Clove Hitches out toward the sides, but leave out the 8 outside cords on each side.
16. Do a pattern of increasing Square Knots inside the inverted V: a row of 1, increasing to a row of 9.

To finish: Tie Overhand Knots in all the hanging cords at random intervals. Decide on your hem length and tie Coil Knots of 6–8 wraps near the bottom. I've left the ends raggy.

Make laces for the center front and sides to adjust dress by the method shown on page 60. The sides lace in and out of the ends of the Clove Hitch bars—the 8 rows in the back and the bottom 8 rows in the front. Start the laces at the top so that the ends pull tight at the waistband.

For the front, start the lace with the top bar of Clove Hitches and work it down the center front, also ending at the waist

Note: If you've made your dress with cotton seine twine, it's pretty stiff. Give it a bath in fabric softener.

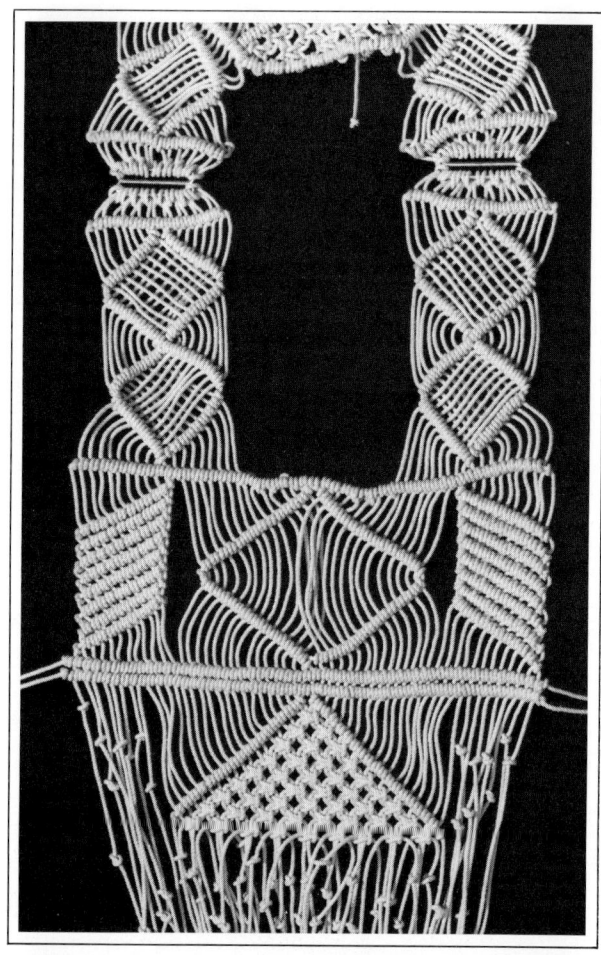

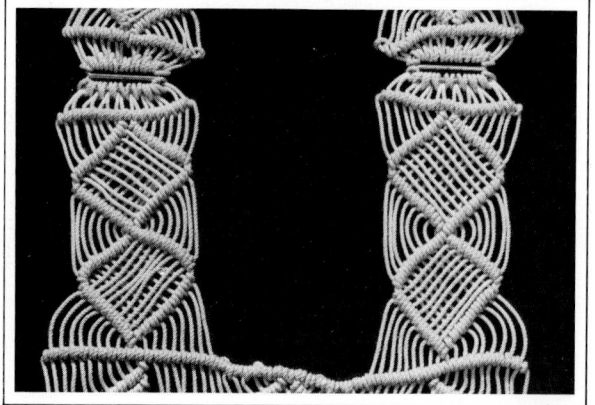

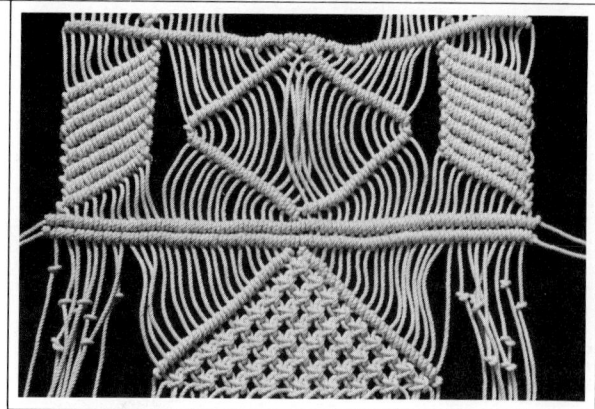

Project 25: Bikini

For this project you're pretty much on your own—it's definitely only for those who have pretty much mastered the craft and can improvise enough to fit it to their own size. It's very comfortable and, because it's made with polypropylene cord, you can actually wear it in the water.

If you've built up your confidence with past projects, try it. It's a difficult project, but good practice for all the things you're going to make on your own now that you've finished this book!

Pertinent Information

Size: Top is 17" wide and 5" deep (plus Square Knot sennits which tie in back and around neck). See the drawing of the dimensions for the bottom. This bikini should fit size 7–9.

Materials: Polypropylene Mason Line #18

For top: 50 cords 80"
         8 cords 40"
8 tile beads
8 crow beads
5 brass rings (1" diam.)

For bottom: 2 cords 160" 16 cords 100"
                8 cords 50"   40 cords 40"
              12 cords 80"   40 cords 40"
              several cords about 100"
              4 brass rings 1½" diameter
              ¼ yard white nylon or silk for lining

When I said you were on your own for this one, I meant it: these directions are very general.

Bikini Top

1. Using an 80" cord as holding cord, do a spiral pattern according to the directions on page 50, adding more 80" cords as needed spiraling out and around as many times as needed to fit, until you've added 24 cords.

Do a spiral pattern in the opposite direction for the other cup of the bikini top.

2. Measure the distance you need between the center of the cups and pin the spirals to the knotting surface at this distance.

3. There are 48 cords coming out of each spiral. Take 12 cords from the left and right and set them aside for the side panels on each side.

Take 20 cords from the bottom and the insides of the spirals to use to tie over the center ring. Take 16 cords nearest the top on each side to use for the top rings.

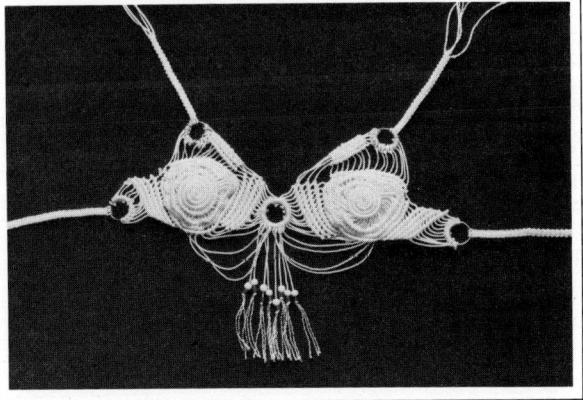
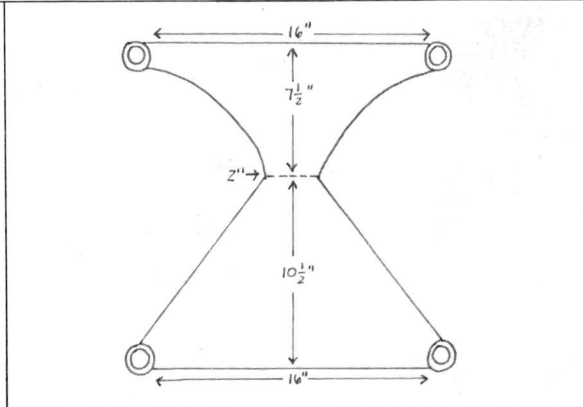

4. Take the 12 side cords on each side and tie 4 rows of Clove Hitches as shown; then Clove Hitch all the cords to 1 brass ring on each side. Cut and burn ends of cords.
5. Take the cords to be used for the center and tie 4 rows of Clove Hitches on each side as shown. Clove Hitch the tying cords from the rows and some of the rest of the bottom cords onto the center ring. Leave big loops in the bottom cords for a decorative effect. Cut and burn ends of cords. (Bead a few of the center cords as shown, if you like.)
6. Use the holding cords used for the Clove Hitch rows in the center and Clove Hitch some of the cords of the top section, making 4 rows on each side. Clove Hitch all the top cords onto the top rings. Cut cords and burn ends.
7. Mount 2 40" cords on each ring for Square Knot sennits of 4", leaving the ends long to tie the top behind the back and around the neck.

Bikini Bottom

To begin: Draw yourself a pattern, full scale, as shown here. Pin the paper pattern to your knotting surface and pin the 4 brass rings firmly in place.

Wind a 160" cord back and forth 8 times between the top 2 rings, and wind the other between the bottom 2 rings, keeping the cords taut. Mount 4 30" cords on each of the top 2 rings with the Reverse Lark's Head. Pin them in the curve shown and Clove Hitch them to the bottom rings. This is the "framework" of the bikini bottom.

Front of bikini bottom:

1. Mount the 12 80" cords with the Double Lark's Head method to the top cord (of the 8) in the center front of the bikini and Clove Hitch them down over the other 7 cords (page 23). Use the last 2 pairs of horizontal cords as double-thick holding cords (you'll have 6 rows of Clove Hitches).
2. With these 24 working cords, do a pattern of increasing Square Knots from 1 to 6. Continue with alternate rows of 5 and 6 Square Knots until you reach the bottom of the front section, then decrease to 4 in a row as the center curves in.

When you start to decrease the pattern of Square Knots, use the cords you are leaving out and Clove Hitch them over the outside 4 "framework" cords on each side, finishing with Overhand Knots.

3. Add a 100" cord, just above the point where the Square Knot pattern started to decrease, to the outside of the 4 "framework" cords with the Double Lark's Head. Clove Hitch it over the 4 cords, loop it through the first "hole" in the side of the Square Knot pattern, bring it back and again Clove Hitch it over the outside 4 cords, this time from the inside out. Turn, and repeat this sequence (adding new cords as necessary), until you have looped through all the holes in the sides of the Square Knot pattern.
4. Now mount 10 40" cords on each side of the center Square Knot pattern with the Double Lark's Head as in step 1. Clove Hitch these cords over the 8 horizontal cords in the same manner; then leave space and Clove Hitch them over the outside 4 cords, finishing with Overhand Knots.
5. Add a 100" cord to the left and right of these 10 cords and Clove Hitch back and forth from the top 8 to the bottom 4, adding new cords as needed (as in step 4) until you reach the brass side rings. Add extra cords as needed (page 58).

Back of bikini bottom:

Repeat the same sequence used for front, but use 16 100" cords for the center pattern of Square Knots (steps 1 and 2). Your alternating Square Knot pattern will be rows of 7 and 8.

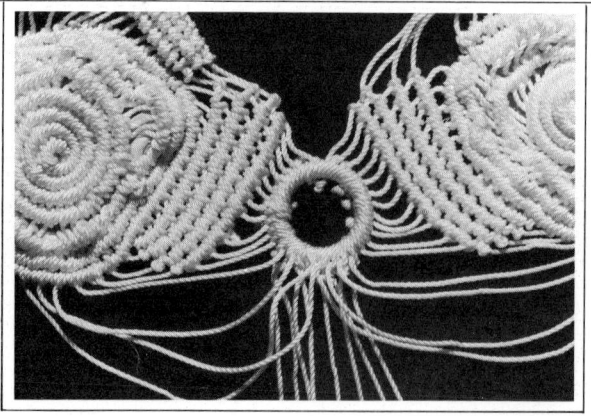
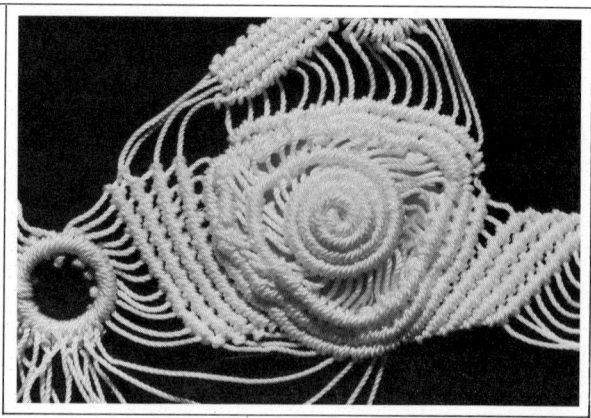

To finish bikini bottom: At the center bottom you will have 4 Square Knots from the front and the back. Take each corresponding pair of cords, front and back, and join them with double Overhand Knots.

Readjust the tension on the 8 outside "framework" cords, by re-tying the Clove Hitches over the brass rings.

Add a short Square Knot sennit with the 40″ cords to each brass ring, for tying the bikini at the sides.

Cut and burn all ends.

Unless you're very daring, line the bikini.

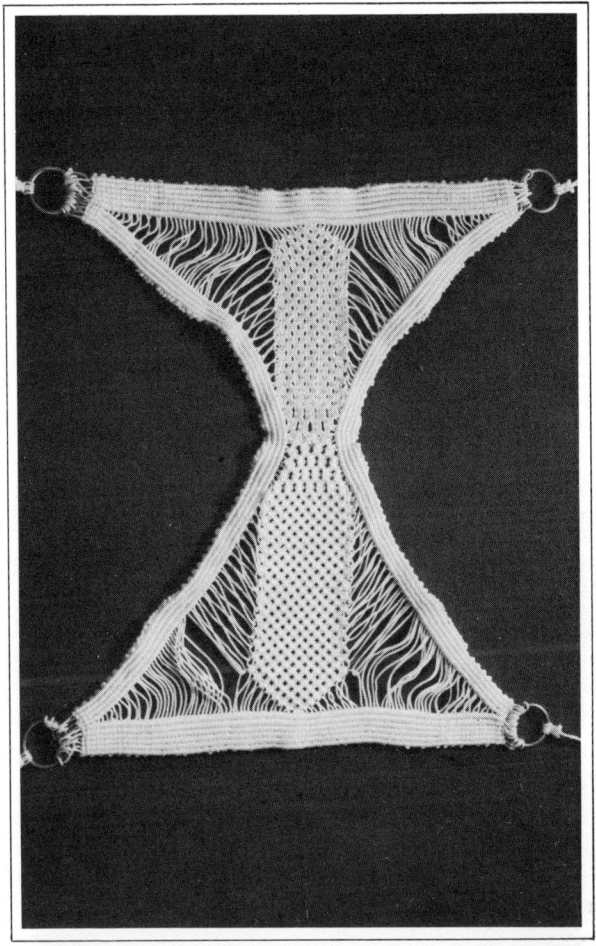

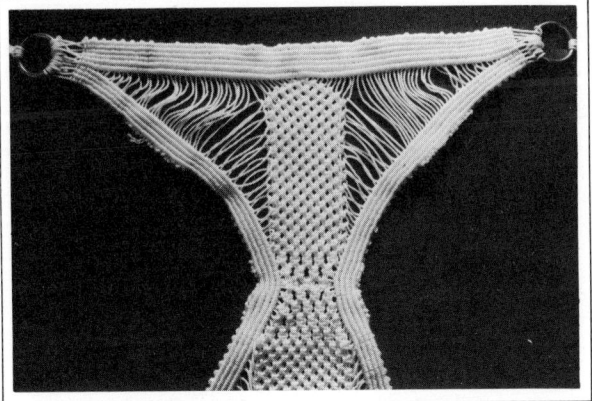

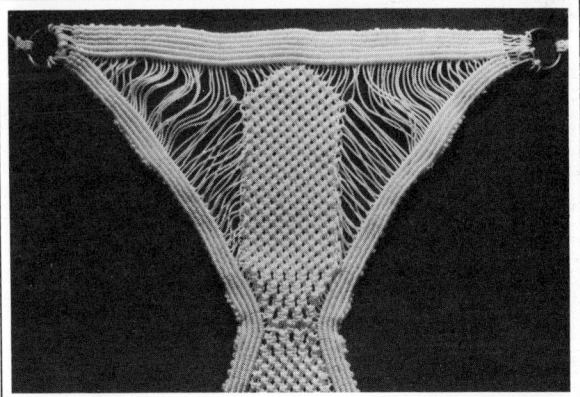

Bibliography

Handbook of Knots   Raoul Graumont
Cornell Maritime Press, Inc.   1945
Cambridge, Md.

Introducing Macramé   Eirian Short
Watson-Guptill Publications   1970
New York, N.Y.

Macramé: Creative Design in Knotting
   Dona Z. Meilach
Crown Publishers, Inc.   1971
New York, N.Y.

Macramé: Creative Knotting   Imelda Manalo Pesch
Sterling Publishing Company   1970
New York, N.Y.

Macramé: The Art of Creative Knotting
   Virginia I. Harvey
Van Nostrand Reinhold Company   1967
New York, N.Y.

Practical Macramé   Eugene Andes
Van Nostrand Reinhold Company   1971
New York, N.Y.

Square Knot Book No. 3   P. C. Herwig
P. C. Herwig Co. 4th Edition   1970
Brooklyn, N.Y.

Square Knot Handicraft Guide
   Raoul Graumont and Elmer Wenstrom
Cornell Maritime Press, Inc.   1949
Cambridge, Md.

Step-By-Step Macramé   Mary Walker Phillips
Golden Press   1970
New York, N.Y.

Threads in Action   Virginia I. Harvey
Threads in Action Publication   1970–1971
Freeland, Wash.

List of Suppliers

Cord

AAA Cordage Co.
3238 N. Clark St.
Chicago, Ill. 60657

Baehm Paper & Twine Co., Inc.
53 Murray St.
New York, N.Y. 10007

Briggs & Little's Woolen Mill Ltd.
York Mills, Harvey Station,
N. B., Canada

Wm. Condon & Sons Limited
65 Queen St.
Charlottetown,
P.E.I., Canada

Craft Yarns of Rhode Island, Inc.
Post Office Box 385
Pawtucket, R.I. 02862

Creative Handweavers
P. O. Box 26480
Los Angeles, Calif. 90026

Frederick J. Fawcett Incorporated
129 South St.
Boston, Mass. 02111

Fibre Yarn Co.
840 Avenue of the Americas
New York, N.Y.

House of Yarns and Fabrics
Box 98
Hampton, N.H. 03842

Lily Mills Company
Shelby, N.C. 28150

Macramé & Weaving Supply Co.
63 East Adams St.
Chicago, Ill. 60603

Manhattan Marine
116 Chambers St.
New York, N.Y.

Norden Products
P.O. Box 1
Glenview, Ill. 60025

Paternayen Bros., Inc.
312 E. 95 St.
New York, N.Y. 10028

Puritan Mills
P.O. Box 22185
Louisville, Ky. 40222

Warp, Woof & Potpourri
514 North Lake Ave.
Pasadena, Calif. 91101

Yarn Center
868 Avenue of the Americas
New York, N.Y. 10001

The Yarn Depot, Inc.
545 Sutter St.
San Francisco, Calif. 94102

United Chambers Trading Corp.
83 Chambers St.
New York, N.Y.

Beads

American Handicrafts (Tandy)
(headquarters store)
1011 Foch St.
Fort Worth, Texas 76101

Bead and Gem
920 Broadway
New York, N.Y.

Bead Game
505-B North Fairfax Ave.
Los Angeles, Calif. 90036

Bethlehem Imports
1169 Cushman
San Diego, Calif. 92110

Ellis Imports
44 W. 37 St.
New York, N.Y. 10018

Glori Bead Shoppe
172 W. 4 St.
New York, N.Y.

Gloria's Glass Garden
Box 1990
Beverley Hills, Calif. 90213

Rhinestone Imports
61 W. 37 St.
New York, N.Y. 10018

Sheru Bead Curtain & Jewelry Designers
49 W. 38 St.
New York, N.Y. 10018

Walbead Inc.
38 W. 37 St.
New York, N.Y. 10018

Findings & Miscellany

Del Trading Post
Mission, S.D. 57555
(feather cones, feathers, imitation bone beads)

P. C. Herwig Co.
Square Knot Headquarters
264 Clinton St.
Brooklyn, N.Y. 11201

Jewelart Inc.
7753 Densmore Ave.
Van Nuys, Calif. 91406

Macramania
886 Ninth Ave.
New York, N.Y. 10019

Plume Trading and Sales Co., Inc.
155 Lexington Ave.
New York, N.Y. 10016
(feather cones, feathers, imitation bone beads)

The Weavers Loft
320 Blue Bell Road
Williamstown, N.J. 08094

Other Sources of Supplies

Variety stores
Five and dime stores
Needlecraft and drapery sections of department stores
Army-Navy surplus stores
Stationers
Hobby and craft stores
Marine supply stores
Upholsterer supply stores
Hardware stores

About the Author

Laura Torbet was art director for a New York firm before starting her own graphic design studio, specializing in posters, brochures, bags, and book jackets. She began doing macramé in 1970 just for pleasure, and was soon selling her beaded macramé jewelry to department stores and boutiques across the country. Her work has been featured in *Vogue, Harper's Bazaar, Women's Wear Daily, Glamour,* and *New York.* She also has a line of kits which correspond to some of the projects in this book under the name DESIGNWORKS, which are available at needlecraft and hobby stores or by writing to The Design Works, 6 So. Fullerton Ave., Montclair, N.J. 07042. Laura Torbet also makes leatherwork, jewelry, and works at an odd assortment of "unclassifiable" crafts.

TT
840
.T67

53093

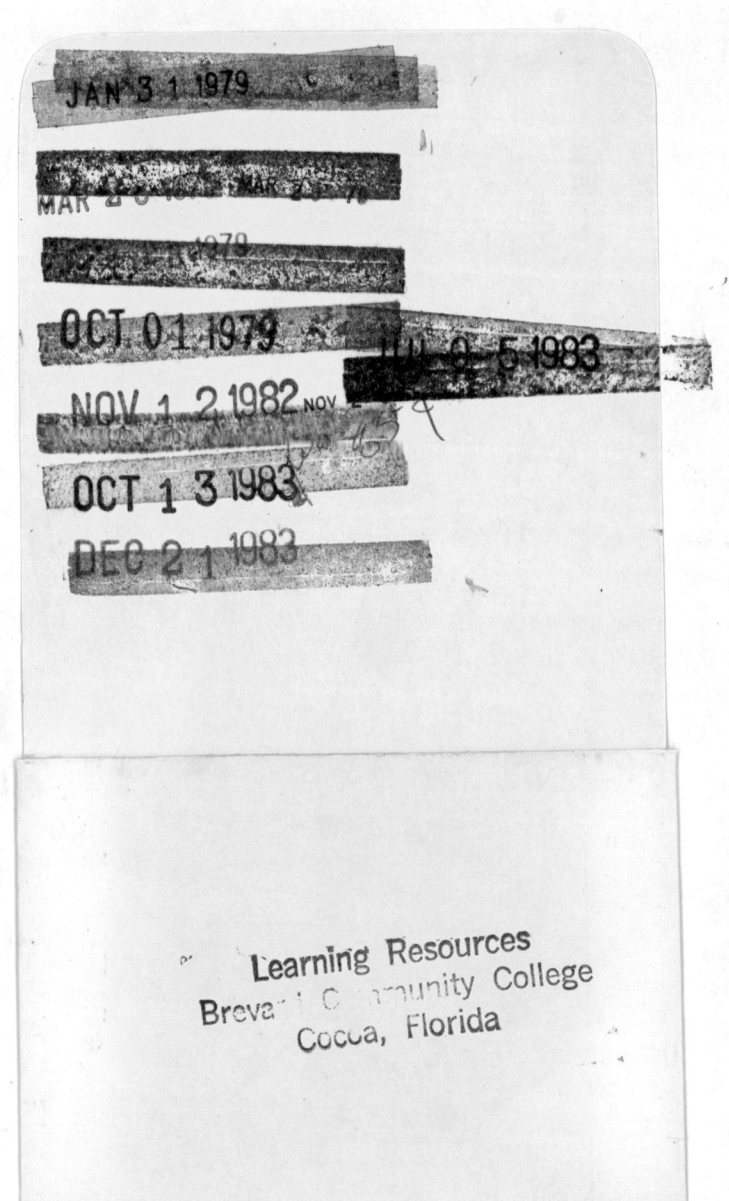